Financial Records & Accounts

Tutorial

NVQ Accounting Unit 5
AAT Diploma Pathway Unit 5

David Cox

osborne
BOOKS

Published by Osborne Books Limited
Unit 1B Everoak Estate
Bromyard Road
Worcester WR2 5HP
Tel 01905 748071
Email books@osbornebooks.co.uk
Website www.osbornebooks.co.uk

Design by Richard Holt
Cover image from Getty Images

Printed by the Bath Press, Bath

British Library Cataloguing in Publication Data
A catalogue record for this book is available from the British Library

ISBN 978 1872962 924

Contents

Acknowledgements

The author wishes to thank the following for their help with the editing and production of the book: Jean Cox, Michael Fardon, Michael Gilbert, Claire McCarthy and Liz Smith. Particular thanks go to Roger Petheram of Worcester College of Technology for reading the text, commenting upon it, checking answers, and always being prepared to discuss any aspect of the book.

The publisher is indebted to the Association of Accounting Technicians for its generous help and advice to its authors and editors during the preparation of this text, and for permission to reproduce extracts from the relevant Accounting Standards.

Author

David Cox has had more than twenty years' experience teaching accountancy students over a wide range of levels. Formerly with the Management and Professional Studies Department at Worcester College of Technology, he now lectures on a freelance basis and carries out educational consultancy work in accountancy studies. He is author and joint author of a number of textbooks in the areas of accounting, finance and banking.

Introduction

Osborne tutorials

Financial Records & Accounts Tutorial has been written to provide a study resource for students taking courses based on the NVQ Level 3 Accounting and on the Diploma Pathway Unit 5 'Maintaining financial records and preparing accounts'.

Financial Records & Accounts Tutorial commences with the recording of business transactions in double-entry accounts, develops through the extended trial balance, and leads to the final accounts of sole traders and partnerships. The emphasis in the text is on the extended trial balance and, from that, the preparation of final accounts in the conventional format used by accountants. Other topics included are:

– the preparation of final accounts from incomplete records
– the record keeping and accounting treatment of fixed asset acquisition and disposal
– the regulatory framework of accounting
– the use of control accounts
– journal entries for year-end transfers and the correction of errors
– changes in the ownership structure of partnerships

Financial Records & Accounts Tutorial provides the student with the theoretical background to the subject while at the same time including plenty of opportunity to put theory into practice. The aim has been to introduce the right amount of material at the right level.

Osborne workbooks

If you are taking the NVQ route you will need *Financial Records & Accounts Workbook,* which contains practice questions and assessment material. For the Diploma Pathway, the equivalent book is *Financial Accounting Workbook.* Visit the 24-hour online shop at www.osbornebooks.co.uk for your copy.

Osborne Tutor Packs

The answers to the material in the *Workbooks* are available in separate *Tutor Packs.* Contact the Osborne Books Sales Office on 01905 748071 or visit the website for details of how to obtain Tutor Packs.

surfing with www.osbornebooks.co.uk

The Osborne Books website is constantly developing its range of facilities for tutors and students. Popular features include free downloadable resources and the on-line shop. Log on and try us!

UNIT 5: MAINTAINING FINANCIAL RECORDS AND PREPARING ACCOUNTS

This unit relates to the maintenance of accounts from the drafting of the initial trial balance through to the preparation of information required to produce a set of final accounts.

The **first element** is concerned with the records for capital items, how to deal with acquisitions, on-going depreciation and the rules for disposal.

The **second element** requires you to collect relevant information for preparing the final accounts and to present the information to your supervisor in the form of a trial balance or an extended trial balance.

The **third element** requires you to prepare final accounts for sole traders and partnerships. You must also be responsible for communication in relation to the handling of queries, for making suggestions for improvements and maintaining confidentiality.

Element 5.1

Maintaining records relating to capital acquisition and disposal

Performance Criteria

		chapter
A	Record relevant details relating to capital expenditure in the appropriate records	10
B	Ensure that the organisation's records agree with the physical presence of capital items	10
C	Correctly identify and record all acquisition and disposal costs and revenues in the appropriate records	10
D	Correctly calculate and record depreciation charges and other necessary entries and adjustments in the appropriate records	10
E	Ensure that the records clearly show the prior authority for capital expenditure and disposal and the approved method of funding and disposal	10
F	Correctly calculate and record the profit and loss on disposal in the appropriate records	10
G	Ensure that the organisation's policies and procedures relating to the maintenance of capital records are adhered to	10
H	Identify and resolve or refer to the appropriate person any lack of agreement between physical items and records	10
I	Make suggestions for improvements in the way the organisation maintains its capital records where possible to the appropriate person	10

Element 5.2

Collecting and collating information for the preparation of final accounts

Performance Criteria

		chapter
A	Correctly prepare reconciliations for the preparation of final accounts	11
B	Identify any discrepancies in the reconciliation process and either take steps to rectify them or refer them to the appropriate person	11
C	Accurately prepare a trial balance and open a suspense account to record any imbalance	3,12
D	Establish the reasons for any imbalance and clear the suspense account by correcting the errors, or reduce them and resolve outstanding items to the appropriate person	12
E	Correctly identify, calculate and record appropriate adjustments	6,7,8,12,14,15
F	Make the relevant journal entries to close off the revenue accounts in preparation for the transfer of balances to the final accounts	12
G	Conduct investigations into business transactions with tact and courtesy	6,7,8,11,12,13
H	Ensure that the organisation's policies, regulations, procedures and timescales relating to preparing final accounts are observed	4,6,7,8,9,12,13

Element 5.3

Preparing the final accounts of sole traders and partnerships

Performance Criteria

		chapter
A	Prepare final accounts of sole traders in proper form, from the trial balance	5,6,7,8
B	Prepare final accounts of partnerships in proper form and in compliance with partnership agreement, from the trial balance	14,15
C	Observe the organisation's policies, regulations, procedures and timescales in relation to preparing final accounts of sole traders and partnerships	5,6,7,8,13,14,15
D	Identify and resolve or refer to the appropriate person discrepancies, unusual features or queries	5,6,7,8,9,13,14,15

Note
For the 'Knowledge and Understanding' requirements of this Unit, pleased refer to the index for individual subjects.

1 The accounting system

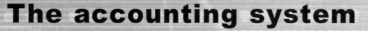

this chapter covers . . .

Before studying financial records and accounts in detail, it is important to take an overview of the accounting system. Every organisation is unique and therefore no one accounting system will be exactly the same as another. This chapter provides:

- an introduction to business transactions
- an explanation of how the transactions are recorded in an accounting system
- an introduction to some of the terms used in accounting

PERFORMANCE CRITERIA COVERED

unit 5: MAINTAINING FINANCIAL RECORDS AND PREPARING ACCOUNTS

KNOWLEDGE AND UNDERSTANDING – THE BUSINESS ENVIRONMENT

5   the methods of recording information for the organisational accounts of sole traders and partnerships

7   the need to present accounts in the correct form

9   the importance of maintaining the confidentiality of business transactions

KNOWLEDGE AND UNDERSTANDING – THE ORGANISATION

31   the ways the accounting systems of an organisation are affected by its organisational structure, its administrative systems and procedures and the nature of its business transactions

ACCOUNTING AND THE ACCOUNTING SYSTEM

what is accounting?

Accounting is essential to the recording and presentation of business activities in the form of *financial accounts*. Accounting involves:

- recording business transactions in financial terms

- reporting financial information to the owner and managers of the business and other interested parties

- advising the owner how to use the financial reports to assess the past performance of the business, and to make decisions for the future

the role of the accountant

The accountant's job is to check, summarise, present, analyse and interpret the accounts for the benefit of the owner/owners and other interested parties. There are two types of specialist accountant:

- *financial accountant*, mainly concerned with external reporting

- *management accountant*, mainly concerned with internal reporting

The function of the *financial accountant* is concerned with financial transactions, and with taking further the information produced by whoever 'keeps the books'. The financial accountant extracts information from the accounting records in order to provide a method of control, for instance over debtors, creditors, cash and bank balances. The role also requires the preparation of year end final accounts.

The *management accountant* obtains information about costs – eg the cost of materials, labour, expenses and overheads – and interprets it and prepares reports for the owners or managers of the business. In particular, the management accountant will be concerned with financial decision-making, planning and control of the business.

manual and computer accounts

This book is concerned with the preparation of the accounting records and their use in the end-of-period final accounts.

Financial accounting records are kept in handwritten form and in many cases on computer. Computer accounting systems are sensibly backed up by handwritten records, in case of computer disasters such as total loss of data. The main record in a handwritten system is *the ledger* which, at one time, would be a weighty leather-bound volume, neatly ruled, into which the book-keeper would handwrite each business transaction into individual accounts.

Computers are now relatively cheap and affordable. The major advantage of computer accounting is that it is a very accurate method of recording business transactions. The word 'ledger' has survived into the computer age but, instead of being a bound volume, it is used to describe data files held on a computer disk.

Whether business transactions are recorded by hand, or by using a computer, the basic principles remain the same. In the first few chapters of this book we will concentrate on these basic principles.

keeping accounts – practical points

When maintaining financial accounts you should bear in mind that they should be kept:

- accurately
- up-to-date
- confidentially:
  - not revealed to people outside the business (unless authorisation is given)
  - revealed only to those within the business who are entitled to the information

Maintaining financial accounts is a discipline, and you should develop disciplined accounting skills as you study with this book. In particular, when attempting Skills Tests and Examinations you should:

- be neat in the layout of your work
- use ink (in accounting, the use of pencil shows indecision)
- not use correcting fluid (errors should be crossed through neatly with a single line and the correct version written on the line below)

The reason for not using correcting fluid in handwritten accounts is because the accounts should always be available for auditing (checking by accountants): correcting fluid may hide errors, but it can also conceal fraudulent transactions.

the stages of the accounting system

The diagram on the next page should now be studied carefully.

The stages of the accounting system are covered in your earlier studies. Topics such as prime documents, books of prime entry, and some aspects of double-entry book-keeping will have been explained in Osborne Books' introductory texts. In this book we will focus on the double-entry accounts system, the trial balance in its 'extended' form, and the preparation of final accounts for sole traders and partnerships. If you should at any time lose sight of where your studies are taking you, refer back to this chapter, and the diagram, and it should help to place your work in context.

the accounting system

PRIME DOCUMENTS
invoices – issued and received

credit notes – issued and received

bank paying-in slips

cheques issued

BACS documents

sources of accounting information

BOOKS OF PRIME (ORIGINAL) ENTRY
day books

journal

cash books (also used in double-entry)

gathering and summarising accounting information

DOUBLE-ENTRY BOOK-KEEPING
sales ledger – accounts of debtors

purchases ledger – accounts of creditors

main (nominal) ledger

– 'nominal' accounts for sales, purchases, expenses, capital, loans etc

– 'real' accounts for items, eg fixed assets

cash books

– cash book for bank and cash transactions

– petty cash book

recording the dual aspect of business transactions in the accounting system

TRIAL BALANCE
a summary of the balances of all the accounts – 'extended' to produce data for final accounts

arithmetical checking of double-entry book-keeping

FINAL ACCOUNTS
• profit and loss account

and

• balance sheet

statement measuring profit (or loss) for an accounting period

statement of assets, liabilities and capital at the end of an accounting period

We will now look at each of the stages of the accounting system in turn.

PRIME DOCUMENTS

Business transactions generate documents. In this section we link the main documents to the type of transaction involved.

sales and purchases – the invoice

When a business buys or sells goods or services the seller prepares an invoice stating:

- the amount owing
- when it should be paid
- details of the goods sold or service provided

cash sales and credit sales – debtors and creditors

An invoice is prepared by the seller for:

- *cash sales* – where payment is immediate, whether by cash or by cheque. (note that not all cash sales will require an invoice to be prepared by the seller – shops, for instance, normally issue a receipt for the amount paid)
- *credit sales* – where payment is to be made at a later date (often 30 days later)

A *debtor* is a person who owes you money when you sell on credit.

A *creditor* is a person to whom you owe money when you buy on credit.

return of goods – the credit note

If the buyer returns goods which are bought on credit (they may be faulty or incorrect) the seller will prepare a credit note which is sent to the buyer, reducing the amount of money owed. The credit note, like the invoice, states the money amount and the goods and services to which it relates.

bank transactions – cheques, giro credits, BACS

Businesses need to pay in money, draw out cash and make payments. Paying-in slips and cheques are used as prime documents for bank account transactions as are documents generated by the BACS inter-bank computer payments system (eg debtors paying direct into the bank).

BOOKS OF PRIME ENTRY

Many businesses issue and receive large quantities of invoices, credit notes and banking documents, and it is useful for them to list these in summary form, during the course of the working day. These summaries are known as *books of prime (or original) entry*. These books of prime entry include:

- *sales day book* – a list of sales made, compiled from invoices issued

- *purchases day book* – a list of purchases made, compiled from invoices received

- *sales returns day book* – a list of 'returns in', ie goods returned by customers, compiled from credit notes issued

- *purchases returns day book* – a list of 'returns out', ie goods returned by the business to suppliers, compiled from credit notes received

- *cash book* – the business' record of the bank account and the amount of cash held, compiled from receipts, paying-in slips and cheques

- *petty cash book* – a record of low-value cash purchases made by the business, compiled from petty cash vouchers

- *journal* – a record of non-regular transactions, which are not recorded in any other primary accounting record (this is covered in Chapter 10)

DOUBLE-ENTRY ACCOUNTS: THE LEDGER

The basis of many accounting systems is the *double-entry book-keeping system* which is embodied in a series of records known as the *ledger*. This is divided into a number of separate *accounts*.

double-entry book-keeping

Double-entry book-keeping involves making two entries in the accounts for each transaction: for instance, if you are paying wages by cheque you will make an entry in bank account and an entry in wages account. If you are operating a manual accounting system you will make the two entries by hand, if you are operating a computer accounting system you will make *one* entry on the keyboard, but indicate to the machine where the other entry is to be made by means of a numerical code.

accounts

The books of prime entry are the sources for the entries you make in the accounts. The ledger into which you make the entries is divided into separate accounts, eg a separate account for sales, purchases, each type of business expense, each debtor, each creditor, and so on. Each account is given a specific name, and a number for reference purposes.

computer accounts

As noted earlier, many small businesses and all large businesses use computers to handle their business transactions. Using an accounting program, transactions are input into the computer and stored on disk. The separate accounts are represented by data files held on disk. The principles of double-entry book-keeping remain the same; an input code is used to identify the two accounts involved in each transaction.

division of the ledger

Because of the large number of accounts involved, the ledger has traditionally been divided into a number of sections. These same sections are used in computer accounting systems.

- *sales ledger* – personal accounts of debtors, ie customers to whom the business has sold on credit
- *purchases ledger* – personal accounts of creditors, ie suppliers to whom the business owes money
- *cash books* – a cash book comprising cash account and bank account, and a petty cash book for petty cash account (low-value purchases); note that the cash books are also primary accounting records for cash transactions
- *main (or nominal) ledger* – the remainder of the accounts: *nominal accounts*, eg sales, purchases, expenses, and *real accounts* for items owned by the business

Note that, when control accounts (see Chapter 11) are in use, the sales ledger and purchases ledger are *subsidiary ledgers* to the main ledger. They are then referred to as 'subsidiary (sales) ledger' and 'subsidiary (purchases) ledger' respectively. The diagrams in Chapter 11 – on pages 189 and 190 – show the relationship between main ledger and the subsidiary ledgers.

TRIAL BALANCE

Double-entry book-keeping, because it involves making two entries for each transaction, is open to error. What if the person keeping the books writes £45 in one account and £54 in another? The trial balance – explained fully in

Chapter 3 – effectively checks the entries made over a given period and will pick up most errors. It sets out the *balances* of all the double-entry accounts, ie the totals of the accounts to date. As well as being an arithmetical check, it is the source of valuable information which is used – in the *extended trial balance* – to help in the preparation of the *final accounts* of the business.

FINAL ACCOUNTS

The final accounts of a business comprise the profit and loss account and the balance sheet.

profit and loss account

income	minus	**expenses**	equals	**profit**

The profit and loss account of a business calculates the profit due to the owner(s) of the business after the cost of purchases and other expenses have been deducted from the sales income.

The figures for these calculations – sales, purchases, expenses of various kinds – are taken from the double-entry system. Profit and loss accounts, which are discussed in more detail in Chapters 4 and 5, are invariably presented in a vertical format:

	income	£
minus	**expenses**	£
equals	**profit**	£

balance sheet

The balance sheet is so called because it balances in numerical (money) terms:

assets	minus	**liabilities**	equals	**capital**
what a business owns		*what a business owes*		*how the business has been financed*

The double-entry system contains figures for:

assets   items the business owns, which can be:

- fixed assets – items bought for use in the business, eg premises, vehicles, computers
- current assets – items used in the everyday running of the business, eg stock, debtors (money owed by customers), and money in the bank

liabilities   items that the business owes, eg bank loans and overdrafts, and creditors (money owed to suppliers)

capital   money or assets introduced by the owner(s) of the business; capital is in effect owed by the business to the owner

Balance sheets, which are explained in Chapters 4 and 5, are – like profit and loss accounts – usually presented in a vertical format:

	assets	£
minus	**liabilities**	£
equals	**capital**	£

the accounting equation

The balance sheet illustrates a concept important to accounting theory, known as the *accounting equation*. This equation has been explained above, namely:

assets   minus   **liabilities**   equals   **capital**

Every business transaction will change the balance sheet and the equation, as each transaction has a *dual effect* on the accounts. However, the equation will always balance. Consider the following transactions:

Transaction	Effect on accounting equation
1. Business pays creditor	decrease in asset (bank) decrease in liability (money owed to creditor)
2. Business buys a computer	increase in asset (computer) decrease in asset (bank)
3. The owner introduces new capital by paying a cheque into the bank	increase in asset (bank) increase in capital (money owed by business to owner)

How is the equation affected by these particular transactions?

Transaction 1   Assets and liabilities both decrease by the amount of the payment; capital remains unchanged.

Transaction 2   Assets remain the same because the two transactions cancel each other out in the assets section: value is transferred from the asset of bank to the asset of computer.

Transaction 3   Both sides of the equation increase by the amount of the capital introduced.

The equation always balances, as will the balance sheet of a business.

In conclusion, every business transaction has a *dual aspect*, as two entries are involved: this is the basis of the theory of double-entry book-keeping.

Chapter Summary

- Accounting is used to record business transactions in financial terms

- Financial accounts are used by the owner(s) and managers of the business and also by other interested parties.

- The accounting system comprises a number of specific stages of recording and presenting business transactions
  - prime documents
  - books of prime (or original) entry
  - the double-entry system of ledgers
  - the trial balance and extended trial balance
  - final accounts

- The balance sheet uses the accounting equation:

  assets − liabilities = capital

Key Terms

In the course of this chapter a number of specific accounting terms have been introduced. You should now study this section closely to ensure that you are clear about these terms:

accounts	financial records, where business transactions are entered
ledger	the set of accounts of a business
assets	items owned by a business
liabilities	items owed by a business
capital	the amount of the owner's (or owners') stake in the business
debtors	individuals or businesses who owe money in respect of goods or services supplied by the business
creditors	individuals or businesses to whom money is owed by the business
purchases	goods bought, either on credit or for cash, which are intended to be resold later
credit purchases	goods bought, with payment to be made at a later date
cash purchases	goods bought and paid for immediately
petty cash	low-value cash purchases, often for expenses
sales	the sale of goods, whether on credit or for cash, in which the business trades

credit sales	goods sold, with payment to be received at an agreed date in the future
cash sales	goods sold, with immediate payment received in cash, by cheque, by credit card, or by debit card
turnover	the total of sales, both cash and credit, for a particular time period
profit	the gain made by a business from selling goods or services during a particular time period
expenses	the costs of running the business, eg wages, rent, rates, telephone, etc
trial balance	list of the balances of all the double-entry account

Student Activities

1.1 Write out and complete the following sentences.

(a) The set of double-entry accounts of a business is called the ....

(b) A .... is a person who owes you money when you sell on credit.

(c) A .... is a person to whom you owe money when you buy on credit.

(d) The .... is a list of sales made, compiled from invoices issued.

(e) The business' record of bank account and amount of cash held is kept in the ....

(f) Accounts such as sales, purchases, expenses are kept in the ....

(g) The accounting equation is: .... minus .... equals ....

1.2 Distinguish between:

  (a) assets and liabilities

  (b) debtors and creditors

  (c) purchases and sales

  (d) credit purchases and cash purchases

1.3 Show the dual aspect, as it affects the accounting equation (assets – liabilities = capital), of the following transactions (which follow one another) for a particular business (ignore VAT):

  (a) owner starts in business with capital of £8,000 in the bank

  (b) buys a computer for £4,000, paying by cheque

  (c) obtains a loan of £3,000 by cheque from a friend

  (d) buys a van for £6,000, paying by cheque

1.4 Fill in the missing figures:

	Assets	Liabilities	Capital
	£	£	£
(a)	20,000	0	....
(b)	15,000	5,000	....
(c)	16,400	....	8,850
(d)	....	3,850	10,250
(e)	25,380	....	6,950
(f)	....	7,910	13,250

1.5 The table below sets out account balances from the books of a business. The columns (a) to (f) show the account balances resulting from a series of transactions that have taken place over time. You are to compare each set of adjacent columns, ie (a) with (b), (b) with (c), and so on and state, with figures, what accounting transactions have taken place in each case. (Ignore VAT).

	(a) £	(b) £	(c) £	(d) £	(e) £	(f) £
Assets						
Office equipment	–	2,000	2,000	2,000	2,000	2,000
Van	–	–	–	10,000	10,000	10,000
Bank	10,000	8,000	14,000	4,000	6,000	3,000
Liabilities						
Loan	–	–	6,000	6,000	6,000	3,000
Capital	10,000	10,000	10,000	10,000	12,000	12,000

2 Double-entry book-keeping

We saw in Chapter 1 that book-keeping is the basic recording of business transactions in financial terms. Before studying financial accounts in detail it is important to study the principles of double-entry book-keeping, as these form the basis of all that we shall be doing in the rest of the book.

In Chapter 1 we looked briefly at the dual aspect of accounting – each time there is a business transaction there are two effects on the accounting equation. This chapter shows how the dual aspect is used in the principles of book-keeping. In particular, we shall be looking at accounts used when:

* starting a business
* dealing with cash and bank transactions
* paying expenses and receiving income
* buying and selling goods
* dealing with returned goods, carriage costs and discounts
* dealing with Value Added Tax

PERFORMANCE CRITERIA COVERED

unit 5: MAINTAINING FINANCIAL RECORDS AND PREPARING ACCOUNTS

KNOWLEDGE AND UNDERSTANDING – ACCOUNTING PRINCIPLES AND THEORY

24   the principles of double-entry accounting

DOUBLE-ENTRY ACCOUNTS

In this book we will use a simple account layout shown as follows:

Dr	Bank Account			Cr
2004		£	2004	£
22 April Sales		450	23 April Wages	7,900

This layout is often known in accounting jargon as a 'T' account; it separates in a simple way the two sides of the account – debit (Dr) and credit (Cr). Note that each side records three items – the date, the nature of the transaction and the money amount.

debits and credits

The principle of double-entry book-keeping is that for every business transaction:

- one account is *debited* with the money amount of the transaction, and
- one account is *credited* with the money amount of the transaction

Debit entries are on the left-hand side of the appropriate account, while credit entries are on the right. The rules for debits and credits are:

- *debit entry* – the account which gains value, or records an asset, or an expense
- *credit entry* – the account which gives value, or records a liability, or an income item

This is illustrated as follows:

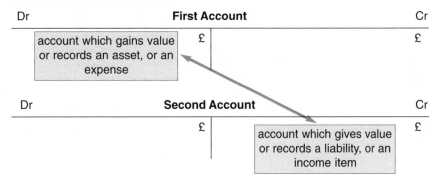

When one entry has been identified as a debit or credit, the other entry will be on the *opposite* side of the other account.

DOUBLE-ENTRY INVOLVING BANK ACCOUNT

In order to see how accounts are used, we will look at the business transactions undertaken by a new business which was set up by Jayne Hampson on 1 September 2004 (and is not registered for VAT):

1 Sep	Started in business with capital of £5,000: a cheque from Jayne Hampson paid into the business bank account
4 Sep	Bought office equipment £2,500, paying by cheque
7 Sep	Paid rent of office £500, by cheque
10 Sep	Received commission of £100, by cheque
14 Sep	Withdrew £250 from the bank for own use (drawings)
16 Sep	Received a loan of £1,000 from James Henderson by cheque

All of these transactions involve the bank, and the business will enter them in its *bank account*. The bank account records money in the form of bank receipts and payments, ie cheques, standing orders, direct debits, bank giro credits, credit card transactions, and debit card transactions. (Most businesses also use a *cash account* to record transactions which involve money in the form of cash.)

With both bank account and cash account, the rules for debit and credit are:

- *money in* is recorded on the debit side
- *money out* is recorded on the credit side

Using these rules, the bank account of Jayne Hampson's business, after entering the transactions listed above, appears as:

Dr			**Bank Account**		Cr
2004		£	2004		£
1 Sep	Capital	5,000	4 Sep	Office equipment	2,500
10 Sep	Commission	100	7 Sep	Rent paid	500
16 Sep	J Henderson: loan	1,000	14 Sep	Drawings	250

Money in   Money out

Note: the bank account shows the firm's record of how much has been paid into, and drawn out of, the bank – it may not be exactly the same as the record of receipts and payments kept by the bank.

To complete the double-entry book-keeping transactions we need to:

- identify on which side of the bank account the transaction is recorded – debit (money in), or credit (money out)

- record the other double-entry transaction on the *opposite side* of the appropriate account

- note that business transactions involving cash will be entered in the cash account

The other accounts involved can now be recorded, and we shall look at the principles involved for each transaction.

CAPITAL ACCOUNT

Capital is the amount of money invested in the business by the owner (or owners). The amount is *owed* by the business back to the owner, although it is unlikely to be repaid immediately as the business would cease to exist. A *capital account* is used to record the amount(s) paid into the business; the book-keeping entries are:

- **capital introduced**
    - *debit* bank account, as in the case of Jayne Hampson, or cash account (or a fixed asset account – see below – where these form part of the capital)
    - *credit* capital account

example transaction

1 Sep 2004   Started in business with capital of £5,000, a cheque paid into the bank.

Dr		Capital Account		Cr
2004	£	2004		£
		1 Sep	Bank	5,000

Note: The dual aspect is that bank account has gained value and has been debited already (see page 16); capital account records a liability (to the owner) and is credited. Note that the business is a *separate entity* from the owner, and this book-keeping entry looks at the transaction from the point of view of the business. The introduction of capital into a business is often the very first business transaction entered into the books of account.

FIXED ASSETS

Fixed assets are items purchased by a business for use on a semi-permanent basis. Examples are premises, motor vehicles, machinery and office equipment. All of these are bought by a business with the intention that they will be used for some time. Without fixed assets, it would be difficult to continue in business, eg without machinery it would prove difficult to run a factory; without delivery vans and lorries it would be difficult to transport the firm's products to its customers.

When a business buys fixed assets, the expenditure is referred to as *capital expenditure*. This means that items have been bought for use in the business for some years to come. By contrast, *revenue expenditure* is where the items bought will be used by the business quite quickly. For example, the purchase of a car is capital expenditure, while the cost of repair of the car is revenue expenditure.

The importance of the difference between capital expenditure and revenue expenditure is covered in Chapter 9.

fixed assets and double-entry book-keeping

When fixed assets are bought, a separate account for each type of fixed asset is used, eg premises account, motor vehicles account, machinery account, etc. The book-keeping entries are:

* **purchase of a fixed asset**
    - *debit* fixed asset account (using the appropriate account)
    - *credit* bank account (or cash account)

example transaction

4 Sep 2004   Bought office equipment £2,500, paying by cheque.

Dr			Office Equipment Account		Cr
2004		£	2004		£
4 Sep	Bank	2,500			

The other part of the dual aspect of this transaction is a credit to bank account: this has been entered already (see account on page 16). Notice how the name of the other account involved in the double-entry transaction is always used in the details column as a description – this helps to cross-reference transactions.

EXPENSES

Businesses pay various running expenses, such as rent, wages, electricity, telephone, vehicle running expenses, etc. These day-to-day expenses of running the business are termed revenue expenditure. A separate account is used in the accounting system for each main class of revenue expenditure, eg rent paid account, wages account, etc.

The book-keeping entries are:

* **payment of an expense**
    – *debit* expense account (using the appropriate account)
    – *credit* bank account (or cash account)

example transaction

7 Sep 2004   Paid rent of office £500, by cheque.

Dr			Rent Paid Account		Cr
2004		£	2004		£
7 Sep	Bank	500			

Note: The accounting rules followed are that we have debited the account which has gained value (rent – the business has had the use of the office for a certain time). The account which has given value (bank) has already been credited (see page 16).

INCOME

From time-to-time a business may receive amounts of income, such as rent received, commission received, or fees received. These are recorded in separate accounts for each category of income, eg rent received account, commission received account. The book-keeping entries are:

- **receipt of income**
  - *debit* bank account (or cash account)
  - *credit* income account (using the appropriate account)

---

example transaction

10 Sep 2004   Received commission of £100, by cheque.

Dr		Commission Received Account		Cr
2004	£	2004		£
		10 Sep Bank		100

Note: We have already debited the account which has gained value (bank – see page 16) and credited the account which has given value (commission received).

OWNER'S DRAWINGS

Drawings is the term used when the owner takes money, in cash or by cheque (or sometimes goods), from the business for personal use. A drawings account is used to record such amounts; the book-keeping entries for withdrawal of money are:

- **owner's drawings**
  - *debit* drawings account
  - *credit* bank account (or cash account)

---

example transaction

14 Sep 2004   Withdrew £250 from the bank for own use.

Dr		Drawings Account	Cr
2004	£	2004	£
14 Sep Bank	250		

The other part of the dual aspect of this transaction is a credit to bank account: this entry has been made already (see page 16).

LOANS

When a business or organisation receives a loan, eg from a relative or from the bank, it is the cash account or bank account which gains value, while a loan account (in the name of the lender) records the liability.

- **loan received**
    - *debit* bank account (or cash account)
    - *credit* loan account (in name of the lender)

example transaction

16 Sep 2004   Received a loan of £1,000 from James Henderson by cheque

Dr		James Henderson: Loan Account		Cr
2004	£	2004		£
		16 Sep Bank		1,000

The debit entry has already been made in bank account (see page 16).

FURTHER TRANSACTIONS

Using the accounts which we have seen already, here are some further transactions:

- **loan repayment**
    - *debit* loan account
    - *credit* bank account (or cash account)
- **sale of a fixed asset, or return of an unsuitable fixed asset**
    - debit bank account (or cash account)
    - credit fixed asset account
- **withdrawal of cash from the bank for use in the business**
    - *debit* cash account
    - *credit* bank account
- **payment of cash held by the business into the bank**
    - *debit* bank account
    - *credit* cash account

PURCHASES AND SALES

purchases account and sales account

Buying and selling goods or services are common business transactions. They are recorded in *purchases account* and *sales account* respectively. These two accounts are used to record the purchase and sale of the goods or services in which the business trades. For example, a shoe shop will buy shoes from the manufacturer and will record this in purchases account; as shoes are sold, the transactions will be recorded in sales account.

The normal entry on a purchases account is on the debit side – the account has gained value, ie the business has bought goods for resale. The normal entry on a sales account is on the credit side – the account has given value, ie the business has sold goods.

When a business buys an item for use in the business, eg a computer, this is debited to a separate account, because a fixed asset (see page 18) has been purchased. Likewise, when a fixed asset is sold, it is not entered in the sales account.

Case Study

TEMESIDE TRADERS: PURCHASES AND SALES

situation

To show the double-entry book-keeping for purchases and sales, we will look at some financial transactions undertaken by Temeside Traders, a business which started trading on 1 October 2004:

1 Oct	Started in business with capital of £7,000 paid into the bank
2 Oct	Bought goods for £5,000, paying by cheque
5 Oct	Sold some of the goods for £3,000, a cheque being received
6 Oct	Bought equipment for use in the business, £700, paying by cheque
12 Oct	Bought goods for £2,800, paying by cheque
13 Oct	Sold some of the goods for £5,000, a cheque being received
15 Oct	Paid rent £150, by cheque

Note: Temeside Traders is not yet registered for Value Added Tax

solution

The entries into the book-keeping system are shown on the next page.

Dr		Bank Account			Cr
2004		£	2004		£
1 Oct	Capital	7,000	2 Oct	Purchases	5,000
5 Oct	Sales	3,000	6 Oct	Equipment	700
13 Oct	Sales	5,000	12 Oct	Purchases	2,800
			15 Oct	Rent paid	150

Dr		Capital Account			Cr
2004		£	2004		£
			1 Oct	Bank	7,000

Dr		Purchases Account			Cr
2004		£	2004		£
2 Oct	Bank	5,000			
12 Oct	Bank	2,800			

Dr		Sales Account			Cr
2004		£	2004		£
			5 Oct	Bank	3,000
			13 Oct	Bank	5,000

Dr		Equipment Account			Cr
2004		£	2004		£
6 Oct	Bank	700			

Dr		Rent Paid Account			Cr
2004		£	2004		£
15 Oct	Bank	150			

Notes:

- A purchases account and a sales account are used to record the two different movements of the goods or services in which a business trades.
- The equipment is a fixed asset, so its purchase is entered to a separate equipment account.
- The purchases and sales made in the transactions above are called cash purchases and cash sales, because payment is immediate.

CREDIT PURCHASES AND SALES

credit transactions

We have just looked at the book-keeping for cash purchases and cash sales, ie where payment is made immediately. However, in business, many transactions for purchases and sales are made on credit, ie the goods or services are bought or sold now, with payment to be made at a later date. It is an important aspect of double-entry book-keeping to record the credit transaction as a purchase or a sale, and then record the second entry in an account in the name of the creditor or debtor, ie to record the amount owing by the firm to a creditor, or to the firm by a debtor.

Businesses usually record credit transactions in appropriate books of prime entry:

- credit purchases are entered in the purchases day book
- credit sales are entered in the sales day book

At regular intervals – daily, weekly or monthly – the totals and amounts from the day books are transferred into the double-entry accounts.

credit purchases

Credit purchases are goods obtained from a supplier, with payment to take place at a later date. From the buyer's viewpoint, the supplier is a *creditor.*

The book-keeping entries are:

- **credit purchase**
  - *debit* purchases account
  - *credit* creditor's (supplier's) account

When payment is made to the creditor the book-keeping entries are:

- **payment made to creditor**
  - *debit* creditor's account
  - *credit* bank account or cash account

Many businesses keep their creditors' accounts as subsidiary accounts and use a *purchases ledger control account* as part of the double-entry system. The use of control accounts is covered in Chapter 11.

credit sales

With credit sales, goods or services are sold to a customer who is allowed to settle the account at a later date. From the seller's viewpoint, the customer is a *debtor.*

The book-keeping entries are:

- **credit sale**
  - *debit* debtor's (customer's) account
  - *credit* sales account

When payment is received from the debtor the book-keeping entries are:

- **payment received from debtor**
  - *debit* bank account or cash account
  - *credit* debtor's account

Many businesses keep their debtors' accounts as subsidiary accounts and use a *sales ledger control account* as part of the double-entry system. The use of control accounts is covered in Chapter 11.

Case Study

WYVERN WHOLESALERS: CREDIT TRANSACTIONS

situation

A local business, Wyvern Wholesalers, has the following transactions:

2004

18 Sep	Bought goods, £250, on credit from Malvern Manufacturing, with payment to be made in 30 days' time
21 Sep	Sold goods, £175, on credit to Strensham Stores, payment to be made in 30 days' time
16 Oct	Paid £250 by cheque to Malvern Manufacturing
20 Oct	Received a cheque for £175 from Strensham Stores

Notes:

- *Wyvern Wholesalers is not registered for Value Added Tax*
- *day books are not used*

solution

These transactions will be recorded in the book-keeping system as follows (previous transactions on accounts, if there are any, are not shown here) :

Dr			Purchases Account			Cr
2004		£	2004			£
18 Sep	Malvern Manufacturing	250				

Dr			Sales Account			Cr
2004		£	2004			£
			21 Sep	Strensham Stores		175

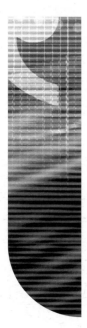

Dr			Malvern Manufacturing		Cr
2004		£	2004		£
16 Oct	Bank	250	18 Sep	Purchases	250

Dr			Strensham Stores		Cr
2004		£	2004		£
21 Sep	Sales	175	20 Oct	Bank	175

Dr			Bank Account		Cr
2004		£	2004		£
20 Oct	Strensham Stores	175	16 Oct	Malvern Manufacturing	250

Note: the name of the other account involved has been used in the details column as a description.

balancing off accounts

In the Case Study above, after the transactions have been recorded in the books of Wyvern Wholesalers, the accounts of Malvern Manufacturing and Strensham Stores have the same amount entered on both debit and credit side. This means that nothing is owing to Wyvern Wholesalers, or is owed by it, ie the accounts have a 'nil' balance. In the course of trading, accounts will often *not* have a nil balance. We will explain in Chapter 3 how to 'balance' an account to show the 'total' of that account.

fixed assets bought on credit

Fixed assets are often purchased on credit terms. As with the purchase of goods for resale, an account is opened in the name of the creditor, as follows:

- **purchase of a fixed asset on credit**
  - *debit* fixed asset account
  - *credit* creditor's (supplier's) account

When payment is made to the creditor the book-keeping entries are:

- **payment made to creditor**
  - *debit* creditor's account
  - *credit* bank account or cash account

The book of prime entry for the purchase of fixed assets on credit is the journal – see Chapter 12.

PURCHASES RETURNS AND SALES RETURNS

From time-to-time goods bought or sold are returned, perhaps because the wrong items have been supplied (eg wrong type, size or colour), or because the goods are unsatisfactory. The book-keeping entries for returned goods are explained below.

purchases returns

Purchases returns (or *returns out*) is where a business returns goods to a creditor (supplier).

The book-keeping entries are:

- – *debit* creditor's (supplier's) account
- – *credit* purchases returns (or returns outwards) account

Purchases returns are normally kept separate from purchases, ie they are entered in a separate purchases returns account rather than being credited to purchases account.

sales returns

Sales returns (or *returns in*) is where a debtor (customer) returns goods to the business.

The book-keeping entries are:

- – *debit* sales returns (or returns in) account
- – *credit* debtor's (customer's) account

Sales returns are normally kept separate from sales, ie they are entered in a separate sales returns account rather than being debited to sales account.

Businesses usually record returns transactions (of goods or services originally bought/sold on credit) in appropriate books of prime entry:

• purchases returns are entered in the purchases returns day book

• sales returns are entered in the sales returns day book

The totals and amounts from these day books are transferred into the double-entry accounts at regular intervals.

Now read the Case Study which follows on the next page. It shows how the double-entry book-keeping for purchases and sales returns is carried out.

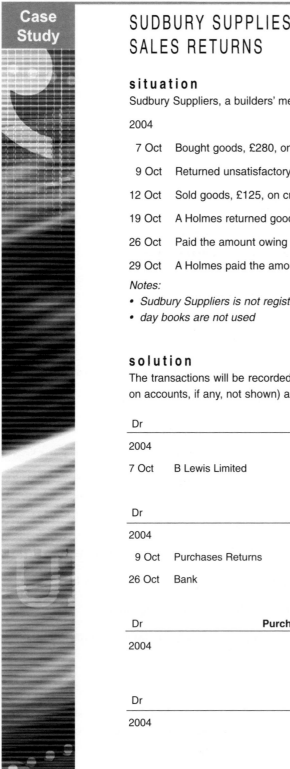

Case Study

SUDBURY SUPPLIES: PURCHASES RETURNS AND SALES RETURNS

situation

Sudbury Suppliers, a builders' merchant, has the following transactions:

2004

7 Oct   Bought goods, £280, on credit from B Lewis Limited

9 Oct   Returned unsatisfactory goods, £30, to B Lewis Limited

12 Oct   Sold goods, £125, on credit to A Holmes

19 Oct   A Holmes returned goods, £25

26 Oct   Paid the amount owing to B Lewis Limited by cheque

29 Oct   A Holmes paid the amount owing in cash

Notes:
* *Sudbury Suppliers is not registered for Value Added Tax*
* *day books are not used*

solution

The transactions will be recorded in the book-keeping system (previous transactions on accounts, if any, not shown) as follows:

Dr		Purchases Account			Cr
2004		£	2004		£
7 Oct	B Lewis Limited	280			

Dr		B Lewis Limited			Cr
2004		£	2004		£
9 Oct	Purchases Returns	30	7 Oct	Purchases	280
26 Oct	Bank	250			

Dr		Purchases Returns Account			Cr
2004		£	2004		£
			9 Oct	B Lewis Limited	30

Dr		Sales Account			Cr
2004		£	2004		£
			12 Oct	A Holmes	125

Dr	A Holmes			Cr
2004	£	2004		£
12 Oct Sales	125	19 Oct	Sales Returns	25
		29 Oct	Cash	100

Dr	Sales Returns Account		Cr
2004	£	2004	£
19 Oct A Holmes	25		

Dr	Bank Account			Cr
2004	£	2004		£
		26 Oct	B Lewis Limited	250

Dr	Cash Account		Cr
2004	£	2004	£
29 Oct A Holmes	100		

CARRIAGE INWARDS AND CARRIAGE OUTWARDS

Carriage inwards is where the buyer pays the carriage (transport) cost of purchases, eg an item is purchased by mail order, and the buyer has to pay the additional cost of delivery (and possibly packing also).

*Carriage outward*s is where the seller pays the carriage charge, eg an item is sold to the customer and described as 'post free'.

Both carriage inwards and carriage outwards are expenses and their cost should be debited to two separate expenses accounts, *carriage inwards account* and *carriage outwards account* respectively:

- **carriage inwards**
  - *debit* carriage inwards account (alternatively, purchases account could be debited)
  - *credit* creditor's account, or bank account/cash account
- **carriage outwards**
  - *debit* carriage outwards account
  - *credit* bank account/cash account

SETTLEMENT DISCOUNT IN THE BOOK-KEEPING SYSTEM

Settlement discount (or cash discount) is an allowance off the invoice amount for quick settlement, eg 2% settlement discount for settlement within seven days. (Do not confuse settlement discount with *trade discount* – an amount sometimes allowed as a reduction in price when goods are supplied to other businesses – or with *bulk discount* – a reduction in price when large quantities of goods are supplied.) A business can be involved with settlement discount in two ways:

- discount allowed to debtors
- discount received from creditors

Case Study

R PATEL: DISCOUNTS ALLOWED AND RECEIVED

situation - discount allowed

R Patel sells TV and video equipment. When settlement discount allowed is taken by one of his customers it is entered into the accounts as shown by the following transactions:

2004

| 12 Oct | Sold goods, £100, on credit to P Henry, allowing her a settlement discount of 2% for payment within 7 days (note: the seller of the goods is not VAT-registered) |
| 16 Oct | P Henry pays £98 by cheque |

solution

Dr			**Sales Account**			Cr
2004		£	2004			£
			12 Oct	P Henry		100

Dr			**P Henry**			Cr
2004		£	2004			£
12 Oct	Sales	100	16 Oct	Bank		98
			16 Oct	Discount Allowed		2
		100				100

Dr			**Bank Account**			Cr
2004		£	2004			£
16 Oct	P Henry	98				

Dr			**Discount Allowed Account**			Cr
2004		£	2004			£
16 Oct	P Henry	2				

Notes:

* *The amount of the payment received from the debtor (P Henry) is debited to the bank account and credited to the debtor's account.*
* *The amount of discount allowed – an expense to the business – is debited to discount allowed account and credited to the debtor's account.*

situation – discount received

R Patel is allowed settlement discount by his creditors. The following transactions show how discount received is entered into the accounts.

2004

20 Oct   Bought goods, £200, on credit from H Singh Limited; 2.5% settlement discount is offered for payment by the end of October (note: the seller of the goods is not registered for VAT)

30 Oct   Paid H Singh Limited £195 by cheque

solution

Dr		Purchases Account			Cr
2004		£	2004		£
20 Oct	H Singh Limited	200			

Dr		H Singh Limited			Cr
2004		£	2004		£
30 Oct	Bank	195	20 Oct	Purchases	200
30 Oct	Discount Received	5			
		200			200

Dr		Bank Account			Cr
2004		£	2004		£
			30 Oct	H Singh Limited	195

Dr		Discount Received Account			Cr
2004		£	2004		£
			30 Oct	H Singh Limited	5

Notes:

* *The business is receiving settlement discount from its creditor, and the amount is entered as: debit creditor's account, credit discount received account.*
* *Discount received account is an income account, because it represents a benefit given to the business by creditors.*

VAT AND DOUBLE-ENTRY ACCOUNTS

When a business is registered for Value Added Tax it is normally able to claim back VAT paid on purchases of goods, fixed assets and expenses – this is known as *input tax.* A VAT-registered business must also charge VAT – *output tax* – whenever it supplies goods and services (except for zero-rated and exempt goods and services). A separate account is opened for VAT.

When a VAT-registered business buys, for example, fixed assets it will enter the amount of input VAT direct to the debit side of VAT account.

example transaction

On 16 April 2004, Osborne Paints Limited, a company which is registered for Value Added Tax, buys a new computer at a cost of £1,000 + VAT of £175, paying by a cheque for £1,175.

This is recorded in the double-entry accounts as:

Dr		**Computer Account**		Cr
2004		£	2004	£
16 Apr	Bank	1,000		

Dr		**Value Added Tax Account**		Cr
2004		£	2004	£
16 Apr	Bank	175		

Dr		**Bank Account**		Cr
2004		£	2004	£
			16 Apr Computer	1,175

Similarly when the business sells its paints to a customer it will charge *output VAT* on the goods. The entries for a sale of £705 (£600 + VAT) will be:

- *debit* customer's account £705 – this is the amount owed
- *credit* VAT account £105 – this is the VAT charged on the sale
- *credit* sales account £600 – this is the value of the goods sold

For more detail on Value Added Tax, please see Chapter 9 (page 144).

- Business transactions are recorded in ledger accounts using double-entry book-keeping principles.

- Each double-entry book-keeping transaction involves a debit entry and a credit entry.

- Entries in the bank account and cash account are:
  - *debit* money in
  - *credit* money out

- Fixed assets are items purchased by a business for use on a semi-permanent basis, eg premises, motor vehicles, machinery and office equipment. The purchase of such items is called *capital expenditure*.

- Running expenses of a business, such as rent paid, wages, electricity, etc are called *revenue expenditure*.

- Other accounts are opened in the book-keeping system for: capital, fixed assets, expenses, income, drawings and loans.

- Purchases account is used to record the purchase of goods in which the business trades: the normal entry is on the debit side.

- Sales account is used to record the sale of goods or services in which the business trades: the normal entry is on the credit side.

- The purchase of goods is recorded as:
  - *debit* purchases account
  - *credit* bank/cash account or, if bought on credit, creditor's account

- The sale of goods or services is recorded as:
  - *debit* bank/cash account or, if sold on credit, debtor's account
  - *credit* sales account

- Purchases returns (or returns out) are recorded as:
  - *debit* creditor's account
  - *credit* purchases returns account

- Sales returns (or returns in) are recorded as:
  - *debit* sales returns account
  - *credit* debtor's account

- 'Carriage' is the expense of transporting goods:
  - *carriage inwards* is the cost of carriage paid on purchases
  - *carriage outwards* is the cost of carriage paid on sales

- Settlement discount allowed (cash discount) is entered in the accounts as:
  - *debit* discount allowed account
  - *credit* debtor's account

- Settlement discount received is entered as:
  - *debit* creditor's account
  - *credit* discount received account

- VAT account will record the amounts of input VAT (VAT on purchases and expenses) and output VAT (VAT on sales of goods and services).

Key Terms	**ledger accounts**	where double-entry book-keeping transactions are recorded
	debit entry	the account which gains value, or records an asset or an expense
	credit entry	the account which gives value, or records a liability, or an income item
	capital	the amount of money invested in the business by the owner (or owners)
	fixed asset	item purchased by a business for use on a semi-permanent basis
	capital expenditure	the purchase of fixed assets for use by the business
	revenue expenditure	the expenses incurred in the day-to-day running of the business
	drawings	money taken from the business by the owner, in the form of cash or cheque (or sometimes goods) for personal use
	purchases account	used to record the purchase – whether on credit or for cash – of the goods in which the business trades
	sales account	used to record the sale – whether on credit or for cash – of the goods in which the business trades
	credit purchases	goods bought, with payment to be made at a later date
	credit sales	goods sold, with payment to be received at an agreed date in the future
	purchases returns	where a business returns goods to a creditor (supplier)
	sales returns	where a debtor (customer) returns goods to the business
	carriage inwards	the cost of carriage paid on purchases
	carriage outwards	the cost of carriage paid on sales
	settlement discount	an allowance off the invoice amount for quick payment
	discount allowed	settlement discount allowed to debtors
	discount received	settlement discount received from creditors

Student Activities

2.1 The payment of wages in cash is recorded in the accounts as:

	Debit	*Credit*
(a)	wages account	drawings account
(b)	cash account	wages account
(c)	capital account	wages account
(d)	wages account	cash account

Answer (a) or (b) or (c) or (d)

2.2 A loan is received by cheque from John Box. This is recorded in the accounts as:

	Debit	*Credit*
(a)	bank account	capital account
(b)	bank account	John Box: loan account
(c)	drawings account	John Box: loan account
(d)	John Box: loan account	bank account

Answer (a) or (b) or (c) or (d)

2.3 The owner of a business withdraws cash for her own use. This is recorded in the accounts as:

	Debit	*Credit*
(a)	drawings account	bank account
(b)	bank account	cash account
(c)	wages account	cash account
(d)	drawings account	cash account

Answer (a) or (b) or (c) or (d)

2.4 James Anderson has kept his bank account up-to-date, but has not got around to the other double-entry book-keeping entries. Rule up the other accounts for him, and make the appropriate entries.

Dr			**Bank Account**			Cr
2004		£		2004		£
2 Feb	Capital	7,500		6 Feb	Computer	2,000
13 Feb	Bank loan	2,500		9 Feb	Rent paid	750
20 Feb	Commission received	145		12 Feb	Wages	425
				23 Feb	Drawings	200
				25 Feb	Wages	380
				27 Feb	Van	6,000

Note: James Anderson is not registered for Value Added Tax

3 Balancing accounts and the trial balance

this chapter covers . . .

With the 'traditional' form of account (the 'T' account) that we have used so far, it is necessary to calculate the balance of each account from time-to-time, according to the needs of the business, and at the end of each financial year.

The balance of an account is the total of that account to date, eg the amount of wages paid, the amount of sales made. In this chapter we shall see how this balancing of accounts is carried out.

We shall then use the balances from each account in order to check the double-entry book-keeping by extracting a trial balance, which is a list of the balances of all the ledger accounts.

PERFORMANCE CRITERIA COVERED

unit 5: MAINTAINING FINANCIAL RECORDS AND PREPARING ACCOUNTS

element 5.2

collecting and collating information for the preparation of final accounts

C   accurately prepare a trial balance and open a suspense account* to record any imbalance

*see Chapter 12 for coverage of suspense accounts

BALANCING THE ACCOUNTS

At regular intervals, often at the end of each month, accounts are balanced in order to show total amounts, for example:

- owing to each creditor
- owing by each debtor
- sales
- purchases
- sales returns (returns in)
- purchases returns (returns out)
- expenses incurred by the business
- fixed assets, eg premises, machinery, etc owned by the business
- capital and drawings of the owner of the business
- other liabilities, eg loans

An exception to this periodic balancing of accounts is the *running balance account* which calculates the balance in a separate column *after each transaction*. A common example of this is the bank statement which prints the 'running balance' in a column on the right-hand side.

METHOD OF BALANCING ACCOUNTS

Set out below is an example of a traditional format double-entry account which has been balanced at the month-end:

Dr			**Bank Account**		Cr
2004		£	2004		£
1 Sep	Capital	5,000	2 Sep	Computer	1,800
4 Sep	J Jackson: loan	2,500	7 Sep	Purchases	500
10 Sep	Sales	750	11 Sep	Drawings	100
			15 Sep	Wages	200
			30 Sep	Balance c/d	5,650
		8,250			8,250
1 Oct	Balance b/d	5,650			

The steps involved in balancing accounts are shown on the next page.

Step 1   The entries in the debit and credit money columns are totalled; these totals are not recorded in ink on the account at this stage, but can be written either as sub-totals in pencil on the account, or noted on a separate piece of paper. In the example on the previous page the debit side totals £8,250, while the credit side is £2,600.

Step 2   The difference between the two totals is the balance of the account and this is entered on the account:

- on the side of the smaller total
- on the next available line
- with the date of balancing (often the last day of the month)
- with the description 'balance c/d', or 'balance carried down'

In the example shown, the balance carried down is £8,250 – £2,600 = £5,650, entered in the credit column.

Step 3   Both sides of the account are now totalled, including the balance which has just been entered, and the totals (the same on both sides) are entered *on the same line* in the appropriate column, and double underlined. The double underline indicates that the account has been balanced at this point using the figures above the total: the figures above the underline should not be added in to anything below the underline.

In the example shown, the totals on each side of the account are £8,250.

Step 4   As we are using double-entry book-keeping, there must be an opposite entry to the 'balance c/d' calculated in Step 2. The same money amount is entered *on the other side of the account* below the double underlined totals entered in Step 3. We have now completed both the debit and credit entry. The date is usually recorded as the next day after 'balance c/d', ie often the first day of the following month, and the description can be 'balance b/d' or 'balance brought down'.

In the example shown, the balance brought down on the bank account on 1 October 2004 is £5,650 debit; this means that, according to the firm's accounting records, there is £5,650 in the bank.

a practical point

When balancing accounts, use a pen and not a pencil (except for Step 1). If any errors are made, cross them through neatly with a single line, and write the corrected version on the line below. Avoid using correcting fluid – it can lead to all sorts of problems (see page 4).

further examples of balancing accounts

Dr			**Wages Account**		Cr
2004		£	2004		£
9 Apr	Bank	750	30 Apr	Balance c/d	2,250
16 Apr	Bank	800			
23 Apr	Bank	700			
		2,250			2,250
1 May	Balance b/d	2,250			

This wages account has transactions on one side only, but is still balanced in the same way. The account shows that the total amount paid for wages is £2,250.

Dr			**B Lewis Limited**		Cr
2004		£	2004		£
10 Apr	Purchases Returns	30	7 Apr	Purchases	280
27 Apr	Bank	250			
		280			280

This account in the name of a creditor has a 'nil' balance after the transactions for April have taken place. The two sides of the account are totalled and, as both debit and credit side are the same amount, there is nothing further to do, apart from entering the double underlined total.

Dr			**A Holmes**		Cr
2004		£	2004		£
1 Apr	Balance b/d	105	10 Apr	Bank	105
10 Apr	Sales	125	13 Apr	Sales Returns	25
			30 Apr	Balance c/d	100
		230			230
1 May	Balance b/d	100			

This is the account of a debtor and, at the start of the month, there was a debit balance of £105 brought down from March. After the various transactions for April, there remains a debit balance of £100 owing at 1 May.

Dr			Office Equipment Account		Cr
2004		£	2004		£
13 Apr	Bank	2,000			

This account has just the one transaction and, in practice, there is no need to balance it. The account clearly has a debit balance of £2,000, which represents office equipment (a fixed asset).

Dr			Malvern Manufacturing Company		Cr
2004		£	2004		£
29 Apr	Bank	250	17 Apr	Purchases	250

This creditor's account has a 'nil' balance, with just one transaction on each side. All that is needed here is to double underline the amount on both sides.

CONTROL ACCOUNTS

There is one further type of account to mention before looking at the accounts listed in the trial balance – a control account.

A control account is a summary account or master account, which records the totals of entries to a particular set of accounts.

Sales ledger control account, for instance, shows the total of all the accounts in the sales ledger and tells the owner of the business how much in total is owing from debtors.

Purchases ledger control account shows the total of all the accounts in the purchases ledger and tells the owner of the business how much in total is owing to creditors.

The individual debtor and creditor accounts are known as 'subsidiary' accounts.

The use of control accounts is covered in more detail in Chapter 11.

control accounts and the trial balance

The trial balance (see next page) is the listing of all the account balances in two columns: debit balances on the left, credit balances on the right.

It is the balances of the control accounts which are taken to the trial balance rather than the individual debtor and creditor balances, which would clutter it up and make it very long. The description of the control accounts in the trial balance is simply 'debtors' (a debit balance on the left) and 'creditors' (a credit balance on the right). This is illustrated in the diagram below.

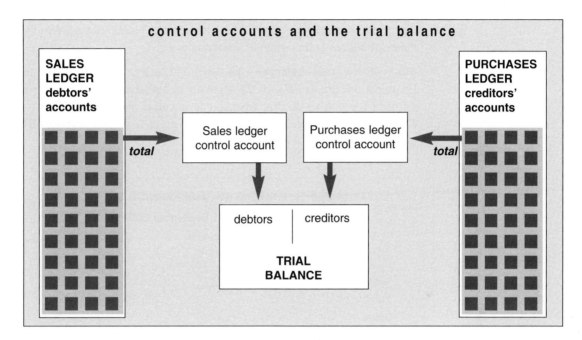

EXTRACTING A TRIAL BALANCE

A trial balance is taken from the accounting records, either manually or by generation of a computer report, in order to check the accuracy of the double-entry book-keeping, ie that the total of the debit entries equals the total of the credit entries.

A trial balance is a list of the balances of every account from the ledger, setting out debit balances and credit balances in separate columns.

A trial balance is extracted at regular intervals – often at the end of each month. An example is shown on the next page. Note that:

- The debit and credit columns have been totalled and are the same amount. Thus the trial balance proves that the accounting records are *arithmetically* correct – the total of the debits equals the total of the credits. (For types of errors, see page 45.)

- The heading for a trial balance gives the name of the business whose accounts have been listed and the date on which it was extracted.

- The balance for each account listed in the trial balance is the figure brought down after the accounts have been balanced.

- As well as showing the name of each account, a trial balance may quote an account number (eg a computer produced trial balance), or a 'folio' reference to the individual ledger, eg: ML = main ledger, SL = sales ledger, PL = purchases ledger, CB = cash book. You do not need to use these references at this stage in your studies.

- Most of the trial balances that you will see in Skills Tests and Examinations are listed with the accounts in alphabetical order. There is no need for you to do this when preparing trial balances – unless, of course, you are instructed to do so, or are given a printed accounts list already in alphabetical order with the amounts to be filled in.

TARA SMITH, TRADING AS "THE FASHION SHOP" Trial balance as at 31 December 2004		
	Dr	Cr
	£	£
Opening stock	12,500	
Purchases	105,000	
Sales		155,000
Administration expenses	6,200	
Wages	23,500	
Rent paid	750	
Telephone	500	
Interest paid	4,500	
Travel expenses	550	
Premises	100,000	
Shop fittings	20,000	
Debtors	10,500	
Bank	5,450	
Cash	50	
Capital		75,000
Drawings	7,000	
Loan from bank		50,000
Creditors		14,500
Value Added Tax		2,000
	296,500	296,500

DEBIT AND CREDIT BALANCES – GUIDELINES

Certain accounts always have a debit balance, while others always have a credit balance. You should already know these, but the lists set out below will act as a revision guide, and will also help in your understanding of trial balances.

debit balances

* cash account

* purchases account

* sales returns account (returns in)

* fixed asset accounts, eg computers, motor vehicles, machinery, etc

* expenses accounts, eg wages, telephone, rent paid, etc

* drawings account

* debtors' accounts (most businesses use a *sales ledger control account* – as mentioned earlier – the balance of which gives the total of debtors: this balance is entered in the trial balance as 'debtors')

credit balances

* sales account

* purchases returns account (returns out)

* income accounts, eg rent received, commission received, fees received, etc

* capital account

* loan account, eg loan from bank

* creditors' accounts (most businesses use a *purchases ledger control account* – as mentioned earlier – the balance of which gives the total of creditors: this balance is entered in the trial balance as 'creditors')

Note that:
* *Bank account* can be either debit or credit – it will be debit when the business has money in the bank, and credit when it is overdrawn.
* *Value Added Tax account* can be either debit or credit – it will be debit when VAT is due to the business and credit when the business owes VAT to HM Revenue & Customs.

IF THE TRIAL BALANCE DOESN'T BALANCE . . .

If the trial balance fails to balance, ie the two totals are different, there is an error (or errors):

- *either* in the addition of the trial balance
- *and/or* in the double-entry book-keeping

The procedure for finding the error(s) is as follows:

- check the addition of the trial balance

- check that the balance of each account has been correctly entered in the trial balance, and under the correct heading, ie debit or credit

- check that the balance of every account in the ledger has been included in the trial balance

- check the calculation of the balance on each account

- calculate the amount that the trial balance is wrong, and then look in the accounts for a transaction for this amount: if one is found, check that the double-entry book-keeping has been carried out correctly

- halve the amount by which the trial balance is wrong, and look for a transaction for this amount: if it is found, check the double-entry book-keeping

- if the amount by which the trial balance is wrong is divisible by nine, then the error may be a reversal of figures, eg £65 entered as £56, or £45 entered as £54

- if the trial balance is wrong by a round amount, eg £10, £100, £1,000, the error is likely to be in the calculation of the account balances

- if the error(s) is still not found, it is necessary to check the book-keeping transactions since the date of the last trial balance, by going back to the prime documents (invoices, cheques, etc) and the primary accounting records (day books and cash books)

ERRORS NOT SHOWN BY A TRIAL BALANCE

As mentioned earlier, a trial balance does not prove the complete accuracy of the accounting records. There are six types of errors that are not shown by a trial balance.

error of omission

Here a business transaction has been completely omitted from the accounting records, ie both the debit and credit entries have not been made.

reversal of entries

With this error, the debit and credit entries have been made in the accounts but on the wrong side of the two accounts concerned. For example, a cash sale has been entered wrongly as a debit to sales account, and as a credit to cash account. (This should have been entered as a debit to cash account, and a credit to sales account.)

mispost/error of commission

Here, a transaction is entered to the wrong person's account. For example, a sale of goods on credit to A T Hughes has been entered as a debit to A J Hughes' account and as a credit to sales account. Here, double-entry book-keeping has been completed but, when A J Hughes receives a statement of account, he or she will soon complain about being debited with goods not ordered or received.

error of principle

This is when a transaction has been entered in the wrong type of account. For example, the cost of fuel for vehicles has been entered as a debit to motor vehicles account, and as a credit to bank account. The error is that motor vehicles account represents fixed assets – the transaction should have been debited to the expense account for motor vehicle running expenses.

error of original entry (or transcription)

Here, the correct accounts have been used, and the correct sides: what is wrong is that the amount has been entered incorrectly in *both* accounts. This could be caused by a 'bad figure' on an invoice or a cheque, or it could be caused by a 'reversal of figures', eg an amount of £45 being entered in both accounts as £54. Note that where both debit and credit entries have been made incorrectly the trial balance will still balance; if one entry has been made incorrectly and the other is correct, then the error will be shown.

compensating error

This is where two errors cancel each other out. For example, if the balance of purchases account is calculated wrongly at £10 too much, and a similar error has occurred in calculating the balance of sales account, then the two errors will compensate each other, and the trial balance will not show them.

Correction of errors is covered fully in Chapter 12.

IMPORTANCE OF THE TRIAL BALANCE

A business will extract a trial balance on a regular basis to check the arithmetical accuracy of the book-keeping. More importantly, the trial balance is used as a basis for the production of the *final accounts* of a business. These final accounts, which are prepared once a year (often more frequently) comprise:

- profit and loss account
- balance sheet

The final accounts show the owner(s) how profitable the business has been, what the business owns, and how the business is financed. The preparation of final accounts is an important aspect of accounting and one which we shall be developing in the remainder of this book.

In the next chapter we will see how the two-column trial balance is 'extended' and the figures entered into further columns in preparation for the production of the final accounts.

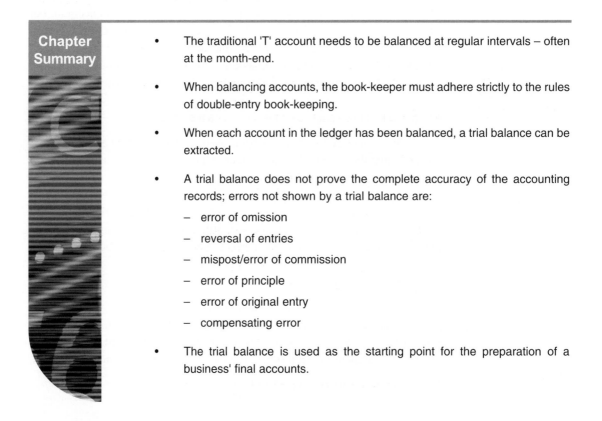

Chapter Summary

- The traditional 'T' account needs to be balanced at regular intervals – often at the month-end.

- When balancing accounts, the book-keeper must adhere strictly to the rules of double-entry book-keeping.

- When each account in the ledger has been balanced, a trial balance can be extracted.

- A trial balance does not prove the complete accuracy of the accounting records; errors not shown by a trial balance are:
    - error of omission
    - reversal of entries
    - mispost/error of commission
    - error of principle
    - error of original entry
    - compensating error

- The trial balance is used as the starting point for the preparation of a business' final accounts.

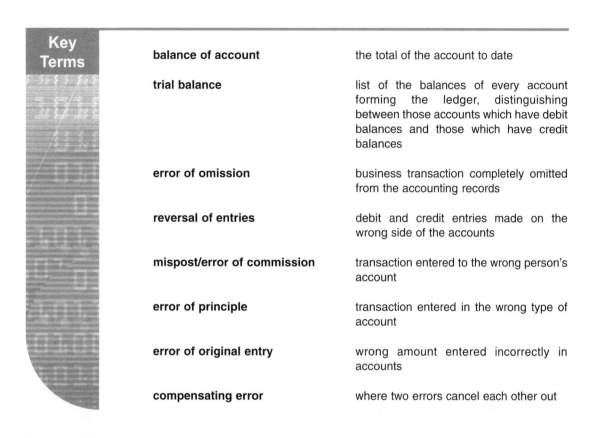

Key Terms		
	balance of account	the total of the account to date
	trial balance	list of the balances of every account forming the ledger, distinguishing between those accounts which have debit balances and those which have credit balances
	error of omission	business transaction completely omitted from the accounting records
	reversal of entries	debit and credit entries made on the wrong side of the accounts
	mispost/error of commission	transaction entered to the wrong person's account
	error of principle	transaction entered in the wrong type of account
	error of original entry	wrong amount entered incorrectly in accounts
	compensating error	where two errors cancel each other out

Student Activities

3.1   A firm's bank account is as follows:

Dr			Bank Account			Cr
2004		£	2004			£
1 Jan	Capital	1,000	9 Jan	Computer		500
19 Jan	Sales	650	12 Jan	Purchases		400
			27 Jan	Purchases		350
			29 Jan	Electricity		75

At 31 January 2004, the balance of the account is:

(a)   credit £325

(b)   debit £1,650

(c)   debit £325

(d)   credit £1,325

Answer (a) or (b) or (c) or (d)

3.2   Which one of the following accounts normally has a debit balance?

(a)   capital account

(b)   purchases account

(c)   sales account

(d)   purchases returns account

Answer (a) or (b) or (c) or (d)

3.3   Which one of the following accounts normally has a credit balance?

(a)   purchases account

(b)   premises account

(c)   capital account

(d)   wages account

Answer (a) or (b) or (c) or (d)

3.4   The following are the business transactions of Andrew Johnstone, a retailer of computer software, for the months of January and February 2004:

Transactions for January

1 Jan	Started in business with £10,000 in the bank
4 Jan	Paid rent on premises £500, by cheque
5 Jan	Bought shop fittings £1,500, by cheque
7 Jan	Bought stock of computer software £5,000, on credit from Comp Supplies Limited
11 Jan	Software sales £1,000 paid into bank
12 Jan	Software sales £1,250 paid into bank
16 Jan	Software sales £850 on credit to Rowcester College
20 Jan	Paid Comp Supplies Limited £5,000 by cheque
22 Jan	Software sales £1,450 paid into bank
25 Jan	Bought software £6,500 on credit from Comp Supplies Limited
27 Jan	Rowcester College returns software £100

Transactions for February

2 Feb	Paid rent on premises £500 by cheque
4 Feb	Software sales £1,550 paid into bank
5 Feb	Returned faulty software, £150 to Comp Supplies Limited
10 Feb	Software sales £1,300 paid into bank
12 Feb	Rowcester College pays the amount owing by cheque
15 Feb	Bought shop fittings £850 by cheque
19 Feb	Software sales £1,600 paid into bank
22 Feb	Paid Comp Supplies Limited the amount owing by cheque
24 Feb	Bought software £5,500 on credit from Comp Supplies Limited
25 Feb	Software sales £1,100 paid into bank
26 Feb	Software sales £1,050 on credit to Rowcester College

You are to:

(a)   record the January transactions in the books of account, and balance each account at 31 January 2004

(b)   draw up a trial balance at 31 January 2004

(c)   record the February transactions in the books of account, and balance each account at 29 February 2004

(d)   draw up a trial balance at 29 February 2004

Notes

*   *Andrew Johnstone is not registered for Value Added Tax*
*   *day books are not required*
*   *Andrew Johnstone's accounting system does not use control accounts*
*   *make sure that you leave plenty of space for each account – particularly sales, purchases and bank*

4 Final accounts – the extended trial balance

this chapter covers . . .

So far we have looked at the techniques of recording different types of financial transactions in the books of account. The financial accountant will use the information from the accounting system, summarised in the two-column trial balance, to produce the final accounts of the business: profit and loss account and balance sheet.

These final accounts can be produced from a more elaborate form of trial balance known as the extended trial balance (ETB). This sets out debit and credit columns for:

- the ledger balances
- adjustments to the figures
- the final accounts where the figures are used: profit and loss account and balance sheet

Later in the chapter we study the link between double-entry book-keeping and the final accounts.

PERFORMANCE CRITERIA COVERED

unit 5: MAINTAINING FINANCIAL RECORDS AND PREPARING ACCOUNTS

element 5.2

collecting and collating information for the preparation of final accounts

H   ensure that the organisation's policies, regulations, procedures and timescales relating to preparing final accounts are observed

KNOWLEDGE AND UNDERSTANDING – ACCOUNTING PRINCIPLES AND THEORY

24   the principles of double-entry accounting

27   the function and form of a trial balance and an extended trial balance

FINAL ACCOUNTS

At regular intervals the owner of a business and other interested parties need to know how the business is progressing. To meet this need, final accounts are prepared which comprise the accounting statements of:

- *profit and loss account* – showing the profitability and performance of the business during the accounting period
- *balance sheet* – showing what the business is worth (in terms of assets, liabilities, and capital) at the end of the accounting period

Note that, for businesses that buy and sell goods, profit and loss account usually incorporates a trading account (see Chapter 5, page 66). The whole account may then be entitled *trading and profit and loss account*; however it often continues to be referred to as *profit and loss account*.

In this chapter we will see how the figures for the final accounts are prepared by means of the *extended trial balance* which takes the figures from the two-column trial balance explained in the last chapter and sets them out in columns ready for the preparation of the profit and loss account and balance sheet. To illustrate this process we will look at the accounts of a sole trader boutique owner, Tara Smith.

In the next chapter we will take the extended trial balance and will use it to produce final accounts in the conventional format used by accountants. This is a very important aspect of your Unit 5 studies, and one that we shall be continuing to develop throughout most of the rest of the book.

ACCOUNTING PERIODS

There is a link between the final accounts: a profit and loss account covers a specific time period, and a balance sheet shows the state of the business on the last day of that time period. For example:

- profit and loss account **for the year ended** 31 December 2004
- balance sheet **as at** 31 December 2004

The time period covered by the profit and loss account is known as an *accounting period*. Generally, for each business, an accounting period covers the same length of time, for example the year ended 31 December 2004, year ended 31 December 2005, and so on. The last day of one accounting period is immediately followed by the first day of the next accounting period. While accounting periods can cover any length of time, the most common are:

- *monthly or quarterly* – used within a business to monitor activity and profitability in the accounting period, and the state of the business, in terms of assets and liabilities, at the end of the period

- *half-yearly* – often produced by public limited companies as information for their shareholders

- *annually* – the most common accounting period, used by virtually every business from sole traders and partnerships, through to the largest public limited companies

FINAL ACCOUNTS AND THE TRIAL BALANCE

As we have seen in earlier chapters, the book-keeping system records day-to-day financial transactions. At regular intervals a trial balance is extracted to prove the arithmetical accuracy of the book-keeping. It is the trial balance that provides the starting point in the preparation of final accounts. There are two trial balance formats:

- the two-column trial balance (shown opposite)

- the trial balance *extended* into a number of columns (see page 55)

Note that the profit and loss account is an 'account' in terms of double-entry book-keeping. This means that an amount recorded in this account must be recorded elsewhere in the book-keeping system, eg a debit to profit and loss is recorded as a credit to another account, in order to complete double-entry. By contrast, the balance sheet is not an account, but is a statement of account balances remaining after the profit and loss account has been prepared.

To understand the preparation of the extended trial balance you should now read the Tara Smith Case Study which follows.

TARA SMITH: THE EXTENDED TRIAL BALANCE

situation

Tara Smith runs a designer fashion shop in town. Her book-keeper has just extracted the year end trial balance shown below. You will see that the trial balance includes the stock value at the *start* of the year, while the end-of-year stock valuation is noted *after* the trial balance. For the purposes of financial accounting, the stock of goods for resale is valued by the business (and may be verified by the auditor) at the end of each financial year, and the valuation is subsequently entered into the book-keeping system (see page 57).

We will go through the process of preparing the final accounts using an extended trial balance (ETB) – this is the next stage on from the trial balance shown below and is often presented in a spreadsheet format. We will go through this process before explaining adjustments for items such as accruals, prepayments, depreciation of fixed assets, bad debts written off, and provision for doubtful debts (each of which will be dealt with in Chapters 6 to 8).

TARA SMITH, TRADING AS "THE FASHION SHOP"
Trial balance as at 31 December 2004

	Dr £	Cr £
Opening stock	12,500	
Purchases	105,000	
Sales		155,000
Administration expenses	6,200	
Wages	23,500	
Rent paid	750	
Telephone	500	
Interest paid	4,500	
Travel expenses	550	
Premises	100,000	
Shop fittings	20,000	
Debtors	10,500	
Bank	5,450	
Cash	50	
Capital		75,000
Drawings	7,000	
Loan from bank		50,000
Creditors		14,500
Value Added Tax		2,000
	296,500	296,500

Note: closing stock was valued at £10,500

The layout on page 55 shows how an extended trial balance uses columns and rows to prepare the final accounts of Tara Smith. The steps to complete the extended trial balance are as follows:

step 1 Enter the trial balance details into the account name and ledger balances columns. Total the debit and credit columns of ledger balances to show that the trial balance proves the arithmetical accuracy of the book-keeping. Note that the blank lines after premises and shop fittings will be used for depreciation amounts – dealt with in Chapter 7.

step 2 Transfer to the profit and loss columns the rows for
* opening stock at the start of the year
* purchases made by the business
* sales made by the business (together with any small amounts of income)

- overheads (revenue expenditure) of the business, such as administration expenses, wages, rent paid, interest paid, travel expenses

Ensure that debit balances from the trial balance rows are entered in the debit column of profit and loss account; credit balances are entered in the credit column.

step 3

Transfer to the balance sheet columns the remaining rows from the trial balance (keeping debit and credit figures in the correct columns). These figures represent:

- assets (amounts owned by the business) such as premises, shop fittings, debtors, bank, cash

- liabilities (amounts owed by the business) such as bank overdraft, creditors, loans, Value Added Tax due to HM Revenue & Customs

- capital (the amount of the owner's finance in the business)

- drawings (the amount withdrawn from the business by the owner during the year)

step 4

Deal with adjustments – in this example, the only adjustment is for the valuation of closing stock (at 31 December 2004). In the adjustments columns the amount of closing stock is credited to the profit and loss account and debited to the balance sheet (see page 57 for the book-keeping entries for closing stock). Transfer the adjustment for closing stock to:

- profit and loss – credit column
- balance sheet – debit column

Now total the debit and credit adjustment columns; note that the totals are the same, ie they balance. We shall be using the other adjustment items (eg accruals and prepayments) in the next few chapters.

In the profit and loss columns, total the money amounts and then, just like balancing an account, enter the amount required to make both debit and credit sides equal: here it is £12,000. If the amount is entered on the debit side, it represents the net profit of the business for the accounting period; if on the credit side, it is a loss. For Tara Smith, it is a profit of £12,000 for the financial year.

step 5

Enter the net profit or loss in the balance sheet columns, but on the opposite side to that in profit and loss. For example, with Tara Smith's business, the amount of the net profit row is £12,000, which is *debited* in the profit and loss column and *credited* in the balance sheet column.

Now total the debit and credit balance sheet columns. They balance with the same total – here £153,500 – which proves that the balance sheet balances.

points to note about the extended trial balance

Each account balance from the trial balance is entered into the final accounts once only – either to profit and loss account (income and expenses), or to balance sheet (assets, liabilities, capital and drawings). The additional items of closing stock and net profit or loss are entered into both final accounts – this ensures that the double-entry book-keeping rules of one debit and one credit entry for each transaction are maintained.

There are blank rows below the items of premises and shop fittings. These are intentionally left blank and will eventually show depreciation amounts (see Chapter 7).

EXTENDED TRIAL BALANCE   TARA SMITH TRADING AS "THE FASHION SHOP"   31 DECEMBER 2004

Account name	Ledger balances		Adjustments		Profit and loss		Balance sheet	
	Dr £	Cr £	Dr £	Cr £	Dr £	Cr £	Dr £	Cr £
Opening stock	12,500				12,500			
Purchases	105,000				105,000			
Sales		155,000				155,000		
Administration expenses	6,200				6,200			
Wages	23,500				23,500			
Rent paid	750				750			
Telephone	500				500			
Interest paid	4,500				4,500			
Travel expenses	550				550			
Premises	100,000						100,000	
Shop fittings	20,000						20,000	
Debtors	10,500						10,500	
Bank	5,450						5,450	
Cash	50						50	
Capital		75,000						75,000
Drawings	7,000						7,000	
Loan from bank		50,000						50,000
Creditors		14,500						14,500
Value Added Tax		2,000						2,000
Closing stock: Profit and loss				10,500		10,500		
Closing stock: Balance sheet			10,500				10,500	
Accruals								
Prepayments								
Depreciation								
Bad debts								
Provision for doubtful debts:adjustment								
Net profit/loss					12,000			12,000
	296,500	296,500	10,500	10,500	165,500	165,500	153,500	153,500

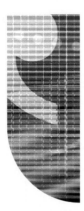

Revenue expenditure (the payment of expenses and overheads) is shown in the profit and loss account, while *capital expenditure* (the cost of fixed assets, such as premises, vehicles and equipment) is shown in the balance sheet. Note that if, for example, the cost of buying a new vehicle was wrongly recorded as an overhead in profit and loss account, then

- net profit would be understated (or even a net loss sustained)
- the balance sheet would not show the value of a fixed asset owned by the business

This means that both accounting statements would fail to show the correct state of the business' finances. Thus it is important to show revenue expenditure in the profit and loss account, and capital expenditure in the balance sheet – we will look in more detail at these two types of expenditure in Chapter 9.

EXTENDED TRIAL BALANCE – A 'PRO-FORMA'

The extended trial balance gives an understanding of the principles of final accounts by showing

- the profit (or loss) made by the business during the accounting period
- the assets, liabilities and capital of the business at the end of the accounting period

The extended trial balance format is often used by accountancy firms as a first step towards preparing year-end accounts for their clients. When the adjustments have been completed and the accounts have been finalised, it provides a posting sheet for making transfers in the main ledger (see the book-keeping entries in the section which follows).

To help with your practice of extended trial balances, a set layout or pro-forma is included in the Appendix (page 341). This may be photocopied (it is advisable to enlarge it up to A4 size); alternatively, the layout can be downloaded from the website www.osbornebooks.co.uk

Note that the layout used for the extended trial balance includes space for a number of other adjustments (eg accruals and prepayments) – these will be covered in the later chapters.

DOUBLE-ENTRY BOOK-KEEPING AND THE FINAL ACCOUNTS

We have already noted that the profit and loss account (which often incorporates a trading account) forms part of the double-entry book-keeping system. Therefore, each amount recorded in this account must have an opposite entry in the main (or nominal) ledger. In preparing the profit and loss account we are, in effect, emptying each account that has been storing up a record of transactions during the course of the financial year and transferring it to profit and loss account.

purchases, sales and stock

In the accounts of Tara Smith the balance of purchases account will be transferred to profit and loss account as follows *(debit* profit and loss account; *credit* purchases account):

Dr		**Purchases Account**	Cr
2004	£	2004	£
31 Dec Balance b/d (ie total for year)	105,000	31 Dec Profit and loss account	105,000

The account now has a nil balance and is ready to receive the transactions for next year.

The balances of sales account (and also, where used, sales returns and purchases returns accounts) will be cleared to nil in a similar way and the amounts transferred to profit and loss account, as debits or credits as appropriate.

Stock account, however, is dealt with differently. Stock is valued for financial accounting purposes at the end of each year (it is also likely to be valued more regularly in order to provide management information). Only the annual stock valuation is recorded on stock account, and the account is not used at any other time. After the book-keeper has extracted the trial balance, but *before* preparation of the profit and loss account, the stock account appears as follows:

Dr		**Stock Account**	Cr
2004	£	2004	£
31 Dec Balance b/d	12,500		

This balance, which is the opening stock valuation for the year, is transferred to the profit and loss account to leave a nil balance, as follows *(debit* profit and loss account; *credit* stock account):

Dr		**Stock Account**	Cr
2004	£	2004	£
31 Dec Balance b/d	12,500	31 Dec Profit and loss account	12,500

The *closing* stock valuation for the year – for Tara Smith it is £10,500 – is now recorded on the account as an asset *(debit* stock account; *credit* profit and loss account):

Dr			Stock Account		Cr
2004		£	2004		£
31 Dec	Balance b/d	12,500	31 Dec	Profit and loss account	12,500
31 Dec	Profit & loss account	10,500	31 Dec	Balance c/d	10,500
2005					
1 Jan	Balance b/d	10,500			

The closing stock figure is shown on the balance sheet as a current asset, and will be the opening stock in next year's profit and loss account. In the extended trial balance the closing stock figure is normally put through the adjustments columns; however, some trial balances in Skills Tests and Examinations may already incorporate the closing stock adjustments – see Student Activity 4.6 on page 63 for an example of this.

overheads

The overheads or expenses of running the business are transferred from the double-entry accounts to the profit and loss account. For example, the wages account of Tara Smith has been storing up information during the year and, at the end of the year, the total is transferred to profit and loss account *(debit* profit and loss account; *credit* wages account):

Dr			Wages Account		Cr
2004		£	2004		£
31 Dec	Balance b/d (ie total for year)	23,500	31 Dec	Profit and loss account	23,500

The wages account now has a nil balance and is ready to receive transactions for 2005, the next financial year.

net profit

After the profit and loss account has been completed, the amount of net profit (or net loss) is transferred to the owner's capital account. The book-keeping entries are:

- net profit
    - *debit* profit and loss account
    - *credit* capital account

- net loss
    - *debit* capital account
    - *credit* profit and loss account

A net profit increases the owner's stake in the business by adding to capital account, while a net loss decreases the owner's stake.

At the same time the account for drawings, which has been storing up the amount of drawings during the year is also transferred to capital account:

- *debit* capital account
- *credit* drawings account

Thus the total of drawings for the year is debited to capital account.

When these transactions are completed, the capital account for Tara Smith appears as:

Dr			**Capital Account**		Cr
2004		£	2004		£
31 Dec	Drawings for year	7,000	31 Dec	Balance b/d	75,000
31 Dec	Balance c/d	80,000	31 Dec	Profit and loss account (net profit for year)	12,000
		87,000			87,000
2005			2005		
			1 Jan	Balance b/d	80,000

Note: Although the balance of capital account at the end of the year, £80,000, does not appear on the extended trial balance, the constituent figures are shown, ie capital £75,000, net profit £12,000, drawings £7,000.

balance sheet

Unlike profit and loss account, the balance sheet is not part of the double-entry accounts. The balance sheet is made up of those accounts which remain with balances at the end of the financial year, after the profit and loss account transfers have been made. Thus it consists of asset and liability accounts, not forgetting the asset of closing stock, together with the owner's capital and drawings.

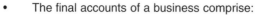

Chapter Summary

- The final accounts of a business comprise:
  - profit and loss account (which often incorporates a trading account)
  - balance sheet

- The extended trial balance method of preparing final accounts starts with the trial balance and then transfers each account balance to one of the final accounts.

- Each account balance from the trial balance is entered into the final accounts once only; the additional items of closing stock and net profit or loss are entered into both final accounts – this ensures that the double-entry rules of one debit and one credit entry for each transaction are maintained.

- The profit and loss account forms part of the double-entry system; amounts entered must have the opposite entry recorded in the appropriate general (or nominal) ledger account.

- The balance sheet is not part of the double-entry system; it lists the balances of accounts for assets, liabilities and capital at a particular date.

- The extended trial balance gives an understanding of the principles of final accounts. It is often used by accountancy firms as a first step towards preparing year-end accounts for their clients.

Key Terms

final accounts	accounting statements, comprising the profit and loss account and balance sheet, produced at least once a year, which give information to the owner(s) and other interested parties on how the business is progressing
profit and loss account	shows the net profit (or net loss) of the business for the accounting period
trading account	used by businesses that buy and sell goods; a part of profit and loss account
balance sheet	shows the assets, liabilities and capital of the business at the end of the accounting period
extended trial balance	a spreadsheet format used to produce the final accounts

Student Activities

Extended trial balance format: a blank photocopiable extended trial balance is included in the Appendix (page 341)– it is advisable to enlarge it up to full A4 size. Alternatively you can set up a computer spreadsheet – but remember to allow for all the rows shown on the pro-forma – they will be needed in later chapters.

4.1   Which one of the following does not appear in the profit and loss account?

(a)   salaries

(b)   vehicles

(c)   fuel for vehicles

(d)   net profit

Answer (a) or (b) or (c) or (d)

4.2   Net profit is:

(a)   assets minus liabilities

(b)   debtors minus creditors

(c)   closing bank balance minus opening bank balance

(d)   income minus expenses

Answer (a) or (b) or (c) or (d)

4.3   You are to fill in the missing figures for the following businesses:

	Income	Expenses	Net profit or loss*	Assets	Liabilities	Capital
	£	£	£	£	£	£
Business A	100,000	60,000	....	250,000	150,000	....
Business B	80,000	....	10,000	200,000	....	100,000
Business C	....	50,000	20,000	....	40,000	50,000
Business D	60,000	....	(15,000)	130,000	....	70,000
Business E	90,000	100,000	....	....	60,000	40,000

* Note: net loss is indicated by brackets

4.4 Complete the table below for each item (a) to (g) indicating with a tick:
- whether the item would normally appear in the debit or credit column of the trial balance
- in which final account the item would appear at the end of the accounting period and whether as a debit or credit in the extended trial balance

	TRIAL BALANCE		FINAL ACCOUNTS			
			PROFIT & LOSS		BALANCE SHEET	
	Debit	Credit	Debit	Credit	Debit	Credit
(a) Salaries						
(b) Purchases						
(c) Debtors						
(d) Sales returns						
(e) Discount received						
(f) Motor vehicle						
(g) Capital						

4.5 The following trial balance has been extracted by Nick Johnson on 31 December 2004:

	Dr £	Cr £
Opening stock	25,000	
Purchases	210,000	
Sales		310,000
Administration expenses	12,400	
Wages	41,000	
Rent paid	7,500	
Telephone	1,000	
Interest paid	9,000	
Travel expenses	1,100	
Premises	200,000	
Machinery	40,000	
Debtors	31,000	
Bank	900	
Cash	100	
Capital		150,000
Drawings	14,000	
Loan from bank		100,000
Creditors		29,000
Value Added Tax		4,000
	593,000	593,000

Note: closing stock was valued at £21,000

You are to prepare the final accounts of Nick Johnson for the year ended 31 December 2004, using the extended trial balance method.

Note: please retain the extended trial balance as it will be used in the next chapter as the starting point for a further Student Activity.

4.6 The following trial balance has been extracted by the book-keeper of Alan Harris at 30 June 2004:

	Dr £	Cr £
Opening stock	13,250	
Capital		70,000
Premises	65,000	
Motor vehicle	5,250	
Purchases	55,000	
Sales		85,500
Administration expenses	850	
Wages	9,220	
Rent paid	1,200	
Telephone	680	
Interest paid	120	
Travel expenses	330	
Debtors	1,350	
Creditors		6,400
Value Added Tax		1,150
Bank	2,100	
Cash	600	
Drawings	8,100	
Closing stock – trading and profit and loss account		18,100
Closing stock – balance sheet	18,100	
	181,150	181,150

Tutorial note: this trial balance already incorporates the closing stock adjustments

You are to prepare the final accounts of Alan Harris for the year ended 30 June 2004, using the extended trial balance method.

Note: please retain the extended trial balance as it will be used in the next chapter as the starting point for a further Student Activity.

5 Sole trader final accounts

this chapter covers . . .

In the previous chapter we looked at how the extended trial balance (ETB) format is a first step towards preparing year-end final accounts. In this chapter we take the ETB further to develop final accounts in the conventional format – or proper form – used by accountants.

Maintaining Financial Records and Preparing Accounts focuses on preparing the final accounts of sole traders and partnerships. In this chapter we look at sole traders as a type of business organisation and see the proper form in which the final accounts of a sole trader are presented. Partnership final accounts are considered later in the book (Chapters 14 and 15).

PERFORMANCE CRITERIA COVERED

unit 5: MAINTAINING FINANCIAL RECORDS AND PREPARING ACCOUNTS

element 5.3

preparing the final accounts of sole traders and partnerships

A   prepare final accounts of sole traders in proper form, from the trial balance

C   observe the organisation's policies, regulations, procedures and timescales in relation to preparing final accounts of sole traders and partnerships

D   identify and resolve or refer to the appropriate person discrepancies, unusual features or queries

SOLE TRADERS

Sole traders are people in business on their own: they run shops, factories, farms, garages, local franchises, etc. The businesses are generally small because the owner usually has a limited amount of capital. Profits are often small and, after the owner has taken out drawings, are usually ploughed back into the business.

People set up as sole traders for various reasons:

- the owner has independence and can run the business, often without the need to consult others
- in a small business with few, if any, employees, personal service and supervision by the owner are available at all times
- the business is easy to establish legally – either using the owner's name, or a trading name such as 'The Fashion Shop' or 'Wyvern Plumbers'

The disadvantages of a sole-trader business are:

- the owner has unlimited liability for the debts of the business – this means that if the sole trader should become insolvent, the owner's personal assets may be used to pay creditors
- expansion is limited because it can only be achieved by the owner ploughing back profits, or by borrowing from a lender such as a bank
- the owner usually has to work long hours and it may be difficult to find time to take holidays; if the owner should become ill the work of the business will either slow down or stop altogether

FINAL ACCOUNTS AND THE TRIAL BALANCE

final accounts

The final accounts of a sole trader comprise:

- trading and profit and loss account
- balance sheet

These final accounts can be produced more often than once a year in order to give information to the sole trader on how the business is progressing. However, it is customary to produce annual accounts for the benefit of the Inland Revenue, bank manager and other interested parties. In this way the profit and loss account covers an accounting period of a financial year (which can end at any date – it doesn't have to be the calendar year), and the balance sheet shows the state of the business at the end of the accounting period.

trial balance

The starting point for preparing final accounts is the trial balance prepared by the book-keeper: all the figures recorded on the trial balance are used in the final accounts. The book-keeper's two-column trial balance is often developed into an extended trial balance – as we saw in the last chapter.

The extended trial balance gives an understanding of the principles of final accounts and is often used by accountancy firms as a first step towards preparing year end accounts for their clients. The way in which accountants present final accounts is often described as being in the conventional format, or in proper form.

Shortly we will use the extended trial balance of Tara Smith (seen in the previous chapter on page 55) in a Case Study to prepare her sole trader final accounts in proper form, using the conventional format.

TRADING AND PROFIT AND LOSS ACCOUNT

income   minus   **expenses**   equals   **net profit (or loss)**

The trading and profit and loss account shows the income a business has received over a given period for goods sold or services provided (together with any small amounts of other income, eg rent received). It also sets out the expenses incurred – the cost of the product, and the overheads (eg wages, administration expenses, rent, and so on). The difference between income and expenses is the *net profit* of the business. If expenses are greater than income, then a loss has been made. The net profit (or loss) belongs to the owner of the business. For a business that trades in goods, a figure for *gross profit* shows the profit made before overheads are deducted.

Note that where an extended trial balance is being used, profit can be checked against the figure shown in the ETB's profit and loss account columns.

BALANCE SHEET

assets   minus   **liabilities**   equals   **capital**

The balance sheet gives a 'snapshot' of the business at a particular date – the end of the financial year. A typical business balance sheet will show:

assets	What the business owns:
	– fixed assets, eg premises, vehicles, computers
	– current assets, eg closing stock of goods for resale, debtors, bank and cash balances
liabilities	What the business owes:
	– current liabilities, eg creditors, overdrafts, VAT due
	– long-term liabilities, eg long-term bank loans
net assets	The total of fixed and current assets, less current and long-term liabilities. The net assets are financed by the owner of the business, in the form of capital. Net assets therefore equals the total of the 'financed by' section – the balance sheet 'balances'.
capital	Where the money to finance the business has come from, eg the owner's investment, business profits.

Case Study

TARA SMITH:
FROM ETB TO FINAL ACCOUNTS IN PROPER FORM

situation

Please refer to the extended trial balance of Tara Smith's business on page 55. We will use this ETB to prepare Tara Smith's sole trader final accounts in proper form, using the conventional format.

solution

The ETB does not present the final accounts in the proper form, as used by accountants. While accountancy firms often use the ETB as a first step, the figures have to be taken from the profit and loss account columns of the ETB and presented in vertical format – running down the page.

Tara Smith's profit and loss account is shown in proper form on page 69. Study it carefully and see how the figures can be identified on the ETB shown on page 55. Note that the profit and loss account incorporates a trading account – included because Tara's business trades in goods – which gives a figure for *gross profit*, which is the profit made before overheads are deducted.

Tara Smith's balance sheet is shown in proper form on page 71. Study it carefully and see how the figures can be identified on the ETB shown on page 55.

Notes to explain various aspects of Tara's profit and loss account and balance sheet are given on pages 68 and 70.

Trading account shows gross profit for the accounting period. **Profit and loss account** shows net profit for the accounting period. Note that 'profit and loss account' is often used as a general heading which includes both of these financial statements.

The amounts for **sales** and **purchases** include only items in which the business trades – eg a clothes shop buying clothes from the manufacturer and selling to the public. Note that items bought for use in the business, such as a new till for the shop, are not included with purchases but are shown as assets on the balance sheet.

Cost of sales represents the cost to the business of the goods which have been sold in this financial year. Cost of sales is:

	opening stock	(stock bought previously)
plus	purchases	(purchased during the year)
minus	closing stock	(stock left unsold at the end of the year)
equals	cost of sales	(cost of what has actually been sold)

Gross profit is calculated as:

sales – cost of sales = gross profit

If cost of sales is greater than sales, the business has made a gross loss.

Overheads, or expenses, are the running costs of the business – known as *revenue expenditure.* The categories of overheads or expenses used vary according to the needs of each business.

Net profit is calculated as:

gross profit – overheads = net profit

If overheads are more than gross profit, the business has made a net loss.

The net profit is the amount the business earned for the owner during the year, and is subject to taxation. The owner can draw some or all of the net profit for personal use in the form of drawings. Part of the profit might well be left in the business in order to help build up the business for the future.

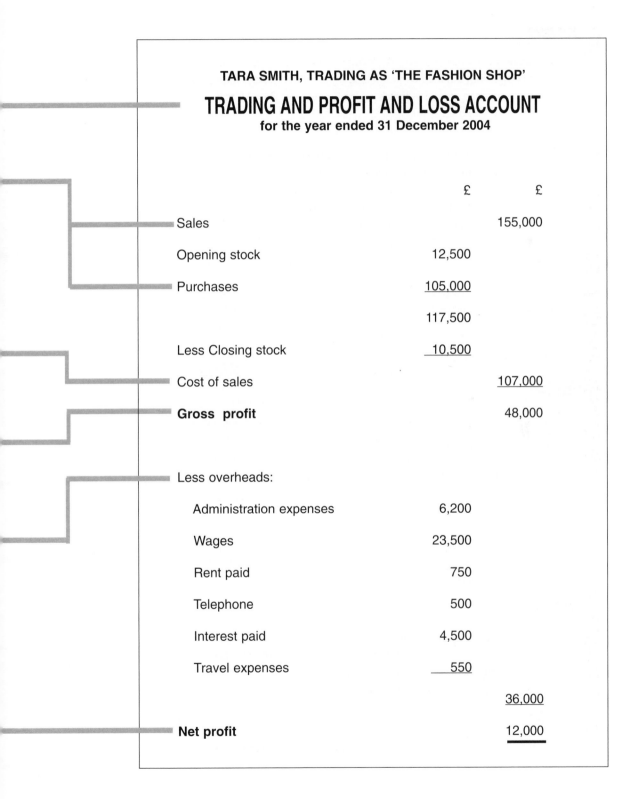

TARA SMITH, TRADING AS 'THE FASHION SHOP'

TRADING AND PROFIT AND LOSS ACCOUNT
for the year ended 31 December 2004

	£	£
Sales		155,000
Opening stock	12,500	
Purchases	105,000	
	117,500	
Less Closing stock	10,500	
Cost of sales		107,000
Gross profit		48,000
Less overheads:		
Administration expenses	6,200	
Wages	23,500	
Rent paid	750	
Telephone	500	
Interest paid	4,500	
Travel expenses	550	
		36,000
Net profit		12,000

Fixed assets comprise the long-term items owned by a business which are not bought with the intention of selling them off in the near future, eg premises, machinery, motor vehicles, office equipment, shop fittings, etc.

Current assets comprise short-term assets which change regularly, eg stock of goods for resale, debtors, bank balances and cash. These items will alter as the business trades, eg stock will be sold, or more will be bought; debtors will make payment to the business, or sales on credit will be made; the cash and bank balances will alter with the flow of money paid into the bank account, or as withdrawals are made.

Current liabilities are due for repayment within twelve months of the date of the balance sheet, eg creditors, and bank overdraft (which is usually repayable on demand, unlike a bank loan which is negotiated for a particular time period).

Working capital is the excess of current assets over current liabilities, ie current assets minus current liabilities = working capital. Without adequate working capital, a business will find it difficult to continue to operate. Working capital is also often referred to as *net current assets*.

Long-term liabilities are where repayment is due in more than one year from the date of the balance sheet; they are often described by terms such as 'bank loan,' 'long-term loan,' or 'mortgage.'

Net assets is the total of fixed and current assets, less current and long-term liabilities. The net assets are financed by the owner of the business, in the form of capital. Net assets therefore equals the total of the 'financed by' section – the balance sheet 'balances'.

Capital is the owner's investment, and is a liability of a business, ie it is what the business owes the owner.

TARA SMITH, TRADING AS 'THE FASHION SHOP'

BALANCE SHEET
as at 31 December 2004

	£	£	£
Fixed assets			
Premises			100,000
Shop fittings			20,000
			120,000
Current assets			
Stock (closing)		10,500	
Debtors		10,500	
Bank		5,450	
Cash		50	
		26,500	
Less Current liabilities			
Creditors	14,500		
Value Added Tax	2,000		
		16,500	
Working capital (or **Net current assets**)			10,000
			130,000
Less Long-term liabilities			
Loan from bank			50,000
NET ASSETS			80,000
FINANCED BY			
Capital			
Opening capital			75,000
Add net profit			12,000
			87,000
Less drawings			7,000
Closing capital			80,000

PREPARATION OF FINAL ACCOUNTS FROM A TRIAL BALANCE

The trial balance contains the basic figures necessary to prepare the final accounts but, as we saw in the previous chapter (pages 56-59), the figures are transferred from the double-entry accounts of the business. Nevertheless, the trial balance is a suitable summary from which to prepare the final accounts. The information needed for the preparation of each of the final accounts needs to be picked out from the trial balance in the following way:

- go through the trial balance and write against the items the final account in which each appears

- 'tick' each figure as it is used – each item from the trial balance appears in the final accounts once only

- the closing stock figure is sometimes listed in the trial balance, but is more usually shown as a note; it appears twice in the final accounts – in the trading account, and in the balance sheet (as a current asset)

If this routine is followed with the trial balance of Tara Smith, it appears as follows . . .

Trial balance of Tara Smith as at 31 December 2004	Dr £	Cr £		
Opening stock	12,500		T	✔
Purchases	105,000		T	✔
Sales		155,000	T	✔
Administration expenses	6,200		P & L (*expense*)	✔
Wages	23,500		P & L (*expense*)	✔
Rent paid	750		P & L (*expense*)	✔
Telephone	500		P & L (*expense*)	✔
Interest paid	4,500		P & L (*expense*)	✔
Travel expenses	550		P & L (*expense*)	✔
Premises	100,000		BS (*fixed asset*)	✔
Shop fittings	20,000		BS (*fixed asset*)	✔
Debtors	10,500		BS (*current asset*)	✔
Bank	5,450		BS (*current asset*)	✔
Cash	50		BS (*current asset*)	✔
Capital		75,000	BS (*capital*)	✔
Drawings	7,000		BS (*capital*)	✔
Loan from bank		50,000	BS (*long-term liability*)	✔
Creditors		14,500	BS (*current liability*)	✔
Value Added Tax		2,000	BS (*current liability*)	✔
	296,500	296,500		
Note: closing stock was valued at £10,500			T	✔
			BS (*current asset*)	✔

Note: T = trading account; P & L = profit and loss account; BS = balance sheet

In the trial balance illustrated here, items are grouped together – for example, all the profit and loss account overheads and expenses are listed together. This has been done to help you at these early stages in the preparation of final accounts.

However, this grouping into categories will not always be the case. In particular, in Skills Tests and Examinations, you will often find that the items listed in the trial balance appear in alphabetical order. This does have the effect of, for example, putting administration expenses (a profit and loss account overhead) next to bank (which appears in the balance sheet). It is time well spent to go through the trial balance carefully and to indicate where each item appears in the final accounts.

FINAL ACCOUNTS: POINTS TO NOTE

trading account and gross profit

The final accounts that we have prepared in conventional format in this chapter include a trading account. This shows the gross profit, which is the profit of the business before overheads are deducted. However, the extended trial balance format that we have used does not easily show gross profit. Both formats show the net profit of the business.

Note that the trading account, whilst an account in its own right, is often referred to under the general heading of profit and loss account.

balance sheet assets and the order of liquidity

In the balance sheet it is customary to list the assets – fixed assets and current assets – in an 'increasing order of liquidity'. In accounting, liquidity means nearness to cash, so the most permanent assets – ie those that are furthest away from cash – are listed first. Thus premises, which would take time to turn into cash, heads the list, with other fixed assets – such as shop fittings, machinery and vehicles – following. For current assets, the usual order is to start with stock, then debtors, bank (if not overdrawn), and cash. In this way, the assets are listed from the most fixed (usually premises) to the most liquid (cash itself).

The reason for this order is historical – nineteenth-century business owners wanted to impress upon readers of their accounts the solid assets that they owned. The top line of the balance sheet was the first to be read and that showed the value of their premises. The following lines listed their other assets. This traditional approach lives on into twenty-first century balance sheets.

adjustments to final accounts

Whilst the starting point for the preparation of final accounts is the book-keeper's two-column trial balance, if we used only the trial balance figures (which record the financial transactions that have taken place) the resultant final accounts would show an inaccurate picture of the state of the business. Adjustments are made with the aim of improving the accuracy of the final accounts in showing the profit, and the assets and liabilities of the business.

The six main adjustments to final accounts are for:

1 closing stock (already covered in this and the previous chapter)

2 accruals

3 prepayments

4 depreciation of fixed assets

5 bad debts written off

6 provision for doubtful debts

These adjustments (except for closing stock) will be covered fully in the next three chapters.

SOLE TRADER FINAL ACCOUNTS: EXAMPLE LAYOUT

An example layout for the final accounts of a sole trader is included in the Appendix (pages 338 and 339), and can also be downloaded from the website www.osbornebooks.co.uk. This format shows:

– the layout for a trading and profit and loss account

– the layout for a balance sheet

Note that when used for partnership final accounts (see Chapter 14), the layout will need to be adjusted to take note of the appropriation of profits and of the partners' capital and current accounts.

FURTHER ITEMS IN FINAL ACCOUNTS

There are a number of further book-keeping items that have to be incorporated into the trading and profit and loss account. These items include:

• carriage in

• carriage out

• sales returns

• purchases returns

- discount received
- discount allowed

carriage in

This is the expense to a buyer of the carriage (transport) costs. For example, if an item is purchased by mail order, the buyer usually has to pay the additional cost of delivery.

In the trading account, the cost of carriage in is added to the cost of purchases. The reason for doing this is so that all purchases are at a 'delivered to your door' price.

carriage out

This is where the seller pays the expense of the carriage charge. For example, an item is sold to the customer and described as 'post free'.

In the profit and loss account, the cost of carriage out incurred on sales is shown as an expense of the business.

sales returns

Sales returns (or *returns in*) is where a debtor returns goods to the business. In final accounts, the amount of sales returns is deducted from the figure for sales in trading account.

purchases returns

Purchases returns (or *returns out*) is where a business returns goods to a creditor.

In final accounts, the amount of purchases returns is deducted from the figure for purchases in trading account.

discount received

Discount received is an allowance offered by creditors on purchases invoice amounts for quick settlement, eg 2% cash discount for settlement within seven days.

In final accounts, the amount of discount received is shown in profit and loss account as income received.

discount allowed

This is an allowance offered to debtors on sales invoice amounts for quick settlement.

In final accounts, the amount of discount allowed is shown in profit and loss account as an expense.

NATASHA MORGAN:
TRADING AND PROFIT AND LOSS ACCOUNT –
FURTHER ITEMS

situation

An extract from the trial balance of Natasha Morgan, sole trader, is as follows:

Trial balance (extract) as at 30 June 2004

	Dr	Cr
	£	£
Opening stock	12,350	
Sales		250,000
Purchases	156,000	
Sales returns	5,400	
Purchases returns		7,200
Carriage in	1,450	
Carriage out	3,250	
Discount received		2,500
Discount allowed	3,700	
Other expenses	78,550	

Note: closing stock was valued at £16,300

Natasha asks for your help in the preparation of the trading and profit and loss account in proper form, using the conventional format.

solution

There are a number of further items to be incorporated into the layout of the trading and profit and loss account. In particular, the calculation of cost of sales is made in the following way:

opening stock

+   purchases

+   carriage in

–   purchases returns

–   closing stock

=   cost of sales

The trading and profit and loss account for Natasha Morgan's business is shown on the next page. Note the use of three money columns.

NATASHA MORGAN, SOLE TRADER
TRADING AND PROFIT AND LOSS ACCOUNT
for the year ended 30 June 2004

	£	£	£
Sales			250,000
Less Sales returns			5,400
Net sales			244,600
Opening stock		12,350	
Purchases	156,000		
Add Carriage in	1,450		
	157,450		
Less Purchases returns	7,200		
Net purchases		150,250	
		162,600	
Less Closing stock		16,300	
Cost of sales			146,300
Gross profit			98,300
Add income: Discount received			2,500
			100,800
Less overheads:			
Discount allowed		3,700	
Other expenses		78,550	
Carriage out		3,250	
			85,500
Net profit			15,300

SERVICE SECTOR BUSINESSES

The final accounts of a service sector business – such as a secretarial agency, solicitor, estate agent, doctor – do not normally include a trading account. This is because the business, instead of trading in goods, supplies services. Thus the final accounts consist of:

- profit and loss account
- balance sheet

The profit and loss account, instead of starting with gross profit from the trading account section, commences with the income from the business activity – such as 'fees', 'income from clients', 'charges', 'work done'. Other items of income – such as discount received – are added, and the overheads are then listed and deducted to give the net profit, or net loss, for the accounting period. An example of a service sector profit and loss account is shown below:

JEMMA SMITH, TRADING AS 'WYVERN SECRETARIAL AGENCY'

PROFIT AND LOSS ACCOUNT

for the year ended 31 December 2004

	£	£
Income from clients		110,000
Less overheads:		
Salaries	64,000	
Heating and Lighting	2.000	
Telephone	2.000	
Rent and Rates	6,000	
Sundry Expenses	3,000	
		77,000
Net profit		33,000

The balance sheet layout of a service sector business is identical to that seen earlier (page 71); the only difference is that there is unlikely to be much, if any, stock in the current assets section.

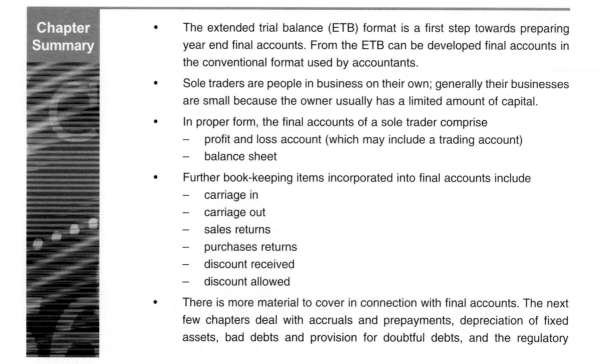

Chapter Summary

- The extended trial balance (ETB) format is a first step towards preparing year end final accounts. From the ETB can be developed final accounts in the conventional format used by accountants.

- Sole traders are people in business on their own; generally their businesses are small because the owner usually has a limited amount of capital.

- In proper form, the final accounts of a sole trader comprise
    - profit and loss account (which may include a trading account)
    - balance sheet

- Further book-keeping items incorporated into final accounts include
    - carriage in
    - carriage out
    - sales returns
    - purchases returns
    - discount received
    - discount allowed

- There is more material to cover in connection with final accounts. The next few chapters deal with accruals and prepayments, depreciation of fixed assets, bad debts and provision for doubtful debts, and the regulatory framework of accounting. Later in the book we will study the preparation of final accounts from incomplete records (Chapter 13), and partnership final accounts (Chapter 14).

Key Terms		
	conventional format	the proper form of final accounts used by accountants
	sole trader	a person who is in business on his/her own
	service sector business	a business which supplies services, eg secretarial agency, solicitor, estate agent
	gross profit	sales minus cost of sales, ie the profit made before overheads are deducted
	net profit	gross profit minus overheads, ie the profit which belongs to the owner of the business
	assets	items owned by the business, split between fixed assets and current assets
	liabilities	items owed by the business, split between current liabilities and long-term liabilities
	capital	the owner's investment in the business

Student Activities

Conventional format: Example layouts of the trading and profit and loss account, and balance sheet in conventional format – or proper form – are included in the Appendix (pages 338 and 339). They may be photocopied for guidance with Student Activities; alternatively, a computer spreadsheet layout can be set up.

5.1 *Please refer back to the extended trial balance of Nick Johnson prepared in Student Activity 4.5.*

You are to prepare the final accounts of Nick Johnson for the year ended 31 December 2004 in proper form, using the conventional format.

5.2 *Please refer back to the extended trial balance of Alan Harris prepared in Student Activity 4.6.*

You are to prepare the final accounts of Alan Harris for the year ended 30 June 2004 in proper form, using the conventional format.

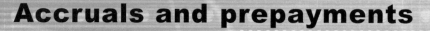

this chapter covers . . .

In the last two chapters we have looked at the preparation of final accounts

- *using the extended trial balance, or spreadsheet, approach*
- *in the proper form with profit and loss account and balance sheet*

There are a number of adjustments which are made to the final accounts at the year end in order to show a more realistic view of the state of the business. This chapter is concerned with the adjustments to be made for accruals and prepayments of expenses and income.

To illustrate the effect of adjustments for accruals and prepayments on final accounts we shall be referring to the final accounts of Tara Smith seen in the previous two chapters.

PERFORMANCE CRITERIA COVERED

unit 5: MAINTAINING FINANCIAL RECORDS AND PREPARING ACCOUNTS

element 5.2

collecting and collating information for the preparation of final accounts

E   correctly identify, calculate and record appropriate adjustments

G   conduct investigations into business transactions with trust and courtesy

H   ensure that the organisation's policies, regulations, procedures and timescales relating to preparing final accounts are observed

element 5.3

preparing the final accounts of sole traders and partnerships

A   prepare final accounts of sole traders in proper form, from the trial balance

C   observe the organisation's policies, regulations, procedures and timescales in relation to preparing final accounts of sole traders and partnerships

D   identify and resolve or refer to the appropriate person discrepancies, unusual features or queries

ACCRUAL OF EXPENSES

An accrual is an amount due in an accounting period which is unpaid at the end of that period, eg an insurance premium or an auditor's bill not yet paid.

In the final accounts, accrued expenses are:

- added to the expense account (eg insurance account, audit account) shown in the trial balance, before it is listed in the profit and loss account
- shown as a current liability in the year-end balance sheet

The reason for dealing with accruals in this way is to ensure that the profit and loss account records the cost that has been incurred for the year, instead of simply the amount that has been paid. In other words, the expense is adjusted to relate to the time period covered by the profit and loss account. The year-end balance sheet shows a liability for the amount that is due, but unpaid.

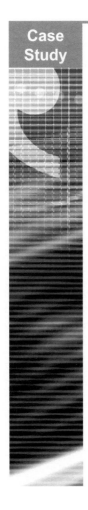

Case Study

TARA SMITH: ACCRUAL OF AN EXPENSE

The trial balance of Tara Smith at 31 December 2004 (see page 53) shows a debit balance for telephone expenses of £500. Before preparing the final accounts, a telephone bill for £100 is received on 4 January 2005, ie early in the new financial year. An examination of the bill shows that it is for costs incurred in 2004, therefore an adjustment needs to be made in the final accounts for 2004 to record this accrued expense.

accruals – the extended trial balance
The accrual is shown in the extended trial balance as follows:

- in the adjustments columns
    - record £100 on the debit side of the telephone row
    - record £100 on the credit side of the accruals row
- on the debit side of the profit and loss column the total cost of the telephone row is now £600 (ie £500 from the trial balance, plus £100 accrual)
- on the credit side of the balance sheet column £100 from the accruals row is shown as a liability of the business

This adjustment is shown on Tara Smith's extended trial balance (page 86): the figures affected by the accrual (and also the prepayment – see below) are shaded for ease of reference.

accruals – the book-keeping records
In the double-entry records, a separate accruals account is opened which shows the amount owing at the end of the financial year. Thus telephone account and accruals account in the records of Tara Smith will appear as follows:

Dr	Telephone Account		Cr
2004	£	2004	£
31 Dec Balance b/d	500	31 Dec Profit and loss account	600
31 Dec Accruals account	100		
	600		600

Dr	Accruals Account		Cr
2004	£	2004	£
31 Dec Balance c/d	100	31 Dec Telephone account	100
2005	£	2005	£
		1 Jan Balance b/d	100

Notes:

- The book-keeper's trial balance showed the debit side balance brought down of £500 on telephone account

- As £100 is owing for telephone expenses at the end of the year, the transfer to profit and loss account is the cost that has been incurred for the year of £600

- The amount of the accrual is transferred to the credit side of accruals account; it is listed on the balance sheet at 31 December 2004 as a liability

Later on, for example on 15 January 2005, the telephone bill is paid by cheque and the accruals account now appears as:

Dr	Accruals Account		Cr
2005	£	2005	£
15 Jan Bank	100	1 Jan Balance b/d	100

The effect of the payment on 15 January is that accruals account now has a 'nil' balance and the bill received on 4 January will not be recorded as an expense in the profit and loss account drawn up at the end of 2005. Where the accruals account contains a number of separate accruals – eg telephone, wages, rates, vehicle expenses – it is essential to keep a note of the amount of each. In this way, we can ensure that each is cleared during the new financial year.

the effect of an accrual on profit

Taking note of the accrual of an expense has the effect of reducing net profit for the accounting period in question. As the expenses have been increased, net profit is reduced. In this case the telephone bill due for the period reduces the net profit of Tara Smith by £100 from £12,000 to £11,900.

PREPAYMENT OF EXPENSES

A prepayment is a payment made in advance of the accounting period to which it relates.

A prepayment is, therefore, the opposite of an accrual: with a prepayment of expenses, some part of the expense has been paid in advance.

In the final accounts, prepaid expenses are:

*   deducted from the expense account shown in the trial balance before it is listed in the profit and loss account
*   shown as a current asset in the year end balance sheet

As with accruals, the reason for dealing with prepaid expenses in this way is to ensure that the profit and loss account records the cost incurred for the year, and not the amount that has been paid – the profit and loss account expense relates to the time period covered by the profit and loss account. The year end balance sheet shows an asset for the amount that has been prepaid.

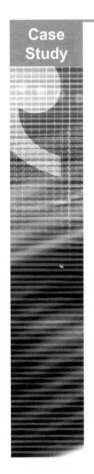

Case Study

TARA SMITH: PREPAID EXPENSES

Tara Smith tells you that the trial balance figure for rent paid of £750 includes £75 of rent for January 2005 paid in advance. An adjustment needs to be made in the final accounts for 2004 to record this prepaid expense.

prepayments – the extended trial balance

The prepayment is shown in the extended trial balance as follows:

*   in the adjustments columns
    *   record £75 on the credit side of the rent paid row
    *   record £75 on the debit side of the prepayments row
*   on the credit side of the profit and loss column the total cost of rent paid is now £675 (ie £750 from the trial balance, less £75 prepaid)
*   on the debit side of the balance sheet column £75 from the prepayments row is shown as an asset of the business

The prepayment adjustment is shown on Tara Smith's extended trial balance (page 86), together with the accrual we have just dealt with – both are shaded for ease of reference.

prepayments – the book-keeping records

In the double-entry records, prepayments must be recorded in an asset account at the end of the financial year.

The expense account for 'rent paid' in the records of Tara Smith will appear as follows:

Dr			Rent Paid Account		Cr
2004		£	2004		£
31 Dec	Balance b/d	750	31 Dec	Profit and loss account	675
			31 Dec	Prepayments account	75
		750			750
2005		£	2005		£
1 Jan	Prepayments account	75			

Dr			Prepayments Account		Cr
2004		£	2004		£
31 Dec	Rent paid account	75	31 Dec	Balance c/d	75
2005		£	2005		£
1 Jan	Balance b/d	75	1 Jan	Rent paid account	75

Notes:

- The trial balance total for rent paid is £750

- As £75 is prepaid at the end of the year, the transfer to profit and loss account is the cost that has been incurred for the year of £675

- The amount of the prepayment is transferred to the debit side of prepayments account; it is listed on the balance sheet at 31 December 2004 as an asset

- At the beginning of the new financial year, amounts held in prepayments account are transferred back to the expense accounts. Thus, for the rent prepaid, the book-keeping entries on 1 January 2005 are:

  – *debit* rent paid account

  – *credit* prepayments account

This now gives rent paid account a debit balance which will be included in the expense for rent paid for the year and will be transferred to profit and loss account on 31 December 2005.

effect on profit

Taking note of the prepayment of an expense has the effect of increasing a previously reported net profit – expenses have been reduced, so net profit is greater.

Case Study

TARA SMITH: ACCRUALS AND PREPAYMENTS IN THE FINAL ACCOUNTS

We will now focus on how the adjustments for accruals and prepayments are shown in the profit and loss account and balance sheet of Tara Smith. Remember that we are taking note of the following items at 31 December 2004:

* telephone accrued £100

* rent prepaid £75

extended trial balance (page 86)

The layout for the extended trial balance includes rows for accruals and prepayments. The columns which are affected are adjustments, profit and loss, and balance sheet – the altered figures are shaded for illustrative purposes. Note that:

* the profit and loss columns show the net figure for each expense after allowing for the accrual or prepayment

* the balance sheet columns show the accrual as a liability and the prepayment as an asset

The effect of taking note of accruals and prepayments is to alter net profit from that shown by the extended trial balance for Tara Smith, seen earlier (page 55):

	£
Net profit (before adjustments)	12,000
Less telephone accrued	100
	11,900
Add rent prepaid	75
Net profit after adjustments	11,975

final accounts: conventional format (pages 87 – 88)

There is no effect on the gross profit; net profit is changed to £11,975 because of the amounts of the accrual and prepayment. In conventional format final accounts, there is no need to show the calculations – they are presented here for illustrative purposes.

In the conventional format balance sheet

* prepayments are included amongst the current assets

* accruals are included amongst the current liabilities

In Tara Smith's final accounts, the accruals and prepayments are shaded for illustrative purposes.

EXTENDED TRIAL BALANCE **TARA SMITH TRADING AS "THE FASHION SHOP"** **31 DECEMBER 2004**

Account name	Ledger balances Dr £	Ledger balances Cr £	Adjustments Dr £	Adjustments Cr £	Profit and loss Dr £	Profit and loss Cr £	Balance sheet Dr £	Balance sheet Cr £
Opening stock	12,500				12,500			
Purchases	105,000				105,000			
Sales		155,000				155,000		
Administration expenses	6,200				6,200			
Wages	23,500				23,500			
Rent paid	750			75	675			
Telephone	500		100		600			
Interest paid	4,500				4,500			
Travel expenses	550				550			
Premises	100,000						100,000	
Shop fittings	20,000						20,000	
Debtors	10,500						10,500	
Bank	5,450						5,450	
Cash	50						50	
Capital		75,000						75,000
Drawings	7,000						7,000	
Loan from bank		50,000						50,000
Creditors		14,500						14,500
Value Added Tax		2,000						2,000
Closing stock: Profit and loss				10,500		10,500		
Closing stock: Balance sheet			10,500				10,500	
Accruals				100				100
Prepayments			75				75	
Depreciation								
Bad debts								
Provision for doubtful debts:adjustment								
Net profit/loss					11,975			11,975
	296,500	296,500	10,675	10,675	165,500	165,500	153,575	153,575

TARA SMITH, TRADING AS "THE FASHION SHOP"

TRADING AND PROFIT AND LOSS ACCOUNT
for the year ended 31 December 2004

	£	£
Sales		155,000
Opening stock	12,500	
Purchases	105,000	
	117,500	
Less Closing stock	10,500	
Cost of sales		107,000
Gross profit		48,000
Less overheads:		
Administration expenses	6,200	
Wages	23,500	
Rent paid 750 – 75 =	675	
Telephone 500 + 100 =	600	
Interest paid	4,500	
Travel expenses	550	
		36,025
Net profit		11,975

note
The calculations in the grey box relate to accrued and prepaid expenses. They are shown here for illustrative purposes. The actual profit and loss account produced would not show these workings, but just the final expense figures.

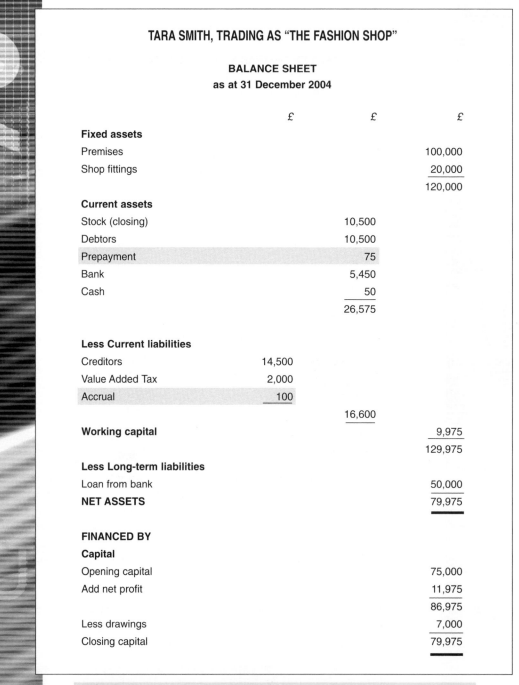

TARA SMITH, TRADING AS "THE FASHION SHOP"

BALANCE SHEET
as at 31 December 2004

	£	£	£
Fixed assets			
Premises			100,000
Shop fittings			20,000
			120,000
Current assets			
Stock (closing)		10,500	
Debtors		10,500	
Prepayment		75	
Bank		5,450	
Cash		50	
		26,575	
Less Current liabilities			
Creditors	14,500		
Value Added Tax	2,000		
Accrual	100		
		16,600	
Working capital			9,975
			129,975
Less Long-term liabilities			
Loan from bank			50,000
NET ASSETS			79,975
FINANCED BY			
Capital			
Opening capital			75,000
Add net profit			11,975
			86,975
Less drawings			7,000
Closing capital			79,975

note

The figures in the grey boxes relate to the prepayment and the accrual as they appear on the balance sheet. The accrual is a current liability because it is still owing and due at the balance sheet date; the prepayment is a current asset as it represents an expense which has already been paid for at the balance sheet date – it is an item of value to the business.

ACCRUALS AND PREPAYMENTS OF INCOME

Just as expenses can be accrued or prepaid at the end of a financial year, income amounts can also be accrued or prepaid.

accrual of income

Here, income of a business is due but unpaid at the end of the financial year. For example, commission might have been earned, but the payment is received after the end of the financial year to which it relates. In the extended trial balance and final accounts, accrual of income is:

- added to the income amount in the trial balance before it is listed in the profit and loss account
- shown as a current asset (eg commission receivable) in the year-end balance sheet

prepayment of income

Here, the income of a business has been paid in advance by the payer. For example, the rent received account for this financial year could include an advance payment received from a tenant in respect of the next financial year. In the extended trial balance and final accounts, prepayment of income is:

- deducted from the income amount in the trial balance before it is listed in the profit and loss account
- shown as a current liability (eg rent received in advance) in the year-end balance sheet

As with expenses, the objective of taking note of accruals and prepayments of income is to ensure that the money amount listed in the profit and loss account relates to the period covered by that account.

PRIVATE EXPENSES AND GOODS FOR OWN USE

Adjustments also have to be made in the final accounts for the amount of any business facilities that are used by the owner for private purposes. These adjustments are for private expenses and goods for own use.

private expenses

Sometimes the owner of a business uses business facilities for private purposes, eg telephone, or car. The owner will agree that part of the expense shall be charged to him or her as drawings, while the other part represents a business expense.

For example, the balance of the telephone account is £600 at the year-end, and the owner agrees that this should be split as one-quarter private use, and three-quarters to the business. The book-keeping entries to record such adjustments are:

- *debit* drawings account
- *credit* telephone account
- *debit* profit and loss account
- *credit* telephone account

The telephone account will be completed at the end of the year as follows:

Dr		Telephone Account		Cr
2004	£	2004		£
31 Dec Balance b/d	600	31 Dec Drawings		150
		31 Dec Profit and loss account		450
	600			600

When using a trial balance to produce the final accounts, private expenses should be adjusted by deducting from the expense account and adding to drawings.

goods for own use

When the owner of a business takes some of the goods in which the business trades for his or her own use, the double-entry book-keeping is:

- *debit* drawings account
- *credit* purchases account

Note that:

- Where a business is VAT-registered, VAT must be accounted for on goods taken by the owner.
- An alternative method of accounting for goods for own use is:
  - *debit* drawings account
  - *credit* sales account

This method is preferred by HM Revenue & Customs for tax purposes; however, either is acceptable for the purpose of financial accounting – which method is used will depend on the custom and practice of the business.

When using a trial balance to produce the final accounts, goods for own use should be adjusted by adding to drawings and deducting from purchases (or adding to sales).

INSURANCE CLAIMS

When a business loses stock as a result of causes such as fire, theft, water damage, a claim is made to the insurance company for the cost of the insured stock. Once the amount of the claim has been agreed with the insurance company, the book-keeping entries are:

– *debit* insurance claims account

– *credit* purchases account

In this way, the figure for purchases is reduced for profit and loss account. If a balance sheet is prepared before payment is received from the insurance company, the insurance claims account will be shown as a current asset.

When payment is received from the insurance company, the book-keeping entries are:

– *debit* bank account

– *credit* insurance claims account

Thus insurance claims account now has a nil balance, and the business has received payment from the insurance company for loss of the stock.

INCOME AND EXPENDITURE ACCOUNTING

In this chapter we have made adjustments for accruals and prepayments to ensure that the profit and loss account shows the correct amount of income and expenses for the financial year, ie what should have been paid, instead of what has actually been paid. In doing this we are adopting the principle of *income and expenditure accounting*. If we simply used the trial balance figures, we would be following the principle of *receipts* and *payments accounting*, ie comparing money coming in, with money going out: this will usually give a false view of the net profit for the year.

The principle of income and expenditure accounting is applied in the same way to purchases and sales, although no adjustments are needed because of the way in which these two are handled in the accounting records. For purchases, the amount is entered into the accounts when the supplier's invoice is received, although the agreement to buy will be contained in the legal contract which exists between buyer and seller. From the accounting viewpoint, it is receipt of the supplier's invoice that causes an accounting entry to be made; the subsequent payment is handled as a different accounting transaction. A business could have bought goods, not paid for them yet, but will have a purchases figure to enter into the profit and loss account – the creditors will soon be wanting payment!

Sales are recorded in a similar way – when the invoice for the goods is sent, rather than when payment is made. This applies the principle of income and expenditure accounting. In this way, a business could have made a large amount of sales, which will be entered in the profit and loss account, but may not yet have received any payments.

The way in which accounts are adjusted to take note of accruals and prepayments is formally recognised in the accruals (or matching) concept, which is discussed in more detail in Chapter 9.

Chapter Summary	• Final accounts are prepared on the income and expenditure basis, rather than the receipts and payments basis.
	• An adjustment should be made at the end of the financial year in respect of accruals and prepayments.
	• In the final accounts, accrued expenses are:
	– added to the expense from the trial balance
	– shown as a current liability in the balance sheet
	• Prepaid expenses are:
	– deducted from the expense from the trial balance
	– shown as a current asset in the balance sheet
	• An accrual of income is:
	– added to the income amount from the trial balance
	– shown as a current asset in the balance sheet
	• A prepayment of income is:
	– deducted from the income amount from the trial balance
	– shown as a current liability in the balance sheet
	• Adjustments also need to be made in the final accounts for:
	– private expenses
	– goods for own use

Key Terms		
	accrual of expenses	an amount due in an accounting period which is unpaid at the end of that period
	prepayment of expenses	a payment made in advance of the accounting period to which it relates
	accrual of income	income of a business due in an accounting period which is unpaid at the end of that period
	prepayment of income	income of a business which has been paid in advance of the accounting period to which it relates
	goods for own use	where the owner of a business takes some of the goods in which the business trades for his/her own use

income and expenditure accounting	recording the amounts that should have been received and paid during an accounting period
receipts and payments accounting	recording the actual amounts that have been received and paid during an accounting period, without taking note of accruals and prepayments

Student Activities

Extended trial balance format: a blank photocopiable pro-forma of the extended trial balance is included in the Appendix (page 341) – it is advisable to enlarge it up to full A4 size.

Conventional format: blank photocopiable pro-formas of the trading and profit and loss account and balance sheet are included in the Appendix (pages 338 and 339) – it is advisable to enlarge them up to full A4 size.

6.1 Wages accrued are shown as a:

(a)   current asset in the balance sheet

(b)   debit balance in accruals account

(c)   fixed asset in the balance sheet

(d)   credit balance in accruals account

Answer (a) or (b) or (c) or (d)

6.2 Rates prepaid are shown as a:

(a)   current liability in the balance sheet

(b)   fixed asset in the balance sheet

(c)   debit balance in prepayments account

(d)   credit balance in prepayments account

Answer (a) or (b) or (c) or (d)

6.3 John Harrington runs an import/export business. At the end of his financial year, on 31 December 2004, the vehicle expenses account is as follows:

Dr			**Vehicle Expenses Account**		Cr
2004		£	2004		£
31 Dec	Balance b/d	1,680			

John Harrington tells you that 25 per cent of vehicle expenses represents his private motoring expenses. He asks you to transfer the amount to his drawings account, before transferring the remainder to profit and loss account. Show the vehicle expenses account after these transactions have been entered.

6.4 Wyvern Stationery Limited has made a claim on its insurance policy for stock damaged by a burst water pipe. The amount of the claim has been agreed today, 17 December 2004, at £845. Show the book-keeping entries to record this and, if the amount is not paid by the end of the financial year on 31 December 2004, how it will be dealt with in the year-end balance sheet.

6.5 Explain how the following would be dealt with in the profit and loss account, and balance sheet of a business with a financial year end of 31 December 2004:

(a)   Wages and salaries paid to 31 December 2004 amount to £55,640. However, at that date £1,120 is owing: this amount is paid on 4 January 2005.

(b)   Rates totalling £3,565 have been paid to cover the period 1 January 2004 to 31 March 2005.

(c)   A computer is rented at a cost of £150 per month. The rental for January 2005 was paid in December 2004 and is included in the total payments during 2004 which amount to £1,950.

6.6 The following trial balance has been extracted by the book-keeper of Don Smith, who runs a wholesale stationery business, at 31 December 2004:

	Dr £	Cr £
Debtors	24,325	
Creditors		15,408
Value Added Tax		4,276
Capital		30,000
Bank		1,083
Rent and rates	10,862	
Electricity	2,054	
Telephone	1,695	
Salaries	55,891	
Motor vehicles	22,250	
Office equipment	7,500	
Motor vehicle expenses	10,855	
Drawings	15,275	
Discount allowed	478	
Discount received		591
Purchases	138,960	
Sales		257,258
Opening stock	18,471	
	308,616	308,616

Notes at 31 December 2004:
* closing stock was valued at £14,075
* rates are prepaid £250
* electricity owing £110
* salaries are owing £365

You are to prepare the final accounts of Don Smith for the year ended 31 December 2004:
* using the extended trial balance method
* in proper form, using the conventional format

6.7 The following trial balance has been extracted by the book-keeper of John Barclay at 30 June 2004:

	Dr	Cr
	£	£
Sales		864,321
Purchases	600,128	
Sales returns	2,746	
Purchases returns		3,894
Office expenses	33,947	
Salaries	122,611	
Motor vehicle expenses	36,894	
Discount allowed	3,187	
Discount received		4,951
Debtors and creditors	74,328	52,919
Value Added Tax		10,497
Opening stock	63,084	
Motor vehicles	83,500	
Office equipment	23,250	
Land and buildings	100,000	
Bank loan		75,000
Bank	1,197	
Capital		155,000
Drawings	21,710	
	1,166,582	1,166,582

Notes at 30 June 2004:
* stock was valued at £66,941
* motor vehicle expenses owing £1,250
* office expenses prepaid £346
* goods costing £250 were taken by John Barclay for his own use

You are to prepare the final accounts of John Barclay for the year ended 30 June 2004:
* using the extended trial balance method
* in proper form, using the conventional format

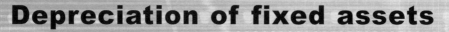

7 Depreciation of fixed assets

Fixed assets, such as machinery and vehicles, lose value as time goes by, largely as a result of wear and tear. This loss in value is known as depreciation. In financial accounting it is necessary to record an estimate of depreciation in the accounting records. In this chapter we will:

- *define depreciation*
- *consider the main methods of calculating depreciation*
- *study the book-keeping entries for depreciation*
- *apply depreciation to the final accounts*
- *investigate the book-keeping entries involved when a fixed asset is sold*

PERFORMANCE CRITERIA COVERED

unit 5: MAINTAINING FINANCIAL RECORDS AND PREPARING ACCOUNTS

element 5.2

collecting and collating information for the preparation of final accounts

E   *correctly identify, calculate and record appropriate adjustments*

G   *conduct investigations into business transactions with trust and courtesy*

H   *ensure that the organisation's policies, regulations, procedures and timescales relating to preparing final accounts are observed*

element 5.3

preparing the final accounts of sole traders and partnerships

A   *prepare final accounts of sole traders in proper form, from the trial balance*

C   *observe the organisation's policies, regulations, procedures and timescales in relation to preparing final accounts of sole traders and partnerships*

D   *identify and resolve or refer to the appropriate person discrepancies, unusual features or queries*

WHAT IS DEPRECIATION?

Depreciation is the estimate of the amount of the loss in value of fixed assets over an estimated time period.

Most fixed assets lose value over time and it is necessary, in order to present a realistic view of the business, to record the amount of the loss in value. This is done by

- showing an expense – called 'depreciation' – in the profit and loss account
- showing the fixed asset at cost price less depreciation to date – called 'provision for depreciation' – in the balance sheet

Depreciation – which is linked to the cost price of the asset – *estimates* the loss in value and the time period over which the loss occurs.

The main factors which cause fixed assets to depreciate are:

- *wear and tear through use*, eg motor vehicles, machinery, etc
- *passage of time*, eg the lease on a building
- *depletion,* eg extraction of stone from a quarry
- *economic reasons*
  - obsolescence, eg a new design of machine which does the job better and faster, making the old machine obsolete
  - inadequacy, eg a machine such as a photocopier no longer has the volume capacity to meet the needs of the business

Fixed assets – including buildings – are depreciated over their useful economic life. The only exception is land, which does not normally depreciate (unless it is a quarry or a mine, when it will have a known useful economic life).

CALCULATING DEPRECIATION

There are several different ways in which we can allow for the loss in value of fixed assets. All of these are *estimates,* and it is only when the asset is sold or scrapped that we will know the accuracy of the estimate. A business can use any acceptable depreciation method; however, once selected, the method would not be changed from one year to the next without good reason.

The two most common methods of calculating depreciation are:

- straight-line method
- reducing balance method

For the calculations of depreciation amounts we will use the following data:

DATA FOR DEPRECIATION OF MACHINE

Cost price (net of VAT)   £2,000

Estimated life   4 years

Estimated scrap value (net of VAT) at end of four years   £400

---

straight-line method of depreciation

With this method, a fixed percentage is written off the *original cost* of the asset each year. For this example, twenty-five per cent will be written off each year by the straight-line method. The depreciation amount (ignoring for the moment any residual or scrap value) for *each year* is:

$$£2,000 \quad x \quad 25\% \quad = \quad £500 \text{ per year}$$

The depreciation percentage will be decided by a business on the basis of what it considers to be the useful economic life of the asset. Thus, twenty-five per cent each year gives a useful economic life of four years (assuming a nil residual value at the end of its life).

Different classes of fixed assets are often depreciated at different rates, eg motor vehicles may be depreciated at a different rate to office equipment. It is important that, once a particular method and rate of depreciation has been selected, depreciation should be applied consistently, ie methods and rates are not changed from year-to-year without good reason.

The method of calculating straight-line depreciation, taking into account the asset's estimated sale proceeds at the end of its useful economic life, is:

$$\frac{\text{cost of asset – estimated residual (scrap or salvage) sale proceeds}}{\text{number of years' expected use of asset}}$$

For example, the machine is expected to have a residual (scrap or salvage) value of £400, so the depreciation amount will be:

$$\frac{£2,000 - £400}{4 \text{ years}} = £400 \text{ per year (ie 20\% per annum on cost)}$$

reducing balance method

With this method, a fixed percentage is written off the reduced balance of the asset each year. The reduced balance is the cost of the asset less the provision for depreciation. For example, the machine is to be depreciated by 33.3% (one-third) each year, using the reducing balance method. The depreciation amounts for the four years of ownership are:

	£
Original cost	2,000
Year 1 depreciation: 33.3% of £2,000	667
Value at end of year 1	1,333
Year 2 depreciation: 33.3% of £1,333	444
Value at end of year 2	889
Year 3 depreciation: 33.3% of £889	296
Value at end of year 3	593
Year 4 depreciation: 33.3% of £593	193
Value at end of year 4	400

Note: the figures have been rounded to the nearest £, and year 4 depreciation has been adjusted by £5 to leave a residual value of £400.

The formula to calculate the percentage of reducing balance depreciation is:

$$r = 1 - \sqrt[n]{\frac{s}{c}}$$

where:

r = percentage rate of depreciation

n = number of years

s = salvage (residual) value

c = cost of asset

In the example above the 33.3% is calculated as:

$$r = 1 - \sqrt[4]{\frac{400}{2,000}}$$

$$r = 1 - \sqrt[4]{0.2}$$ (to find the fourth root press the square root key on the calculator twice)

$$r = 1 - 0.669$$

$$r = 0.331 \text{ or } 33.1\% \text{ (which is close to the 33.3\% used above)}$$

straight-line and reducing balance methods compared

The following tables use the depreciation amounts calculated above.

	1	2	3	4
		straight-line depreciation		
Year	Original cost	Depreciation for year	Provision for depreciation	Net book value (ie column 1-3)
	£	£	£	£
1	2,000	400	400	1,600
2	2,000	400	800	1,200
3	2,000	400	1,200	800
4	2,000	400	1,600	400

Note: Net book value is cost, less provision for depreciation, ie column 1, less column 3.

These calculations will be used in the final accounts (see pages 103-104) as follows: taking year 2 as an example, the profit and loss account will show £400 (column 2) as an expense, while the balance sheet will record £1,200 (column 4) as the net book value.

	1	2	3	4
		reducing balance depreciation		
Year	Original cost	Depreciation for year	Provision for depreciation	Net book value (ie column 1-3)
	£	£	£	£
1	2,000	667	667	1,333
2	2,000	444	1,111	889
3	2,000	296	1,407	593
4	2,000	193	1,600	400

In the final accounts, using year 3 as an example, £296 (column 2) will be shown as an expense in profit and loss account, while £593 (column 4) is the net book value that will be recorded in the balance sheet. We shall look in more detail at how depreciation is shown in the final accounts later in the chapter.

Using these tables, we will now see how the two methods compare:

	straight-line method	reducing balance method
depreciation amount	Same money amount each year – see chart below	Different money amounts each year: more than straight-line in early years, less in later years – see chart below
depreciation percentage	Lower depreciation percentage required to achieve same residual value	Higher depreciation percentage required to achieve same residual value – but can never reach a nil value
suitability	Best used for fixed assets likely to be kept for the whole of their expected lives, eg machinery, office equipment, fixtures and fittings	Best used for fixed assets which depreciate more in early years and which are not kept for the whole of expected lives, eg vehicles

The year-by-year depreciation amounts of the machine in the example are shown on the following bar chart:

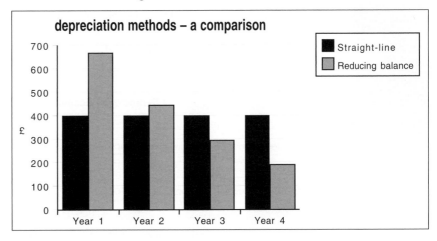

BOOK-KEEPING ENTRIES FOR DEPRECIATION

Once the amounts of depreciation have been calculated using the methods described in the previous section, they can be recorded in the book-keeping system. The usual procedure is to have three accounts:

- *fixed asset account*, which records the cost price of the asset (note that the value of the asset can include certain other capital costs, eg installation costs – see page 151)

- *depreciation account*, which records the amount of depreciation for the asset for the year

- *provision for depreciation account*, which records the amount of depreciation to date for each class of fixed asset in separate provision for depreciation accounts

BOOK-KEEPING ENTRIES FOR DEPRECIATION

A machine is purchased for £2,000 net of VAT on 1 January 2004. It is decided to depreciate it at twenty per cent each year, using the straight-line method. The firm's financial year runs from 1 January to 31 December. The accounting records for the first four years will be:

Dr			Machinery Account			Cr
2004			£	2004		£
1 Jan	Bank		2,000			

This account remains with the balance of £2,000, which is the cost price of the machine. (The other transactions on 1 January 2004 are to bank account and VAT account – these have not been shown.)

Dr			Depreciation Account			Cr
2004			£	2004		£
31 Dec	Provision for depreciation		400	31 Dec	Profit and loss account	400
2005				2005		
31 Dec	Provision for depreciation		400	31 Dec	Profit and loss account	400
2006				2006		
31 Dec	Provision for depreciation		400	31 Dec	Profit and loss account	400
2007				2007		
31 Dec	Provision for depreciation		400	31 Dec	Profit and loss account	400

The depreciation account acts as a 'holding' account for the year's depreciation. The amount is

• credited to depreciation account (and debited to profit and loss account – see later)

• debited to depreciation account (and credited to provision for depreciation account – see next page)

Note that depreciation account may be credited with depreciation amounts for various classes of fixed assets (eg buildings, machinery, vehicles); the amounts are then debited out and credited to the provision for depreciation account for each class of fixed asset.

Dr			Provision for Depreciation Account – Machinery		Cr
2004		£	2004		£
31 Dec	Balance c/d	400	31 Dec	Depreciation account	400
2005			2005		
31 Dec	Balance c/d	800	1 Jan	Balance b/d	400
			31 Dec	Depreciation account	400
		800			800
2006			2006		
31 Dec	Balance c/d	1,200	1 Jan	Balance b/d	800
			31 Dec	Depreciation account	400
		1,200			1,200
2007			2007		
31 Dec	Balance c/d	1,600	1 Jan	Balance b/d	1,200
			31 Dec	Depreciation account	400
		1,600			1,600
2008			2008		
			1 Jan	Balance b/d	1,600

The provision for depreciation account – which is specific to each class of fixed asset – stores up the amounts of depreciation year by year. Notice that, while the asset account of machinery has a debit balance, provision for depreciation account has a credit balance. The difference between the two balances at any time will tell us the net book value of the asset, ie what it is worth according to our accounting records. For example, at 31 December 2006, the net book value of the machine is £800 (£2,000 cost, less £1,200 provision for depreciation).

When a business owns several fixed assets of the same class, eg several machines, it is usual practice to maintain only one asset account and one provision for depreciation account for that class. This does mean that the calculation of amounts of depreciation can become quite complex – particularly when assets are bought and sold during the year. It is good practice to calculate the separate depreciation amount for each machine, or asset, before amalgamating the figures as the year's depreciation charge.

DEPRECIATION AND FINAL ACCOUNTS

profit and loss account

The depreciation amount calculated for each class of asset is listed amongst the overheads in profit and loss account. For example, to consider the machine depreciated in the previous sections, the profit and loss account will show 'depreciation: machinery £400' amongst the overheads. The double-entry book-keeping records the annual amount for depreciation as follows:

– *debit* profit and loss account

– *credit* depreciation account

As we have seen earlier, amounts held in depreciation account are then debited out and credited to the appropriate provision for depreciation accounts.

balance sheet

Each class of fixed asset is shown at cost price, less provision for depreciation (ie accumulated depreciation to date, which is the current year plus the depreciation of previous years). The resulting figure is the net book value of the fixed asset. The usual way of setting these out in a balance sheet (using figures for the machine in the previous section) is:

Balance sheet (extract) .... as at 31 December 2004

	£	£	£
	Cost	Provision for dep'n	Net
Fixed assets			
Machinery	2,000	400	1,600
Vehicles, etc	x	x	x
	x	x	x

Balance sheet (extract) .... as at 31 December 2005

	£	£	£
	Cost	Provision for dep'n	Net
Fixed assets			
Machinery	2,000	800	1,200
Vehicles, etc	x	x	x
	x	x	x

Notice, from the above, how provision for depreciation increases with the addition of each further year's depreciation. At the same time, the net figure reduces – it is this net figure which is added to the other fixed assets to give a sub-total for this section of the balance sheet.

trial balance figures

When preparing final accounts from a trial balance, the trial balance often gives separate figures for the cost of an asset and its provision for depreciation at the start of the year. For example:

Trial balance of .... as at 31 December 2006

	Dr	Cr
	£	£
Machinery at cost	2,000	
Provision for depreciation: machinery		800

If a note to the trial balance then says, for example, to "depreciate machinery for the year at twenty per cent on cost", depreciation of £400 for the year 2006 must be calculated and shown as an expense in profit and loss account. The balance sheet will then show:

Balance sheet (extract) .... as at 31 December 2006

	£	£	£
	Cost	Provision for dep'n	Net
Fixed assets			
Machinery	2,000	1,200	800
Vehicles, etc	x	x	x
	x	x	x

depreciation policies of a business

In Skills Tests and Examinations, information will be given – where it is needed – on the accounting policy for depreciation of the business whose accounts are being prepared. In particular, information will be given on what to do when a fixed asset is bought part of the way through a firm's financial year. The choices here will be to allocate depreciation for the part of the year that it is owned; alternatively the firm may choose to provide for depreciation for the whole year on assets held at the end of the year.

Case Study

TARA SMITH:
DEPRECIATION IN THE FINAL ACCOUNTS

We will now focus on how the depreciation amounts are shown in the profit and loss account and balance sheet. We will continue with the trial balance of Tara Smith and include depreciation adjustments for the year of:

- premises: 2 per cent straight-line, ie £2,000
- shop fittings: 25 per cent reducing balance, ie £5,000

extended trial balance (see next page)
The layout for the extended trial balance includes a pre-printed row allocated for depreciation. Study the extended trial balance on the next page and read the notes that follow.

EXTENDED TRIAL BALANCE — TARA SMITH TRADING AS "THE FASHION SHOP" — 31 DECEMBER 2004

Account name	Ledger balances Dr £	Ledger balances Cr £	Adjustments Dr £	Adjustments Cr £	Profit and loss Dr £	Profit and loss Cr £	Balance sheet Dr £	Balance sheet Cr £
Opening stock	12,500				12,500			
Purchases	105,000				105,000			
Sales		155,000				155,000		
Administration expenses	6,200				6,200			
Wages	23,500				23,500			
Rent paid	750			75	675			
Telephone	500		100		600			
Interest paid	4,500				4,500			
Travel expenses	550				550			
Premises	100,000						100,000	
Provision for depreciation: premises				2,000				2,000
Shop fittings	20,000						20,000	
Provision for depreciation: shop fittings				5,000				5,000
Debtors	10,500						10,500	
Bank	5,450						5,450	
Cash	50						50	
Capital		75,000						75,000
Drawings	7,000						7,000	
Loan from bank		50,000						50,000
Creditors		14,500						14,500
Value Added Tax		2,000						2,000
Closing stock: Profit & loss				10,500		10,500		
Closing stock: Balance sheet			10,500				10,500	
Accruals				100				100
Prepayments			75				75	
Depreciation			7,000		7,000			
Bad debts								
Provision for doubtful debts:adjustment								
Net profit/loss					4,975			4,975
	296,500	296,500	17,675	17,675	165,500	165,500	153,575	153,575

The depreciation is shown in the extended trial balance as follows:

- in the account name column
    - on the blank line below premises write in 'provision for depreciation: premises'
    - on the blank line below shop fittings write in 'provision for depreciation: shop fittings'

- in the adjustments columns
    - record £7,000 (ie £2,000 + £5,000) on the debit side of the depreciation row
    - record £2,000 on the credit side of the provision for depreciation: premises row
    - record £5,000 on the credit side of the provision for depreciation: shop fittings row

- on the debit side of the profit and loss column record the depreciation for the year of £7,000

- on the credit side of the balance sheet column record the £2,000 and £5,000 provision for depreciation on the two classes of assets

Remember that:

- depreciation is the annual charge for depreciation

- provision for depreciation is the accumulated total of depreciation for each class of fixed asset

As this is the first year that Tara Smith has recorded depreciation, both depreciation and provision for depreciation amounts are the same. The figures for depreciation are shaded for ease of reference (note that the extended trial balance already incorporates adjustments for accruals and prepayments of expenses). As a result of depreciation, net profit is reduced by £7,000 (ie £2,000 + £5,000) to £4,975.

final accounts: conventional format (see next 2 pages)

There is no effect on gross profit; net profit is reduced to £4,975 because of the depreciation of £7,000 (ie £2,000 + £5,000).

In conventional format final accounts, the depreciation amounts are:

- listed amongst the overheads in profit and loss account

- deducted from the cost price of fixed assets in the balance sheet

Note that the deduction in the balance sheet is the amount of provision for depreciation (ie accumulated depreciation to date, which is the current year plus the depreciation of previous years).

In Tara Smith's final accounts, the depreciation amounts are shaded for illustrative purposes.

TARA SMITH, TRADING AS "THE FASHION SHOP"

TRADING AND PROFIT AND LOSS ACCOUNT
for the year ended 31 December 2004

	£	£
Sales		155,000
Opening stock	12,500	
Purchases	105,000	
	117,500	
Less Closing stock	10,500	
Cost of sales		107,000
Gross profit		48,000
Less overheads:		
Administration expenses	6,200	
Wages	23,500	
Rent paid	675	
Telephone	600	
Interest paid	4,500	
Travel expenses	550	
Depreciation:		
premises	2,000	
shop fittings	5,000	
		43,025
Net profit		4,975

notes
- The depreciation amounts for the year are debited to profit and loss account, together with the other overheads of the business. They are shown here in a grey box for illustrative purposes.

- In conventional format final accounts, it is usual to show the separate amount of depreciation for each class of fixed asset (as above), rather than the total amount of depreciation.

TARA SMITH, TRADING AS "THE FASHION SHOP"

BALANCE SHEET
as at 31 December 2004

	£	£	£
Fixed assets	Cost	Provision for dep'n	Net
Premises	100,000	2,000	98,000
Shop fittings	20,000	5,000	15,000
	120,000	7,000	113,000
Current assets			
Stock (closing)		10,500	
Debtors		10,500	
Prepayment		75	
Bank		5,450	
Cash		50	
		26,575	
Less Current liabilities			
Creditors	14,500		
Value Added Tax	2,000		
Accrual	100		
		16,600	
Working capital			9,975
			122,975
Less Long-term liabilities			
Loan from bank			50,000
NET ASSETS			72,975
FINANCED BY			
Capital			
Opening capital			75,000
Add net profit			4,975
			79,975
Less drawings			7,000
Closing capital			72,975

note
The figures in the grey box relate to the depreciation of fixed assets as they appear on the balance sheet. The cost of each fixed asset is shown, together with the amount of provision for depreciation (ie accumulated depreciation to date). Cost price, less provision for depreciation equals the net book value (NBV) – shown here as 'net'. It is good practice when preparing balance sheets to total the first two columns and to sub-total the third, as illustrated above.

DEPRECIATION: A NON-CASH EXPENSE

It is very important to realise that depreciation is a non-cash expense: unlike the other overheads in profit and loss account, no cheque is written out, or cash paid, for depreciation. In cash terms, depreciation causes no outflow of money. Nevertheless, it is correct, in the final accounts of a business, to show an allowance for depreciation in the profit and loss account, and to reduce the value of the fixed asset in the balance sheet. This is because the business has had the use of the asset, and needs to record the fall in value as an expense to present a true picture of its financial state. Thus we are led back to the definition of depreciation as "the estimate of the amount of the loss in value of fixed assets over an estimated time period", ie it is an accounting adjustment.

As depreciation is a non-cash expense, it should be noted that depreciation is not a method of providing a fund of cash which can be used to replace the asset at the end of its life. In order to do this, it is necessary to create a separate fund into which cash is transferred at regular intervals. This technique is often known as a sinking fund, and it needs to be represented by a separate bank account, eg a deposit account, which can be drawn against when the new fixed asset is to be purchased.

SALE OF FIXED ASSETS

When a fixed asset is sold or disposed, it is necessary to bring together:
- the original cost of the asset
- provision for depreciation over the life of the asset
- sale proceeds

These figures are transferred from the appropriate accounts in the double-entry book-keeping system to an asset disposal account (also known as a sale of assets account). The disposals account will enable us to calculate the 'profit' or 'loss' on sale of the asset (more correctly the terms are 'over-provision' and 'under-provision' of depreciation, respectively).

The book-keeping transactions are:
- original cost of the asset
    - *debit* disposals account
    - *credit* fixed asset account

- depreciation provided to date
  - *debit* provision for depreciation account
  - *credit* disposals account

Note:

The amount of depreciation for the current accounting period may need to be calculated, eg if disposal takes place part of the way through a financial year and the firm's policy is to charge for part-years.

- sale proceeds
  - *debit* bank/cash account
  - *credit* disposals account

- loss on sale
  - *debit* profit and loss account
  - *credit* disposals account

- profit on sale
  - *debit* disposals account
  - *credit* profit and loss account

Small adjustments for under-provision or over-provision of depreciation will usually be needed because it is impossible, at the start of an asset's life, to predict exactly what it will sell for in a number of years' time.

Case Study

SALE OF FIXED ASSETS

To illustrate the transactions to record the sale of fixed assets, we will use the machine purchased for £2,000 (net of VAT) on 1 January 2004, which is depreciated at twenty per cent each year, using the straight-line depreciation method. On 31 December 2006, the machine is sold for £600 (net of VAT); the company's accounting policy is to depreciate assets in the year of sale. The calculations are:

	£
cost price of machine (net of VAT)	2,000
less provision for depreciation to date	1,200
net book value at date of sale	800
selling price (net of VAT)	600
loss on sale	200

The book-keeping entries (excluding bank account and VAT account) are:

Dr			**Machinery Account**		Cr
2004		£	2006		£
1 Jan	Bank	2,000	31 Dec	Disposals account	2,000

Dr			**Provision for Depreciation Account – Machinery**		Cr
2004		£	2004		£
31 Dec	Balance c/d	400	31 Dec	Depreciation account	400
2005			2005		
31 Dec	Balance c/d	800	1 Jan	Balance b/d	400
			31 Dec	Depreciation account	400
		800			800
2006			2006		
31 Dec	Disposals account	1,200	1 Jan	Balance b/d	800
			31 Dec	Depreciation account	400
		1,200			1,200

Dr			**Disposals Account**		Cr
2006		£	2006		£
31 Dec	Machinery account	2,000	31 Dec	Prov for dep'n account	1,200
			31 Dec	Bank	600
			31 Dec	Profit and loss account	
				(loss on sale)	200
		2,000			2,000

Profit and loss account (extract) .... for the year ended 31 December 2006

	£	£
Gross profit		x
Less overheads:		
Depreciation: machinery	400	
Loss on sale of machinery	200	

Notes:

- In the machinery account, which is always kept 'at cost', the original price of the asset is transferred at the date of sale to disposals account. In this example, a nil balance remains on machinery account; however it is quite likely that the machinery account includes several machines, only one of which is being sold – in this case, there would be a balance on machinery account comprising the cost prices of the remaining machines.

- In provision for depreciation account, the amount of depreciation relating to the machine sold is transferred to disposals account. In this example, as only one machine is owned, the whole balance is transferred. However, if there were machines remaining, only part of the balance would be transferred – the amount remaining on the account relates to the remaining machines.

- Disposals account would balance without the need for a profit and loss account transfer if the depreciation rate used reflected exactly the fall in value of the machine. In practice, this is unlikely to happen, so a transfer to profit and loss account must be made. In this example, it is an under-provision of depreciation (loss on sale), and the profit and loss account lists an extra overhead. If there had been an over-provision of depreciation (profit on sale), an item of additional income would be shown in profit and loss account.

PART-EXCHANGE OF AN ASSET

Instead of selling an old fixed asset for cash, it is quite common to part-exchange it for a new asset. This is exactly the same as if a person trades in their old car for a new (or newer) one.

Once the part-exchange allowance has been agreed, the book-keeping entries for disposal are as detailed earlier except that, instead of sale proceeds, there will be:

– *debit* fixed asset account with the amount of the part-exchange allowance

– *credit* disposals account with the amount of the part-exchange allowance

The remainder of the purchase cost of the new fixed asset paid by cheque is debited to fixed asset account and credited to bank account in the usual way. For a VAT-registered business there will also be amounts to record on the VAT account.

For example, the machine referred to earlier in this section is part-exchanged on 31 December 2006 at an agreed value of £600 (net of VAT) for a new machine costing £2,500 (net of VAT). The balance is paid by cheque.

Machinery account is now be shown as:

Dr			Machinery Account		Cr
2004		£	2006		£
1 Jan	Bank	2,000	31 Dec	Disposals account	2,000
2006					
31 Dec	Disposals account (part-exchange allowance)	600	31 Dec	Balance c/d	2,500
31 Dec	Bank (balance paid by cheque)	1,900			
		2,500			2,500
2007					
1 Jan	Balance b/d	2,500			

Notes:

- This gives two debits (£600 and £1,900) in machinery account for a single machine.
- Disposals account is unchanged, except that the description for the credit transaction of £600 is machinery account, instead of bank. The account is as follows:

Dr			Disposals Account		Cr
2006		£	2006		£
31 Dec	Machinery account	2,000	31 Dec	Prov for dep'n account	1,200
			31 Dec	Machinery account	600
			31 Dec	Profit and loss account	
				(loss on sale)	200
		2,000			2,000

FRS 15: TANGIBLE FIXED ASSETS

Financial Reporting Standard (FRS) No 15, entitled *Tangible fixed assets,* is the accounting standard (see Chapters 9 and 10) which includes the rules for dealing with depreciation in financial accounts.

FRS 15 states that:

- all fixed assets having a known useful economic life are to be depreciated
- any acceptable depreciation method can be used
- depreciation amounts are normally based on the cost of the fixed assets (where assets are revalued, depreciation is based on the revalued amount)

Chapter Summary

- Fixed assets lose value as time goes by as a result of
  - wear and tear
  - passage of time
  - depletion
  - economic reasons, such as obsolescence and inadequacy
- Two common methods of calculating depreciation are the straight-line method and the reducing balance method.
- In terms of book-keeping, the accounts used to record depreciation are:
  - depreciation account, to record the annual charge for depreciation
  - provision for depreciation account, to record the accumulated total of depreciation for each class of fixed asset
- The depreciation amount for each class of fixed asset is included amongst the overheads in profit and loss account, while the value of the asset is shown in the balance sheet at cost price less provision for depreciation.

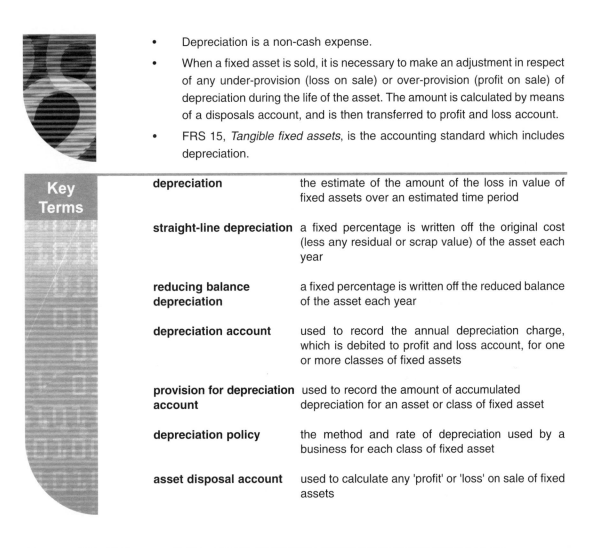

- Depreciation is a non-cash expense.

- When a fixed asset is sold, it is necessary to make an adjustment in respect of any under-provision (loss on sale) or over-provision (profit on sale) of depreciation during the life of the asset. The amount is calculated by means of a disposals account, and is then transferred to profit and loss account.

- FRS 15, *Tangible fixed assets*, is the accounting standard which includes depreciation.

Key Terms		
depreciation	the estimate of the amount of the loss in value of fixed assets over an estimated time period
straight-line depreciation	a fixed percentage is written off the original cost (less any residual or scrap value) of the asset each year
reducing balance depreciation	a fixed percentage is written off the reduced balance of the asset each year
depreciation account	used to record the annual depreciation charge, which is debited to profit and loss account, for one or more classes of fixed assets
provision for depreciation account	used to record the amount of accumulated depreciation for an asset or class of fixed asset
depreciation policy	the method and rate of depreciation used by a business for each class of fixed asset
asset disposal account	used to calculate any 'profit' or 'loss' on sale of fixed assets

Student Activities

7.1 A machine costs £5,000 net of VAT and is expected to last for five years. At the end of this time, it is estimated that it will have a residual (scrap) value of £500 net of VAT. The annual amount of depreciation for a VAT-registered business which uses the straight-line method will be:

(a)   £900

(b)   £1,000

(c)   £1,100

(d)   £1,250

Answer (a) or (b) or (c) or (d)

7.2 The business for which you work depreciates its delivery vans on the reducing balance method. Why do you think this method is used?

7.3 On 1 January 2004, Martin Jackson bought a car for £12,000. In his final accounts, which have a year end of 31 December, he has been depreciating it at 25 per cent per annum using the reducing balance method. On 31 December 2006, he sells the car for £5,500 (cheque received); his accounting policy is to depreciate assets in the year of sale.

You are to show:

(a)   provision for depreciation account for 2004, 2005 and 2006

(b)   a balance sheet extract at 31 December 2004 and 2005

(c)   asset disposal account

Round your answers down to whole £s where appropriate.

7.4 The following list of balances has been extracted from the books of John Henson at 31 December 2004:

	£
Purchases	71,600
Sales	122,000
Opening stock	6,250
Vehicle running expenses	1,480
Rent and rates	5,650
Office expenses	2,220
Discount received	285
Wages and salaries	18,950
Office equipment at cost	10,000
Vehicle at cost	12,000
Debtors	5,225
Creditors	3,190
Value Added Tax	1,720
Capital	20,000
Drawings for the year	13,095
Cash at bank	725

Notes at 31 December 2004:
- stock was valued at £8,500
- depreciation of office equipment for the year £1,000
- depreciation of vehicle for the year £3,000

You are to prepare the final accounts of John Henson for the year ended 31 December 2004:
- using the extended trial balance method
- in proper form, using the conventional format

7.5 A friend of yours has recently started in business: knowing that you are studying Financial Accounts, she seeks your assistance. She has just bought a machine at a cost of £1,000 net of VAT and asks you to advise on depreciation methods. The machine is expected to last for five years after which it will be valueless. She tells you that, if there is a choice of depreciation methods, she would like to use the one "that gives the larger net profit in the early years because the business could make good use of the extra cash". Advise your friend by means of a letter.

7.6 The following trial balance has been extracted by the book-keeper of Hazel Harris at 31 December 2004:

	Dr £	Cr £
Bank loan		75,000
Capital		125,000
Purchases and sales	465,000	614,000
Building repairs	8,480	
Motor vehicle at cost	12,000	
Provision for depreciation on motor vehicles		2,400
Motor expenses	2,680	
Premises at cost	100,000	
Provision for depreciation on premises		4,000
Bank overdraft		2,000
Furniture and fittings at cost	25,000	
Provision for depreciation on furniture and fittings		2,500
Wages and salaries	86,060	
Discounts	10,610	8,140
Drawings	24,000	
Rates and insurance	6,070	
Debtors and creditors	52,130	32,600
Value Added Tax		5,250
General expenses	15,860	
Opening stock	63,000	
	870,890	870,890

Notes at 31 December 2004:
- stock was valued at £88,000
- wages and salaries outstanding: £3,180
- rates and insurance paid in advance: £450
- depreciate premises at 2 per cent using the straight-line method
- depreciate the motor vehicle at 20 per cent using the reducing balance method
- depreciate furniture and fittings at 10 per cent using the straight-line method

You are to prepare the final accounts of Hazel Harris for the year ended 31 December 2004:

- using the extended trial balance method

- in proper form, using the conventional format

Bad debts and provision for doubtful debts

this chapter covers . . .

Most businesses selling their goods and services to other businesses do not receive payment immediately. Instead, they often have to allow a period of credit and, until the payment is received, they have a current asset of debtors. Unfortunately, it is likely that not all debtors will eventually settle the amounts they owe, ie the amounts are bad debts which have to be written off. At the same time a business needs to make a provision for doubtful debts, which allows for debtors who may not pay.

In this chapter we will:

- *distinguish between bad debts and provision for doubtful debts*
- *prepare the accounting entries for bad debts, and consider the effect on the final accounts*
- *prepare the accounting entries to make a provision for doubtful debts, and consider the effect on the final accounts*

PERFORMANCE CRITERIA COVERED

unit 5: MAINTAINING FINANCIAL RECORDS AND PREPARING ACCOUNTS

element 5.2

collecting and collating information for the preparation of final accounts

E   *correctly identify, calculate and record appropriate adjustments*

G   *conduct investigations into business transactions with trust and courtesy*

H   *ensure that the organisation's policies, regulations, procedures and timescales relating to preparing final accounts are observed*

element 5.3

preparing the final accounts of sole traders and partnerships

A   *prepare final accounts of sole traders in proper form, from the trial balance*

C   *observe the organisation's policies, regulations, procedures and timescales in relation to preparing final accounts of sole traders and partnerships*

D   *identify and resolve or refer to the appropriate person discrepancies, unusual features or queries*

BAD DEBTS AND PROVISION FOR DOUBTFUL DEBTS

A bad debt is a debt owing to a business which it considers will never be paid.

Let us consider a business with debtors of £10,000. This total will, most probably, be made up of a number of debtors' accounts. At any one time, a few of these accounts will be bad, and therefore the amount is uncollectable: these are bad debts, and they need to be written off, ie the business will give up trying to collect the debt and will accept the loss.

Provision for doubtful debts (sometimes called provision for bad debts) is the estimate by a business of the likely percentage of its debtors which may go bad during any one accounting period.

There are likely to be some debtors' accounts which, although they are not yet bad, may be giving some concern as to their ability to pay: a provision for doubtful debts) needs to be made in respect of these. The one thing the business with debtors of £10,000 cannot do is to show this debtors' amount as a current asset in the balance sheet: to do so would be to imply to the reader of the balance sheet that the full £10,000 is collectable. Instead, this gross debtors' figure might be reduced in two stages, for example:

- debtors' accounts with balances totalling £200 are to be written off as bad
- a provision for doubtful debts is to be made amounting, in this case, to two per cent of remaining debtors

Thus the debtors figure becomes:

	£
Gross debtors	10,000
Less: bad debts written off	200
	9,800
Less: provision for doubtful debts at two* per cent	196
Net debtors (recorded in balance sheet)	9,604

* Note: The amount of the provision for doubtful debts will vary from business to business, depending on the past experience of receiving payment, the nature of the business and the current economic climate.

Bad debts and provision for doubtful debts is an application of the accounting concept of prudence (see Chapter 9). By reducing the debtors' figure, through the profit and loss account and balance sheet, a more realistic amount is shown of the amount that the business can expect to receive.

TREATMENT OF BAD DEBTS

Bad debts are written off when they become uncollectable. This means that all reasonable efforts to recover the amount owing have been exhausted, ie statements and letters have been sent to the debtor requesting payment and legal action, where appropriate, or the threat of legal action has failed to obtain payment.

In writing off a debtor's account as bad, the business is bearing the cost of the amount due. The debtor's account is closed and the amount (or amounts, where a number of accounts are dealt with in this way) is debited to *bad debts written off* account. This account stores up the amounts of account balances written off during the year (in much the same way as an expense account). At the end of the financial year, the balance of the account is transferred to profit and loss account, where it is described as *bad debts written off.*

In terms of double-entry book-keeping, the transactions are:

– *debit* bad debts written off account

– *credit* debtor's account

At the end of the financial year, bad debts written off account is transferred to profit and loss account:

– *debit* profit and loss account

– *credit* bad debts written off account

For example, the following debtor's account is in the sales ledger:

Dr			T Hughes			Cr
2004		£	2004			£
5 Jan	Sales	55	8 May	Bank		25
			6 Jul	Cash		5

It is now 15 December 2004 and you are reviewing the debtors' accounts before the end of the financial year on 31 December. Your business has sent statements and 'chaser' letters to T Hughes – the last letter was dated 30 September, and was returned marked 'gone away, not known at this address'. Nothing further has been heard from T Hughes. You take the decision to write off this account as a bad debt; the account will be closed off as shown on the next page:

Dr			**T Hughes**		Cr
2004		£	2004		£
5 Jan	Sales	55	8 May	Bank	25
			6 Jul	Cash	5
			15 Dec	Bad debts written off	25
		55			55

The balance is transferred to the 'holding' account, *bad debts written off*, together with other accounts written off. At the end of the financial year, the total of this account is transferred to profit and loss account:

Dr			**Bad Debts Written Off Account**	Cr
2004		£	2004	£
15 Dec	T Hughes	25	31 Dec Profit and loss account	200
15 Dec	A Lane	85		
15 Dec	A Harvey	90		
		200		200

In final accounts, the effect of writing off debts as bad is to reduce the previously reported profit – in the example above, by £200.

Notes:

- If you are preparing final accounts and the figure for bad debts is shown in the trial balance (debit side), simply record the amount as an overhead in profit and loss account – the debtors' figure has been reduced already.

- If the bad debts figure is not already shown in the trial balance, and a note tells you to write off a particular debt as bad, you need to list the amount as an overhead in profit and loss account and reduce the debtors' figure for the balance sheet. To do this with an extended trial balance, use the adjustments columns, debit bad debts, and credit the debtors figure (in the balance sheet columns show net debtors, ie debtors less adjustment).

VAT relief on bad debts

A VAT-registered business can reclaim VAT originally charged on debts which are now being written off. However, in order to claim relief, the debt must be more than six months overdue, ie more than six months from the date the payment was originally due. Thus a sale made on 30-day terms on 1 January would be due for payment on 31 January; if this sale is written off as a bad debt, VAT relief would be available after 31 July.

bad debts recovered

If, by chance, a former debtor whose account has been written off as bad, should make a payment, the book-keeping entries are:

- *debit* cash/bank account
- *credit* debtor's account
- *debit* debtor's account
- *credit* either, bad debts written off account
  or, bad debts recovered account

The latter account, *bad debts recovered*, is used where a business has substantial debtors and is successful in chasing its bad debts. If a recovery is a rare event – perhaps once a year – the practical accounting solution is to credit bad debts written off account. Having recovered payment from the former debtor, if the customer now wishes to buy goods or services, it is prudent to insist on cash payment for some time to come!

TREATMENT OF PROVISION FOR DOUBTFUL DEBTS

Provision for doubtful debts is different from writing off a bad debt because there is only the possibility – not the certainty – of future bad debts. The debtors' figure (after writing off bad debts) is reduced either by totalling the balances of the accounts that may not pay or, more likely, by applying a percentage to the total figure for debtors. The percentage chosen is based on past experience and varies from business to business – for example, a hire purchase company may well use a higher percentage than a bank.

The usual procedure is to have two accounts:

- *provision for doubtful debts: adjustment account*, which records the amount to create, increase or decrease the provision each year
- *provision for doubtful debts account,* which records the accumulated total of the provision

initial creation of a provision for doubtful debts

Making a provision for doubtful debts comes *after* writing off bad debts (if any). The steps are:

step 1   A business, at the end of the financial year, estimates the percentage of its debtors which are doubtful may go bad, say two per cent.

step 2   The provision is calculated (eg £9,800 x 2% = £196)

step 3 The provision is recorded in the book-keeping system:

- *debit* profit and loss account (ie an expense)
- *credit* provision for doubtful debts: adjustment account
- *debit* provision for doubtful debts: adjustment account
- *credit* provision for doubtful debts account

The provision for doubtful debts: adjustment account acts as a 'holding' account, through which transfers to and from profit and loss account are made. The provision for doubtful debts account holds the accumulated total of the provision, which is deducted from debtors in the balance sheet (see below).

step 4 In the final accounts, the amount of the provision is:

- listed in the profit and loss account as an expense
- deducted from the debtors' figure in the current assets section of the balance sheet, as here:

	£	£	£
Current assets			
Stock		x	
Debtors	9,800		
Less provision for doubtful debts	196		
		9,604	
Prepayments		x	
Bank		x	
Cash		x	

Note that the business, in creating a provision for doubtful debts, is presenting a realistic and prudent estimate of its debtor position.

adjustments to provision for doubtful debts

Once a provision for doubtful debts has been created, the only adjustments that need to be made are as a result of:

- a *policy change* in the provision, eg an increase in the fixed percentage from 2% to 5%

- an *arithmetical adjustment* in the provision as a result of a change in the total of debtors, eg increase in debtors of £5,000 will require a proportionally higher provision

If, or when, either of these two situations arises, the adjustment to the existing provision will be:

- either *upwards* (increase in provision percentage, or increase in debtor figure)
- or *downwards* (decrease in provision percentage, or decrease in debtor figure)

increasing the provision

The *increase in the provision* is recorded in the book-keeping system as follows:

– *debit* profit and loss account (ie an overhead)
– *credit* provision for doubtful debts: adjustment account
– *debit* provision for doubtful debts: adjustment account
– *credit* provision for doubtful debts account

For the balance sheet, the balance of provision for doubtful debts account is deducted from the debtors' figure to show net debtors.

decreasing the provision

The *decrease in the provision* is recorded as:

– *debit* provision for doubtful debts: adjustment account
– *credit* profit and loss account (ie income)
– *debit* provision for doubtful debts account
– *credit* provision for doubtful debts: adjustment account

Again, the balance sheet shows the balance of provision for doubtful debts account deducted from the debtors' figure to show net debtors.

Note that provision for doubtful debts and bad debts written off are completely separate adjustments: the two should not be confused. It is quite usual to see in a profit and loss account entries for both bad debts (written off) and provision for doubtful debts (the creation or adjustment of provision for doubtful debts).

Case Study

BOOK-KEEPING FOR PROVISION FOR DOUBTFUL DEBTS

A business decides to create a provision for doubtful debts of five per cent of its debtors. After writing off bad debts, the debtors figures at the end of each of three years are:

2004 £10,000
2005 £15,000
2006 £12,000

book-keeping entries

creating the provision (year 2004):
£10,000 x 5% = £500

– *debit* profit and loss account

– *credit* provision for doubtful debts: adjustment account

– *debit* provision for doubtful debts: adjustment account

– *credit* provision for doubtful debts account

increasing the provision (year 2005):
£5,000 (increase in debtors) x 5% = £250

– *debit* profit and loss account

– *credit* provision for doubtful debts: adjustment account

– *debit* provision for doubtful debts: adjustment account

– *credit* provision for doubtful debts account

decreasing the provision (year 2006):
£3,000 (decrease in debtors) x 5% = £150

– *debit* provision for doubtful debts: adjustment account

– *credit* profit and loss account

– *debit* provision for doubtful debts account

– *credit* provision for doubtful debts: adjustment account

The book-keeping entries for

• provision for doubtful debts: adjustment account

• provision for doubtful debts account

are as follows:

Dr	**Provision for Doubtful Debts: Adjustment Account**			Cr
2004		£	2004	£
31 Dec	Provision for doubtful debts	500	31 Dec Profit and loss account	500
2005			2005	
31 Dec	Provision for doubtful debts	250	31 Dec Profit and loss account	250
2006			2006	
31 Dec	Profit and loss account	150	31 Dec Provision for doubtful debts	150

Dr   **Provision for Doubtful Debts Account**   Cr

2004		£	2004		£
			31 Dec	Prov for doubtful debts:	
31 Dec	Balance c/d	500		adjustment	500
2005			2005		
31 Dec	Balance c/d	750	1 Jan	Balance b/d	500
			31 Dec	Prov for doubtful debts:	
				adjustment*	250
				*(increase in provision)	
		750			750
2006			2006		
31 Dec	Prov for doubtful debts:		1 Jan	Balance b/d	750
	adjustment*	150			
	*(decrease in provision)				
31 Dec	Balance c/d	600			
		750			750
2007			2007		
			1 Jan	Balance b/d	600

the final accounts

The effect of the above transactions on the final accounts is shown as follows:

Year	Profit and loss account		Balance sheet		
	Expense	Income	Debtors	Less provision for doubtful debts	Net debtors
	£	£	£	£	£
2004	500	–	10,000	500	9,500
2005	250	–	15,000	750	14,250
2006	–	150	12,000	600	11,400

The profit and loss account and balance sheet extracts for each year are as follows:

2004

Profit and loss account (extract) for the year ended 31 December 2004

	£	£
Gross profit		x
Less overheads:		
Provision for doubtful debts: adjustment	500	

Balance sheet (extract) as at 31 December 2004

	£	£	£
Current assets			
Stock		x	
Debtors	10,000		
Less provision for doubtful debts	500		
		9,500	

2005

Profit and loss account (extract) for the year ended 31 December 2005

	£	£
Gross profit		x
Less overheads:		
Provision for doubtful debts: adjustment	250	

Balance sheet (extract) as at 31 December 2005

	£	£	£
Current assets			
Stock		x	
Debtors	15,000		
Less provision for doubtful debts	750		
		14,250	

2006

Profit and loss account (extract) for the year ended 31 December 2006

	£	£
Gross profit		x
Add income:		
Provision for doubtful debts: adjustment		150
		x

Balance sheet (extract) as at 31 December 2006

	£	£	£
Current assets			
Stock		x	
Debtors	12,000		
Less provision for doubtful debts	600		
		11,400	

Note:

When preparing final accounts in Student Activities, Skills Tests and Examinations, there will be a note to the trial balance telling you to make an adjustment to the provision for doubtful debts. Sometimes you will be told a percentage figure, eg 'provision for doubtful debts is to be maintained at five per cent of debtors'; alternatively, you may be told the new provision figure (be careful of the wording – distinguish between 'increase the provision to £750' and 'increase the provision by £750').

BAD DEBTS AND PROVISION FOR DOUBTFUL DEBTS IN THE EXTENDED TRIAL BALANCE

bad debts

If bad debts already appear in the trial balance, simply show the amount in the profit and loss column: this will have the effect of reducing net profit. Do not alter the figure for debtors, as it will have been reduced already by the amount written off.

If a note to the trial balance tells you to write off, say, £100 of bad debts, then you will need to include a row on the extended trial balance for bad debts. In the adjustments column, show £100 as a debit to this row, and credit the debtors row. This will give an expense of £100 for profit and loss account, and will reduce debtors for the balance sheet by £100 (show net debtors in the balance sheet column).

provision for doubtful debts

In the extended trial balance layout you will see that, towards the bottom, a row is preprinted for provision for doubtful debts: adjustment. Use this as the 'holding' account to create, or increase, or decrease the provision.

For example, to increase an existing provision of £500 (which will be shown in the trial balance) by, say, £250, record the following in the extended trial balance:

- in the adjustments column
    - *debit* provision for doubtful debts: adjustment account
    - *credit* provision for doubtful debts account
- in the profit and loss column record the £250 amount of the provision for doubtful debts: adjustment as an expense in the debit column
- in the balance sheet column record the provision for doubtful debts as £750, ie the trial balance figure of £500 and the amount of £250 shown in the adjustments column

Where a new provision is to be created the above principles are followed; to reduce an existing provision, then the reverse of the above will be followed.

Remember that, in the extended trial balance:

- provision for doubtful debts: adjustment is shown in the profit and loss account and records the amount to create, increase or decrease the provision each year
- provision for doubtful debts is shown in the credit column of the balance sheet and is the accumulated total of the provision

BAD DEBTS AND PROVISION FOR DOUBTFUL DEBTS IN CONVENTIONAL FORMAT FINAL ACCOUNTS

bad debts

- If bad debts already appear in the trial balance, show the amount as an overhead in profit and loss account. No adjustment is needed to the figure for debtors in the balance sheet.

- If a note to the trial balance tells you to write off a bad debt:
    - show the amount as an overhead in profit and loss account
    - reduce the debtors figure in the balance sheet by the amount

provision for doubtful debts

- Show the amount of the adjustment to be made for the year as either
    - an overhead in profit and loss account (for an increase, and the creation, of a provision), or
    - an income amount in profit and loss account (for a decrease of a provision)
- Deduct from debtors the balance of provision for doubtful debts account (which includes any adjustment just made to profit and loss account) to show net debtors. Note that it is the accumulated total of provision for doubtful debts that is deducted from debtors.

Case Study

TARA SMITH:
BAD DEBTS AND PROVISION FOR DOUBTFUL DEBTS

We will now focus on how the bad debt and provision for doubtful debts amounts are shown in the profit and loss account and balance sheet. We will continue with the trial balance of Tara Smith and include adjustments for the year for:

- bad debts of £100 written off
- provision for doubtful debts of £250 created (note that there is no existing provision)

extended trial balance (see next page)

The columns which are affected are adjustments, profit and loss, and balance sheet – the altered figures are shaded for illustrative purposes.

final accounts: conventional format (pages 131-132)

There is no effect on gross profit; net profit is reduced to £4,625 because of the bad debts of £100 written off and the creation of provision for doubtful debts of £250. In Tara Smith's final accounts, the figures for the adjustments are shaded for illustrative purposes.

EXTENDED TRIAL BALANCE   **TARA SMITH TRADING AS "THE FASHION SHOP"**   **31 DECEMBER 2004**

Account name	Ledger balances		Adjustments		Profit and loss		Balance sheet	
	Dr £	Cr £	Dr £	Cr £	Dr £	Cr £	Dr £	Cr £
Opening stock	12,500				12,500			
Purchases	105,000				105,000			
Sales		155,000				155,000		
Administration expenses	6,200				6,200			
Wages	23,500				23,500			
Rent paid	750			75	675			
Telephone	500		100		600			
Interest paid	4,500				4,500			
Travel expenses	550				550			
Premises	100,000						100,000	
Provision for depreciation: premises				2,000				2,000
Shop fittings	20,000						20,000	
Provision for depreciation: shop fittings				5,000				5,000
Debtors	10,500			100			10,400	
Bank	5,450						5,450	
Cash	50						50	
Capital		75,000						75,000
Drawings	7,000						7,000	
Loan from bank		50,000						50,000
Creditors		14,500						14,500
Value Added Tax		2,000						2,000
Provision for doubtful debts				250				250
Closing stock: Profit & loss			10,500			10,500		
Closing stock: Balance sheet				10,500			10,500	
Accruals				100				100
Prepayments			75				75	
Depreciation			7,000		7,000			
Bad debts			100		100			
Provision for doubtful debts:adjustment			250		250			
Net profit/loss					4,625			4,625
	296,500	296,500	18,025	18,025	165,500	165,500	153,475	153,475

TARA SMITH, TRADING AS "THE FASHION SHOP"

TRADING AND PROFIT AND LOSS ACCOUNT
for the year ended 31 December 2004

	£	£
Sales		155,000
Opening stock	12,500	
Purchases	105,000	
	117,500	
Less Closing stock	10,500	
Cost of sales		107,000
Gross profit		48,000
Less overheads:		
Administration expenses	6,200	
Wages	23,500	
Rent paid	675	
Telephone	600	
Interest paid	4,500	
Travel expenses	550	
Depreciation:		
premises	2,000	
shop fittings	5,000	
Bad debts written off	100	
Provision for doubtful debts	250	
		43,375
Net profit		4,625

note
Bad debts written off for the year, together with the adjustment for an increase in provision for doubtful debts, are included with the other overheads of the business. They are shown here in a grey box for illustrative purposes.

TARA SMITH, TRADING AS "THE FASHION SHOP"

BALANCE SHEET
as at 31 December 2004

	Cost £	Provision for dep'n £	Net £
Fixed assets			
Premises	100,000	2,000	98,000
Shop fittings	20,000	5,000	15,000
	120,000	7,000	113,000
Current assets			
Stock (closing)		10,500	
Debtors	10,400		
Less provision for doubtful debts	250		
		10,150	
Prepayment		75	
Bank		5,450	
Cash		50	
		26,225	
Less Current liabilities			
Creditors	14,500		
Value Added Tax	2,000		
Accrual	100		
		16,600	
Working capital			9,625
			122,625
Less Long-term liabilities			
Loan from bank			50,000
NET ASSETS			72,625
FINANCED BY			
Capital			
Opening capital			75,000
Add net profit			4,625
			79,625
Less drawings			7,000
Closing capital			72,625

notes

- The amount of bad debts written off of £100 has been deducted before debtors are recorded in the balance sheet, ie £10,500 – £100 written off = £10,400.
- The balance of provision for doubtful debts account – here £250 – is deducted from the debtors' figure of £10,400 to give net debtors of £10,150. It is this latter amount that is added in to current assets.

These adjustments are shown here in a grey box for illustrative purposes.

Chapter Summary

- Not all debtors of a business will eventually settle the amounts they owe: such amounts are *bad debts* which have to be written off.

- A *provision for doubtful debts* (or *bad debts*) is made for debtors who may not pay.

- This sequence should be followed:
  - write off bad debts (if any)
  - create (or adjust) provision for doubtful debts

- To write off a bad debt:
  - *debit* bad debts written off account
  - *credit* debtor's account

  At the end of the financial year the bad debts written off account is transferred as an overhead, to profit and loss account.

- A provision for doubtful debts is often based on a fixed percentage of debtors at the year-end.

- For book-keeping purposes, two accounts are used to create, increase or decrease a provision for doubtful debts:
  - provision for doubtful debts: adjustment account, to record the annual change
  - provision for doubtful debts account, to record the accumulated total

- In the balance sheet, provision for doubtful debts is deducted from debtors.

- Having created a provision for doubtful debts, it will usually be adjusted either upwards or downwards in subsequent years in line with the change in the level of debtors.

Key Terms

bad debt	a debt owing to a business which it considers will never be paid
bad debts written off account	the account to which the amounts of account balances written off as bad are transferred
provision for doubtful debts	an estimate by a business of the likely percentage of its debtors which are doubtful and may go bad during any one accounting period
provision for doubtful debts: adjustment account	used to record the annual change in the provision for doubtful debts
provision for doubtful debts account	used to record the accumulated total of the provision for doubtful debts
bad debts recovered	where a former debtor, whose account has been written off as bad, makes payment

Student Activities

8.1   Ken Shah, a debtor of the business where you work, is unable to pay the amount owing and the accounts supervisor has decided to write off his account as a bad debt. This is recorded in the double-entry accounts by:

	Debit	Credit
(a)	bad debts written off	K Shah's account
(b)	K Shah's account	bad debts written off
(c)	cash account	K Shah's account
(d)	sales account	K Shah's account

Answer (a) or (b) or (c) or (d)

(Ignore VAT relief on bad debt write-off)

8.2   A trial balance shows debtors of £48,000 and a provision for doubtful debts of £2,200. It is decided to make the provision for doubtful debts equal to five per cent of debtors. What book-keeping entry will be made on the provision for doubtful debts account?

(a)   debit £200

(b)   debit £2,400

(c)   credit £200

(d)   credit £2,200

Answer (a) or (b) or (c) or (d)

8.3   You are the book-keeper at Waterston Plant Hire. At 31 December 2004, the end of the financial year, the business has gross debtors of £20,210. The owner decides to:

(a)   write off, as bad debts, the accounts of:

P Ross	£55
J Ball	£105
L Jones	£50

(b)   make a provision for doubtful debts of 2.5% of debtors (after writing off the above bad debts)

You are to explain how these transactions will be recorded in the final accounts at the end of the financial year.

8.4   Ross Engineering has an existing provision for doubtful debts of £300, based on 5 per cent of debtors. After writing off bad debts, the amounts of debtors at the end of the next two financial years are found to be:

30 June 2005	£8,000
30 June 2006	£7,000

The business continues to keep the provision for doubtful debts equal to 5 per cent of debtors.

As an accounts assistant at Ross Engineering, you are to show how the provision for doubtful debts will be adjusted at the end of the financial years ended 30 June 2005 and 30 June 2006, and how it will be recorded in the appropriate final accounts.

8.5 The following trial balance has been extracted by the book-keeper of Paul Sanders, who runs an office supplies business, as at 31 December 2004:

	Dr £	Cr £
Purchases and sales	51,225	81,762
Returns	186	254
Opening stock	6,031	
Discounts	324	438
Motor expenses	1,086	
Wages and salaries	20,379	
Electricity	876	
Telephone	1,241	
Rent and rates	4,565	
Sundry expenses	732	
Bad debts written off	219	
Debtors and creditors	1,040	7,671
Value Added Tax		1,301
Bank	3,501	
Cash	21	
Motor vehicles at cost	15,000	
Provision for depreciation on motor vehicles		3,000
Office equipment at cost	10,000	
Provision for depreciation on office equipment		5,000
Capital		25,000
Drawings	8,000	
	124,426	124,426

Notes at 31 December 2004:

* stock was valued at £8,210

* electricity owing £102

* rent prepaid £251

* depreciate motor vehicles at 20 per cent and office equipment at 10 per cent per annum, using the straight-line method

* create a provision for doubtful debts of 5 per cent of debtors

You are to prepare the final accounts of Paul Sanders for the year ended 31 December 2004:

* using the extended trial balance method

* in proper form, using the conventional format

8.6 The following trial balance has been extracted by the book-keeper of James Jenkins, who owns a patisserie and coffee lounge, as at 30 June 2005:

	Dr £	Cr £
Capital		36,175
Drawings	19,050	
Purchases and sales	105,240	168,432
Opening stock	9,427	
Debtors and creditors	3,840	5,294
Value Added Tax		1,492
Returns	975	1,237
Discounts	127	643
Wages and salaries	30,841	
Motor vehicle expenses	1,021	
Rent and rates	8,796	
Heating and lighting	1,840	
Telephone	355	
General expenses	1,752	
Bad debts written off	85	
Motor vehicle at cost	8,000	
Provision for depreciation on motor vehicle		3,500
Shop fittings at cost	6,000	
Provision for depreciation on shop fittings		2,000
Provision for doubtful debts		150
Cash	155	
Bank	21,419	
	218,923	218,923

Notes at 30 June 2005:
- stock was valued at £11,517
- motor vehicle expenses owing £55
- rent prepaid £275
- depreciate the motor vehicle at 25 per cent per annum, using the reducing balance method
- depreciate shop fittings at 10 per cent per annum, using the straight-line method
- the provision for doubtful debts is to be equal to 2.5 per cent of debtors

You are to prepare the final accounts of James Jenkins for the year ended 30 June 2005:
- using the extended trial balance method
- in proper form, using the conventional format

8.7 The accounts supervisor at the firm where you work hands you a cheque for £50 received from a former debtor, James Abel, whose account was written off as bad last year. The cheque is in part settlement of the amount owed by James Abel.

Note: ignore any VAT implications in the transaction.

You are to write up the following accounts, below, using today's date for the transactions:

– bank

– J Abel

– bad debts recovered

Dr		Bank Account		Cr
	£			£

Dr		J Abel		Cr
	£			£

Dr		Bad Debts Recovered Account		Cr
	£			£

this chapter covers . . .

In this chapter we will explain how the regulatory framework of accounting provides the 'rules' to be followed when preparing final accounts. These rules take the form of

- accounting concepts
- accounting standards

If the same rules have been followed, then broad comparisons can be made between the final accounts of different businesses.

We will also see how the accounting 'rules' relating to the valuation of stock are applied.

Later in the chapter we focus on the importance of the distinction between capital expenditure and revenue expenditure.

PERFORMANCE CRITERIA COVERED

unit 5: MAINTAINING FINANCIAL RECORDS AND PREPARING ACCOUNTS

element 5.2

collecting and collating information for the preparation of final accounts

H   ensure that the organisation's policies, regulations, procedures and timescales relating to preparing final accounts are observed

element 5.3

preparing the final accounts of sole traders and partnerships

C   observe the organisation's policies, regulations, procedures and timescales in relation to preparing final accounts of sole traders and partnerships

ACCOUNTING CONCEPTS

There are a number of **accounting concepts** – or 'rules' of accounting – which underlie the preparation of final accounts. These concepts help to make final accounts relevant and reliable to users, and also enable them to be comparable and understandable.

The more important accounting concepts are illustrated in the diagram below.

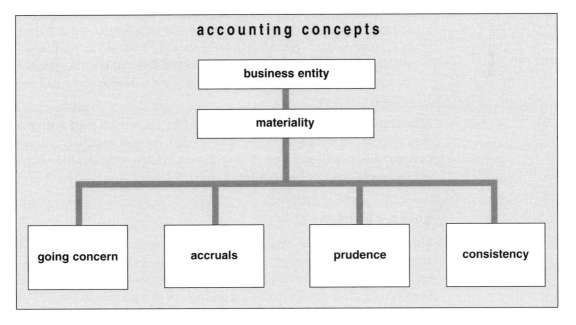

business entity

This refers to the fact that final accounts record and report on the activities of one particular business. They do not include the assets and liabilities of those who play a part in owning or running the business. Thus the owner's personal assets and liabilities are kept separate from those of the business: the main links between the business and the owner's personal funds are capital and drawings.

materiality

Some items in accounts are of such low value that it is not worthwhile recording them separately, ie they are not 'material'.

Examples include:

- Small expense items, such as donations to charities, the purchase of plants for the office, window cleaning, etc, do not justify their own separate expense account; instead they are grouped together in a sundry expenses account.

- End-of-year stocks of office stationery, eg paper clips, staples, photocopying paper, etc, are often not valued for the purpose of final accounts, because the amount is not material and does not justify the time and effort involved. This does mean, however, that the cost of all stationery purchased during the year is charged as an expense to profit and loss account – technically wrong, but not material enough to affect the final accounts.

- Low-cost fixed assets are often charged as an expense in profit and loss account, instead of being classed as capital expenditure, eg a stapler, waste-paper basket, etc. Strictly, these should be treated as fixed assets and depreciated each year over their estimated life; in practice, because the amounts involved are not material, they are treated as profit and loss account expenses.

Materiality depends very much on the size of the business. A large company may consider that items of less than £1,000 are not material; a small company will usually use a much lower figure. What is material, and what is not becomes a matter of judgement.

going concern

This presumes that the business to which the final accounts relate will continue to trade in the foreseeable future. The trading and profit and loss account and balance sheet are prepared on the basis that there is no intention to reduce significantly the size of the business or to liquidate the business. If the business was not a going concern, assets would have very different values, and the balance sheet would be affected considerably. For example, a large, purpose-built factory has considerable value to a going concern business but, if the factory had to be sold, it is likely to have a limited use for other industries, and therefore will have a lower market value. Values based on break-up (realisable) amounts are the opposite of the going concern concept and would require extra depreciation to be charged as an expense to profit and loss account to allow for the reduced value of fixed assets.

accruals (or matching)

This means that expenses and revenues must be matched so that they concern the same goods or services and the same time period. We have already put this concept into practice in Chapter 6, where expenses and revenues were adjusted to take note of prepayments and accruals. The profit and loss account should always show the amount of the expense that should have been incurred, ie the expenditure for the year, whether or not it has been paid.

This is the principle of income and expenditure accounting, rather than using receipts and payments as and when they fall due. Other examples of the accruals concept are:

- debtors
- creditors
- depreciation
- bad debts
- provision for doubtful debts
- opening and closing stock adjustments in the trading account

prudence

This concept, also known as conservatism in accounting, requires that final accounts should always, where there is any doubt, report a conservative figure for profit or the valuation of assets. To this end, profits are not to be anticipated and should only be recognised when it is reasonably certain that they will be realised; at the same time all known liabilities should be provided for. A good example of the prudence concept is where a provision is made for doubtful debts (see Chapter 8) – the debtors have not yet gone bad, but it is expected, from experience, that a certain percentage will eventually need to be written off as bad debts. The valuation of stock (see later in this chapter) also follows the prudence concept. 'Anticipate no profit, but anticipate all losses' is a summary of the concept which, in its application, prevents an over-optimistic presentation of a business through the final accounts.

consistency

This requires that, when a business adopts particular accounting methods, it should continue to use such methods consistently. For example, a business that decides to make a provision for depreciation on machinery at ten per cent per annum, using the straight-line method, should continue to use that percentage and method for future final accounts for this asset. Of course, having once chosen a particular method, a business is entitled to make changes provided there are good reasons for so doing, and a note to the final accounts would explain what has happened. By applying the consistency concept, direct comparison between the final accounts of different years can be made. Further examples of the use of the consistency concept are:

- stock valuation (see later in this chapter)
- the application of the materiality concept

other accounting concepts

Other concepts followed when preparing final accounts include:

- **money measurement** – all items are expressed in the common denominator of money; only by using money can items be added together to give, for example, net profit or a balance sheet total
- **historical cost** – assets and liabilities are initially recorded in the final accounts at historical cost, ie the actual amount of the transaction (note that some businesses may adopt a policy of regular revaluation of assets)
- **dual aspect** – each business transaction is recorded by means of two opposite accounting entries (debit and credit), but of equal values; note that double-entry book-keeping is an example of the dual aspect concept in practice
- **realisation** – business transactions are recorded in the final accounts when the legal title passes between buyer and seller; this may well not be at the same time as payment is made, eg credit sales are recorded when the sale is made, but payment will be made at a later date
- **objectivity** – the presentation of final accounts should be objective, rather than subjective, and should not be influenced by the opinions or personal expectations of the owner of the business concerned, or the accountant preparing the accounts

ACCOUNTING POLICIES

Accounting policies are the methods used by an individual business to show the effect of transactions, and to record assets and liabilities in its accounts. For example, a business will state its accounting policy for the valuation of closing stock – often the phrase used is 'stocks are valued at the lower of cost and net realisable value' (see page 147).

An accounting standard - Financial Reporting Standard No 18, *Accounting policies* (see page 146) - sets out how businesses are to select and report their accounting policies.

'STATEMENTS OF PRINCIPLES' AND ACCOUNTING STANDARDS

Over the last thirty or so years, a framework has been developed to provide the rules of accounting. The intention has been to reduce the variety of alternative accounting treatments. Today, this framework is represented by:

- Statement of Principles for Financial Reporting (SOP)
- Statements of Standard Accounting Practice (SSAPs)
- Financial Reporting Standards (FRSs)

The Accounting Standards Board (ASB) is the organisation responsible for developing these rules of accounting. Its aims are to establish and improve standards of financial accounting and reporting.

Note that SSAPs and FRSs are accounting standards (see next page); Statement of Principles is not an accounting standard, but sets out the principles to be followed when preparing final accounts.

STATEMENT OF PRINCIPLES FOR FINANCIAL REPORTING

The Accounting Standards Board has developed its *Statement of Principles for Financial Reporting* in order to set out the principles that should underlie the preparation and presentation of financial statements (final accounts). Statement of Principles – which is not an accounting standard – comprises eight 'chapters', each dealing with key issues:

1 The objective of financial statements

2 The reporting entity

3 The qualitative characteristics of financial information

4 The elements of financial statements

5 Recognition in financial statements

6 Measurement in financial statements

7 Presentation of financial information

8 Accounting for interests in other entities

Statement of Principles is covered in detail in your later studies (Unit 11). At this level, though, we need to be aware of the characteristics of financial information from Chapter 3 of Statement of Principles. The four characteristics that make financial information useful are identified by Statement of Principles, as shown in the following diagram.

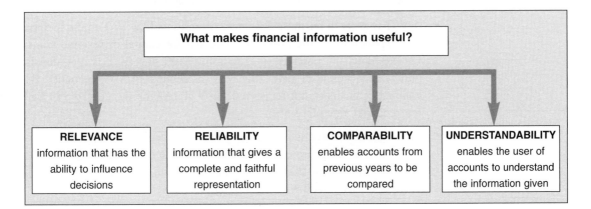

For financial information to be useful it must also be *material* – see also page 139. If information is not material, then it cannot be useful, and will not have any of the four qualitative characteristics.

ACCOUNTING STANDARDS

As noted on the previous page, accounting standards comprise *Statements of Standard Accounting Practice (SSAPs)* and *Financial Reporting Standards (FRSs)*. SSAPs are no longer issued, but those still current come under the control of the Accounting Standards Board. Quite a number of SSAPs have been replaced by FRSs as part of an attempt by the ASB to reduce the number of permissible accounting treatments.

Accountants are required by the ASB to observe the applicable accounting standards, and to disclose and explain significant departures from them.

The accounting standards relevant to your studies are set out below:

SSAP 5 Accounting for Value Added Tax

- VAT is a tax on the supply of goods and services, which is borne by the final consumer but is collected at each stage of the production and distribution chain.

- Most businesses with a turnover (sales) above a certain figure must be registered for VAT.

- At regular intervals, businesses pay the VAT Authority (HM Revenue & Customs):

  – the amount of output tax collected on sales made

  – less the amount of input tax on goods and services purchased

  If the amount of input tax is greater than output tax, the business claims a refund of the difference from HM Revenue & Customs.

- A VAT-registered business does not normally include VAT in the income and expenditure of the business – whether for capital or revenue items. For example, the purchase of goods for £100 plus VAT is recorded in purchases account as £100 (the VAT is debited to VAT account). By contrast, a business not registered for VAT records the cost as £117.50 (current VAT rate of 17.5%).

- Some goods and services (such as postal services, loans of money, sales or lettings of land) are exempt from VAT – the effect of this is that the supplier cannot charge output tax, and can claim back only a proportion of input tax as agreed with the VAT authorities.

- Irrecoverable VAT is where a business registered for VAT cannot reclaim input tax (for example on cars, other than for resale); thus the total cost, including VAT, is entered into the accounts as the expenditure.

- All VAT-registered businesses are required to keep accounting records of their VAT transactions. Such records are normally kept in the form of a VAT account (or VAT control account) in the main ledger:

Dr	VAT Account	Cr
	£	£
input tax on goods and services purchased (figures from books of prime entry: purchases day book, sales returns day book, journal, cash book payments, petty cash book)		**output tax** collected on sales made (figures from books of prime entry: sales day book, purchases returns day book, journal, cash book receipts)
debit balance = amount due to be refunded by the VAT Authority		**credit balance** = amount due to be paid to the VAT Authority

When VAT account is balanced:

– a debit balance means that a refund is due from HM Revenue & Customs (the VAT Authority)

– a credit balance means that a payment is due to be made to HM Revenue & Customs

Refunds and payments are made at regular intervals depending on the terms of the VAT scheme under which the business is registered. Many businesses, for example, make payments, or receive refunds, on a quarterly basis, ie every three months.

SSAP 9 Stocks and long-term contracts

This standard sets out the broad rule that stock should be valued at the lower of cost and net realisable value – see following section.

FRS 15 Tangible fixed assets

- This standard requires that all fixed assets having a known useful economic life are to be depreciated (note that freehold land is not depreciated – unless it is a mine or a quarry). See Chapters 7 and 10.
- The objective of depreciation is to record in profit and loss account the cost of the use of fixed assets during the accounting period. Note that this is an application of the accruals concept (see page 140), where the cost of the fixed asset is spread over its useful economic life.
- Any acceptable depreciation method can be used. A change from one method of depreciation to another is only allowed if the new method gives a fairer presentation in the final accounts.
- Depreciation amounts are normally based on the cost of the fixed assets (where assets are revalued, depreciation is based on the revalued amount).

FRS 18 Accounting policies

The objective of this standard is to ensure that for all material items:

- a business selects the accounting policies most appropriate to its particular circumstances for the purpose of giving a true and fair view
- the accounting policies are reviewed regularly to ensure that they remain appropriate, and are changed when necessary
- sufficient information is disclosed in the financial statements to enable users to understand the accounting policies adopted and how they have been implemented

It is important that a business selects its accounting policies to fit in with the objectives of:

- relevance – the financial information is useful to users of accounts
- reliability – the financial information can be depended upon by users
- comparability – financial information can be compared with that from previous accounting periods
- understandability – users can understand the financial information provided

Note that these four objectives are also referred to in Statement of Principles for Financial Reporting (see page 143).

Two accounting concepts are specifically mentioned by FRS 18:

- going concern (see page 140) – the accounting standard normally requires businesses to prepare final accounts on the basis that they will continue to trade
- accruals (see page 140) – the accounting standard requires the accruals basis (ie accruals and prepayments) of accounting to be used in the preparation of final accounts

VALUATION OF STOCK

The control and valuation of stock is an important aspect in the efficient management of a business. Manual or computer records are used to show the amount of stock held and its value at any time during the year. However, at the end of the financial year it is essential for a business to make a physical *stock-take* for use in the final accounts. This involves stock control personnel going into the stores, the shop, or the warehouse and counting each item. The counted stock for each type of stock held is then valued as follows:

number of items held x stock valuation per item = stock value

The auditors of a business may make random checks to ensure that the stock value is correct.

The value of stock at the beginning and end of the financial year is used to calculate the figure for cost of sales. Therefore, the stock value has an effect on profit for the year.

Stock is valued at:

- either what it cost the business to buy the stock (including additional costs to bring the product or service to its present location and condition, such as delivery charges)

- or the net realisable value – the actual or estimated selling price (less any further costs, such as selling and distribution)

This stock valuation is often described as being *at the lower of cost and net realisable value*. This valuation is taken from SSAP 9 and applies the *prudence concept*. It is illustrated as follows:

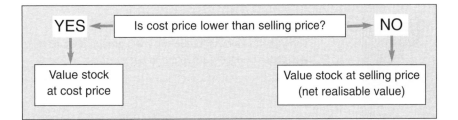

Thus two different stock values are compared:

- cost, including additional costs such as delivery charges

- net realisable value (the amount the stock will sell for), less any further costs such as selling and distribution

The lower of these two values is taken, and *different items or groups of stock are compared separately*. These principles are illustrated in the two Case Studies which follow.

THE CLOTHING STORE: STOCK VALUATION

situation

This shop bought in a range of 'designer' beachwear in the Spring, with each item costing £15 and retailing for £30. Most of the stock is sold but, by Autumn, ten items remain unsold. These are put on the 'bargain rail' at £18 each. On 31 December, at the end of the shop's financial year, five items remain unsold. At what price will they be included in the year-end stock valuation?

Twelve months later, three items still remain unsold and have been reduced further to £10 each. At what price will they now be valued in the year-end stock valuation?

solution

- At 31 December, the five items will be valued at a cost of £15 each, ie 5 x £15 = £75.

- Twelve months later, the three items remaining unsold will be valued at a net realisable value of £10 each, ie 3 x £10 = £30.

Important note: Stock is *never* valued at selling price when selling price is above cost price. The reason for this is that selling price includes profit, and to value stock in this way would bring the profit into the accounts before it has been earned.

PAINT AND WALLPAPER SUPPLIES: STOCK VALUATION

situation

The year-end stocks for the two main groups of stock held by the business 'Paint and Wallpaper Supplies' are found to be:

	Cost	Net Realisable Value
	£	£
Paints	2,500	2,300
Wallpapers	5,000	7,500
	7,500	9,800

Which of the following stock valuations do you think is correct?

(a)   £7,500

(b)   £9,800

(c)   £7,300

(d)   £10,000

solution

Stock valuation (c) is correct, because it has taken the 'lower of cost and net realisable value' for each *group* of stock, ie

Paints (at net realisable value)	£2,300
Wallpapers (at cost)	£5,000
	£7,300

You will also note that this valuation is the lowest of the four possible choices, indicating that stock valuation follows the *prudence concept*.

commonly used stock valuation methods

Businesses use different methods to calculate the cost price of stock. Three commonly-used methods are:

- FIFO (first in, first out) This method assumes that the first stocks received are the first to be used, so that the valuation of stock on hand at any time consists of the most recently acquired stock.

- LIFO (last in, first out) Here it is assumed that the last stocks received are the first to be used, so that the stock on hand is made up of earlier purchases.

- AVCO (average cost) Here the average cost of items held at the beginning of the period is calculated; as new stocks are received a new average cost is calculated (usually based on a weighted average, using the number of units bought as the weighting).

The use of a particular method does not necessarily correspond with the method of physical distribution adopted in a firm's stores. For example, in a car factory one car battery of type X is the same as another, and no-one will be concerned if the storekeeper issues one from the latest batch received, even if the FIFO system has been adopted. However, perishable goods are always physically handled on the basis of first in, first out, even if the accounting stock records use another method.

Having chosen a suitable stock valuation method, a business would continue to use that method unless there were good reasons for making the change. This is in line with the consistency concept of accounting.

Case Study

THE CORNER STORES: VALUATION METHODS

situation

One of the lines stocked by 'The Corner Stores' is tins of baked beans. The following are the purchases and sales of tins of beans for two weeks (note that there was no stock at the beginning of week 1):

Week 1:   100 tins of beans bought at a cost of 25p per tin

50 tins sold at 40p per tin

Week 2:   100 tins of beans bought at a cost of 30p per tin

75 tins sold at 40p per tin

What will be the stock valuation at the end of week 2, using

- FIFO (first in, first out)
- LIFO (last in, first out)
- AVCO (average cost)

and what gross profit has been made on beans over the two week period?

solution

At the end of week 2 there are 75 tins of beans in stock.

FIFO

Using FIFO, the week 2 closing stock consists of 75 tins at the
latest price, ie 30p. Therefore the stock valuation is 75 x 30p   = £22.50

LIFO

With LIFO the closing stock consists of:

50 tins from week 1 at 25p each	= £12.50
25 tins from week 2 at 30p each	= £ 7.50
75 tins	= £20.00

AVCO

We must calculate the average cost as follows:

50 tins in stock at end of week 1 at 25p	= £12.50
100 tins received in week 2 at 30p	= £30.00
150 tins at an average cost of 28.33p (£42.50 ÷ 150)	= £42.50
75 tins in stock at end of week at 28.33p each	= £21.25

The conclusion here is that, even with tins of baked beans, there is a difference in
closing stock valuation depending on the method used:

FIFO	£22.50
LIFO	£20.00
AVCO	£21.25

From these results we can draw a general conclusion that, in times of rising prices,
FIFO always gives the highest valuation, LIFO the lowest, and AVCO comes
somewhere between the two (although not necessarily exactly half-way between the
two).

You may wonder why it is necessary to spend so much time on looking at different stock valuation methods. The method adopted for stock valuation is important because of the effect it has on the profits of the business.

Let us now calculate how much profit this business made on its sales of baked beans. The profit and loss account is set out below.

You will see that as a result of using different closing stock valuations, the gross profit is different. Here, with prices rising, FIFO gives the highest profit, LIFO the lowest, and AVCO is between the two. Do not forget, also, that the closing stock for one accounting period becomes the opening stock for the next, and so the following accounting period will also be affected.

PROFIT AND LOSS ACCOUNT (EXTRACT) FOR THE TWO WEEKS ENDED ....

		£		
Sales	50 tins of baked beans at 40p	20.00		
	75 tins of baked beans at 40p	30.00		
		50.00		

		FIFO £	LIFO £	AVCO £
Purchases	100 tins at 25p	25.00	25.00	25.00
	100 tins at 30p	30.00	30.00	30.00
		55.00	55.00	55.00
Less closing stock		22.50	20.00	21.25
Cost of sales	*minus*	32.50	35.00	33.75
Gross profit		17.50	15.00	16.25

CAPITAL EXPENDITURE AND REVENUE EXPENDITURE

When preparing final accounts it is important to distinguish between *capital expenditure* and *revenue expenditure*.

Capital expenditure can be defined as *expenditure incurred on the purchase, alteration or improvement of fixed assets*. For example, the purchase of a car for use in the business is capital expenditure. Included in capital expenditure are such costs as:

*   delivery of fixed assets
*   installation of fixed assets

- improvement (but not repair) of fixed assets
- legal costs of buying property

Revenue expenditure is *expenditure incurred on running expenses*. For example, the cost of petrol or diesel for the car (above) is revenue expenditure. Included in revenue expenditure are the costs of:

- maintenance and repair of fixed assets
- administration of the business
- selling and distributing the goods or products in which the business trades

Capital expenditure is shown on the balance sheet, while revenue expenditure is charged as an overhead or expense to profit and loss account. It is important to classify these types of expenditure correctly in the accounting system. For example, if the cost of the car was shown as an expense in profit and loss account, then net profit would be reduced considerably, or a net loss recorded; meanwhile, the balance sheet would not show the car as a fixed asset – clearly this is incorrect as the business owns the asset. Note, however, that there is a link between capital expenditure and the profit and loss account: as fixed assets are depreciated, the amount of depreciation is shown as an expense in the profit and loss account. This is an application of the accruals concept, ie the depreciation relates to the time period over which the fixed asset is used.

In some circumstances we must take care to distinguish between capital and revenue expenditure. For example:

- *cost of building an extension to the factory £30,000, which includes £1,000 for repairs to the existing factory*
  - capital expenditure, £29,000
  - revenue expenditure, £1,000 (because it is for repairs to an existing fixed asset)

- *a plot of land has been bought for £20,000, the legal costs are £750*
  - capital expenditure £20,750 (the legal costs are included in the capital expenditure, because they are the cost of acquiring the fixed asset, ie the legal costs are capitalised)

- *the business' own employees are used to install a new air conditioning system: wages £1,000, materials £1,500*
  - capital expenditure £2,500 (an addition to the property). Note that, in cases such as this, revenue expenditure, ie wages and materials purchases, will need to be reduced to allow for the transfer to capital expenditure

- *own employees used to repair and redecorate the premises: wages £500, materials £750*
    - revenue expenditure £1,250 (repairs and redecoration are running expenses)

- *purchase of a new machine £10,000, payment for installation and setting up £250*
    - capital expenditure £10,250 (costs of installation of a fixed asset are capitalised)

Only by allocating capital expenditure and revenue expenditure correctly between the balance sheet and the profit and loss account can the final accounts reflect accurately the financial state of the business. The chart below shows the main items of capital expenditure and revenue expenditure associated with three major fixed assets – buildings, vehicles and computers.

	capital expenditure	*revenue expenditure*
BUILDINGS	• cost of building • cost of extension • carriage on raw materials used • legal fees • labour cost of own employees used on building • installation of utilities, eg gas, water, electricity	• general maintenance • repairs • redecoration • depreciation
VEHICLES	• net cost, including any optional extras • delivery costs • number plates • changes to the vehicle	• fuel • road fund licence • extended warranty • painting company logo • insurance • servicing and repairs • depreciation
COMPUTERS	• net cost • installation and testing • modifications, including memory upgrades, to meet specific needs of business • installation of special wiring • cost of air conditioning to computer room • staff training (where directly related to new equipment) • computer programs (but can be classified as revenue expenditure if cost is low and will have little impact on final accounts)	• floppy discs • printer paper and other consumables • insurance • computer programs (or can be classified as capital expenditure if cost is high and will have a large impact on final accounts) • depreciation

Chapter Summary

- The accounting concepts of business entity, materiality, going concern, accruals, prudence and consistency are fundamental to the relevance and reliability of final accounts.

- *Statement of Principles for Financial Reporting* sets out the principles that should underlie the preparation and presentation of financial statements (final accounts).

- Accounting standards comprise SSAPs and FRSs.

- The usual valuation for stock is at the lower of cost and net realisable value (SSAP 9).

- Commonly used stock valuation methods include:
  - FIFO (first in, first out)
  - LIFO (last in, first out)
  - AVCO (average cost, based on a weighted average)

- Having chosen one stock valuation method, a business should apply it consistently.

- It is important to allocate capital expenditure and revenue expenditure correctly between the balance sheet and the profit and loss account so that the final accounts reflect accurately the financial state of the business.

Key Terms

accounting concepts	part of the 'rules' of accounting
business entity concept	final accounts record and report on the activities of one particular business
materiality concept	items with a low monetary value are not worthwhile recording in the accounts separately
going concern concept	the presumption that the business to which the final accounts relate will continue to trade in the foreseeable future
accruals concept	expenses and revenues are matched so that they concern the same goods or services and the same time period
prudence concept	final accounts should always, where there is any doubt, report a conservative figure for profit or the valuation of assets
consistency concept	when a business adopts particular accounting methods, it should continue to use such methods consistently
accounting policies	methods used by a business to show the effect of transactions, and to record assets and liabilities in its accounts
SSAP	Statement of Standard Accounting Practice; part of the rules of accounting

	FRS	Financial Reporting Standard; part of the rules of accounting
	capital expenditure	expenditure incurred on the purchase, alteration or improvement of fixed assets
	revenue expenditure	expenditure incurred on running expenses

Student Activities

9.1 A business should not change its basis of valuing stock without good reason. This follows the concept of:

(a)   money measurement

(b)   going concern

(c)   prudence

(d)   consistency

Answer (a) or (b) or (c) or (d)

9.2 Explain the appropriate accounting concept in each of the following circumstances.

(a)   A business has a customer who owes £1,000. Despite sending numerous statements of account to the debtor, payment has not been received. It has been decided to make a provision for bad debts in respect of this customer.

(b)   From time-to-time a business buys a pack of blank video tapes in order to record business meetings. The tapes are re-used over a number of years and are sometimes kept as a permanent record of meetings. Accounting policy is to charge the cost of the tapes – £10 for a pack of five tapes – as an expense in profit and loss account.

(c)   As an accounting trainee you are instructed to prepare two sets of a business' final accounts for a particular year, one of which uses straight-line depreciation while the other uses reducing balance depreciation. The owner of the business says that he will use the set which shows the lower profit.

(d)   A business has a financial year end of 31 December 2004. In early February 2005, an electricity bill is received covering the period November 2004 – January 2005. It is decided to apportion two-thirds of the bill to the profit and loss account for 2004 and one-third to the profit and loss account for 2005.

9.3 A discussion is taking place between Jane Smith, a sole trader, who owns a furniture shop, and her husband, John, who solely owns an engineering business. The following points are made:

(a)   John says that, having depreciated his firm's machinery last year on the reducing balance method, for this year he intends to use the straight-line method. By doing this he says that he will deduct less depreciation from profit and loss account, so his net profit will be higher and his bank manager will be impressed. He says he might revert back to reducing balance method next year.

(b)   At the end of her financial year, Jane comments that the stock of her shop had cost £10,000. She says that, as she normally adds 50 per cent to cost price to give the selling price, she intends to put a value of £15,000 for closing stock in the final accounts.

(c)   John's car is owned by his business but he keeps referring to it as my car. Jane reminds him that it does not belong to him, but to the firm. He replies that of course it belongs to him and, furthermore, if the firm went bankrupt, he would be able to keep the car.

(d)   John's business has debtors of £30,000. He knows that, included in this figure is a bad debt of £2,500. He wants to show £30,000 as debtors in the year-end balance sheet in order to have a high figure for current assets.

(e)   On the last day of her financial year, Jane sold a large order of furniture, totalling £3,000, to a local hotel. The furniture was invoiced and delivered from stock that day, before year-end stocktaking commenced. The payment was received early in the new financial year and Jane now asks John if she will be able to put this sale through the accounts for the new year, instead of the old, but without altering the figures for purchases and closing stock for the old year.

(f)   John says that his accountant talks of preparing his accounts on a going concern basis. He asks Jane if she knows of any other basis that can be used, and which it is usual to follow.

You are to take each of the points and state the correct accounting treatment, referring to appropriate accounting concepts.

9.4   Stock is valued at:

(a)   cost price

(b)   net realisable value

(c)   lower of cost and net realisable value

(d)   selling price

Answer (a) or (b) or (c) or (d)

9.5   A stationery supplies business has 500 large ring binders in stock at the end of its financial year on 30 June 2005. The details are

*   cost price £2.20 per ring binder

*   selling price £4.00 each

As the ring binders have not sold well, the owner of the business has decided to overprint them with pictures in order to make them attractive to students starting courses at the local college in September. The cost of the overprinting will be £1 per binder and the 'special offer' price to students will then be £3 per binder.

What is the stock valuation for the 500 binders in stock on 30 June 2005?

(a)   £2,000

(b)   £1,500

(c)   £1,100

(d)   £1,000

Answer (a) or (b) or (c) or (d)

9.6 A furniture shop sells coffee tables amongst the lines that it sells. The stock movements for coffee tables in February 2004 were:

1 February	Stock of 10 tables brought forward at a cost of £30 each
4 February	Sold 2 tables
7 February	Sold 5 tables
10 February	Bought 12 tables at £32 each
12 February	Sold 6 tables
17 February	Sold 4 tables
20 February	Bought 8 tables at £31 each
24 February	Sold 4 tables
27 February	Sold 3 tables

Each table sells at £50.

Stock is valued on the FIFO (first in, first out) basis.

You are to calculate the value of:

(a)   sales for February

(b)   closing stock at 28 February

(c)   cost of sales for February

9.7 A garden supplies shop has the following valuations for each group of stock at the end of its financial year:

	cost	selling price
	£	£
seeds	1,550	1,450
fertilisers and insecticides	2,270	3,560
tools	4,390	6,920

What valuation for closing stock will be used in its final accounts?

9.8 A business has, in error, overcalculated the value of its closing stock by £1,000. Before the error is corrected, what is the effect

(a)   on this year's profit?

(b)   on next year's profit?

9.9 A business has bought an accounting program for its computer system. The cost of the software is £99. Will this be treated as capital expenditure or revenue expenditure? Give reasons for your answer in the form of a memorandum to the owner of the business.

9.10 "Capital expenditure is money spent on fixed assets. As these are recorded on the balance sheet, then it is true to say that capital expenditure has no effect on the profit and loss account."

Discuss this statement, saying whether or not you agree with it and giving reasons for your answer.

10 Accounting for capital transactions

this chapter covers . . .

Capital transactions concern all aspects of the acquisition and disposal of fixed assets. Because of the nature of capital transactions – their high cost and long-term use within the business – management keeps careful control over them. We will examine:

- accounting entries to record acquisition, depreciation, and disposal of fixed assets
- the importance of distinguishing between capital expenditure and revenue expenditure
- acquisition and control of fixed assets, including the use of a fixed asset register
- hire purchase and leasing as methods of financing capital expenditure and their accounting treatment

PERFORMANCE CRITERIA COVERED

unit 5: MAINTAINING FINANCIAL RECORDS AND PREPARING ACCOUNTS

element 5.1

maintaining records relating to capital acquisition and disposal

A record relevant details relating to capital expenditure in the appropriate records

B ensure that the organisation's records agree with the physical presence of capital items

C correctly identify and record all acquisition and disposal costs and revenues in the appropriate records

D correctly calculate and record depreciation charges and other necessary entries and adjustments in the appropriate records

E ensure that the records clearly show the prior authority for capital expenditure and disposal and the approved method of funding and disposal

F correctly calculate and record the profit and loss on disposal in the appropriate records

G ensure that the organisation's policies and procedures relating to the maintenance of capital records are adhered to

H identify and resolve or refer to the appropriate person any lack of agreement between physical items and records

I make suggestions for improvements in the way the organisation maintains its capital records where possible to the appropriate person

CAPITAL TRANSACTIONS

Capital transactions concern all aspects of fixed assets – through purchasing, control and final disposal.

Fixed assets are described in FRS 15, Tangible fixed assets, as assets which 'are held for use in the production or supply of goods or services . . . on a continuing basis in the reporting entity's activities'. Examples of fixed assets include land, premises, vehicles, machinery, office, equipment, etc. These are *tangible fixed assets* which have a physical existence, ie they can be touched and felt.

Assets which have no physical form are called *intangible fixed assets*. An example of an intangible fixed asset is goodwill, which is the difference between the value of a business as a whole and the total value of its separate assets and liabilities (for example, an existing business is bought for £500,000, with the separate assets and liabilities being worth £450,000; goodwill is, therefore, £50,000). Goodwill is the purchase cost of the connections and reputations of a business being acquired. We shall be seeing the use of goodwill in the accounts when we look at changes in partnerships (Chapter 15).

Because of the nature of fixed assets – their high cost and long-term use within the business – management will keep careful control over capital transactions. For example, the purchase of a new computer system costing £100,000 will be authorised by a meeting of senior management; by contrast the purchase of new wastepaper baskets for the office at a cost of £50 will be authorised by the office supervisor.

Before we study the procedures for authorising the purchase, control and final disposal of fixed assets, we will look at a Case Study which shows the accounting entries to record the life of a fixed asset.

Case Study

ACCOUNTING FOR FIXED ASSETS

situation

Eveshore Growers Limited is a co-operative venture which sells fruit, vegetables and flowers grown by its members in the Vale of Eveshore. The company's financial year end is 31 December.

On 4 January 2001 the company buys a Supra XL computer for use in the administration office. The cost is £2,000 + VAT at 17.5% (Eveshore Growers Limited is registered for VAT); the amount is paid by cheque.

The computer is depreciated using the straight-line method at a rate of 25 per cent each year. It is company policy to charge a full year's depreciation in the year of purchase, but none in the year of sale.

By mid-2004 the computer is beginning to show its age and it is decided to replace it by a more up-to-date model. The old computer is sold on 12 July 2004 for £400 + VAT at 17.5%, a cheque being received.

Show the journal and accounting entries to record:

- acquisition of the computer
- depreciation
- disposal

solution

The cost of the fixed asset is £2,000 + VAT (at 17.5%) of £350. This is entered in the journal (see Chapter 12) as the book of prime (or original) entry and recorded in the double-entry accounts:

Date	Details	Folio	Dr	Cr
2001			£	£
4 Jan	Computer	ML	2,000	
	VAT	ML	350	
	Bank	CB		2,350
			2,350	2,350
	Purchase of Supra XL computer			
	for use in the administration office;			
	capital expenditure authorisation			
	number 015/2001			

Tutorial note: the journal is a book of prime entry which is used to list transactions before they are entered into the accounts; its use will be discussed in Chapter 12.

Dr		**Computer Account**		Cr
2001		£	2001	£
4 Jan	Bank	2,000		

Dr		**Value Added Tax Account**		Cr
2001		£	2001	£
4 Jan	Bank	350		

Cash Book (payments)

		Cash	Bank	VAT	Subsidiary (purchases) ledger	Sundry
2001		£	£	£	£	£
4 Jan	Computer		2,350	350		2,000

Note that, as Eveshore Growers Limited is registered for VAT, it will debit its VAT account with the tax. The amount is then included with VAT paid on inputs (purchases and expenses) and set-off against VAT charged on outputs (sales and services).

DEPRECIATION

Depreciation at 25 per cent straight-line per year is as follows:

year ended 31 December 2001	£500	(full year's depreciation)
year ended 31 December 2002	£500	
year ended 31 December 2003	£500	

Note that, following company policy, no depreciation is charged in 2004, being the year of sale.

Depreciation is recorded in the journal (first year only shown) and in the depreciation account, provision for depreciation and profit and loss accounts as follows:

Date	Details	Folio	Dr	Cr
2001			£	£
31 Dec	Profit and loss	ML	500	
	Depreciation	ML		500
	Depreciation charge for year on			
	Supra XL computer			
31 Dec	Depreciation	ML	500	
	Provision for depreciation account –			
	computer	ML		500
	Transfer of depreciation charge for year			
	to provision for depreciation account			

Dr			**Depreciation Account – Computer**		Cr
2001		£	2001		£
31 Dec	Provision for dep'n	500	31 Dec	Profit and loss account	500
2002			2002		
31 Dec	Provision for dep'n	500	31 Dec	Profit and loss account	500
2003			2003		
31 Dec	Provision for dep'n	500	31 Dec	Profit and loss account	500

Dr			Provision for Depreciation Account – Computer		Cr
2001		£	2001		£
31 Dec	Balance c/d	500	31 Dec	Dep'n account: computer	500
2002			2002		
31 Dec	Balance c/d	1,000	1 Jan	Balance b/d	500
			31 Dec	Dep'n account: computer	500
		1,000			1,000
2003			2003		
31 Dec	Balance c/d	1,000	1 Jan	Balance b/d	1,000
			31 Dec	Dep'n account: computer	500
		1,500			1,500
			2004		
			1 Jan	Balance b/d	1,500

PROFIT AND LOSS ACCOUNT (extracts)

for the year ended 31 December 2001

	£	£
Depreciation – computer	500	

for the year ended 31 December 2002

Depreciation – computer	500	

for the year ended 31 December 2003

Depreciation – computer	500	

Notes:
- Each year's profit is reduced by the amount of the depreciation, ie £500
- The fixed asset account for the computer remains with the balance of £2,000, which is the cost price

---

The balance sheet shows for each year the net book value (cost, less provision for depreciation) reducing with each year's depreciation:

BALANCE SHEET (extracts)

as at 31 December 2001

	£	£	£
Fixed assets	Cost	Provision for dep'n	Net
Computer	2,000	500	1,500

as at 31 December 2002

Computer	2,000	1,000	1,000

as at 31 December 2003

Computer	2,000	1,500	500

DISPOSAL

The accounting entries to deal with the disposal of fixed assets have been described in Chapter 7 (pages 110-111). The disposal account brings together

- the original cost of the computer
- provision for depreciation over the asset's life
- sale proceeds

The computer is sold for £400 + VAT at 17.5%; a cheque is received from the buyer. The transaction is recorded in the journal as the book of prime entry, and in the double-entry accounts as follows:

Date	Details	Folio	Dr	Cr
2004			£	£
12 Jul	Disposals	ML	2,000	
	Computer	ML		2,000
	Provision for depreciation account –			
	computer	ML	1,500	
	Disposals	ML		1,500
	Bank	CB	470	
	Disposals	ML		400
	VAT	ML		70
	Profit and loss	ML	100	
	Disposals	ML		100
			4,070	4,070
	Sale of Supra XL computer; loss on sale of £100 transferred to profit and loss account			

Dr			Disposals Account – Computer		Cr
2004		£	2004		£
12 Jul	Computer	2,000	12 Jul	Provision for dep'n	1,500
			12 Jul	Bank	400
			12 Jul	Profit and loss (loss on sale)	100
		2,000			2,000

Dr			Computer Account		Cr
2004		£	2004		£
1 Jan	Balance b/d	2,000	12 Jul	Disposals	2,000

Dr			Provision for Depreciation Account – Computer		Cr
2004		£	2004		£
12 Jul	Disposals	1,500	1 Jan	Balance b/d	1,500

Dr			Value Added Tax Account		Cr
2004		£	2004		£
			12 Jul	Bank	70

Cash Book (receipts)

		Cash	Bank	VAT	Subsidiary (sales) ledger	Sundry
2004		£	£	£	£	£
12 Jul	Disposals – computer		470	70		400

PROFIT AND LOSS ACCOUNT (extract)
for the year ended 31 December 2004

	£	£
Loss on sale of computer	100	

Notes:

• The 'loss on sale' of the computer (more correctly an underprovision of depreciation) is debited to the profit and loss account for the year

• If a 'profit on sale' (or overprovision of depreciation) had been made, ie a debit entry in disposals account, it will be credited to profit and loss account

---

CAPITAL EXPENDITURE AND REVENUE EXPENDITURE

The importance of distinguishing between capital expenditure and revenue expenditure has been highlighted in Chapter 9 (page 151). For example, the purchase of the computer seen in the Case Study is capital expenditure, which is recorded as a fixed asset of the business. Certain costs associated with the delivery and installation of the fixed asset can be capitalised (ie included in the cost of the fixed asset) – for guidance, see the diagram on page 153.

Most fixed assets are depreciated – thus the costs of the assets are spread over the period during which they are used by the business.

ACQUISITION AND CONTROL OF FIXED ASSETS

Because of the often large amounts of money involved, and the non-routine nature of their purchase, the acquisition of fixed assets is monitored and controlled by the business. In particular, their purchase will have to be approved by the business' managers or owners, or by a committee which appraises capital expenditure projects and decides which will be approved. The stages in the acquisition and control of fixed assets are as follows:

application and authorisation

The section of the business that wishes to purchase the fixed asset must submit an application for capital expenditure to the appropriate level of management. For relatively small items, eg the purchase of a filing cabinet, the application may be considered by the manager responsible for the section. More significant items of expenditure, such as the proposed installation of a new computer system, or the purchase and equipping of a new warehouse, will need to be submitted to a meeting of the capital expenditure committee which may, in turn, pass the largest applications to the owners/board of directors.

The form of the application will vary from a single sheet capital expenditure authorisation form, through to a fully documented proposal which includes an assessment of the likely costs and resources to be used over the life of the project. Many businesses require two or three prices or quotations to be obtained, so that they can see that they are getting the best value for money.

Before giving their approval to capital projects, particularly those involving large sums of money, the managers responsible for authorising the expenditure will consider a number of wider issues:

- the expenditure must fit in with the business' plans and budgets
- the method of funding the expenditure must be considered
    - is there sufficient money in the bank account?
    - will a bank overdraft or loan need to be arranged?
    - can old assets be sold or part exchanged to provide some of the money?
    - is leasing or hire purchase (see pages 169-172) to be used?
    - for very large projects, is an increase in capital needed?

- staffing and training implications
  - will there be redundancies?
  - can staff be retrained? at what cost?
  - will new staff need to be employed? at what pay rates?
- productivity of the business
  - will the capital expenditure increase the output of the business?
  - will the quality of output be improved?
- profitability of the business
  - is there a market for the increased output? what will be the sales revenue?
  - by how much will our costs increase?
  - will the business be more profitable?

monitoring and control

Once authorisation has been granted for a particular project, it is important that the actual costs are monitored and controlled against the costs in the original application. For relatively small projects, it is easy to compare the original quotation against the actual price charged. For major projects, where a number of contractors are involved, it will be necessary for the buyer to monitor costs carefully – staff might be appointed specifically for this role. Cost overruns and cost savings need to be investigated to see why they have occurred, and what lessons can be learned for the future.

the use of a fixed asset register

In order to keep a record of fixed assets, many businesses make use of a *fixed asset register* – an extract from which is shown on the next page. This records details of each fixed asset such as:

- fixed asset description and/or serial number (a number often marked on the asset in order to give it a positive identification)
- date of acquisition
- original cost
- depreciation amount for each year of ownership
- net book value (NBV), ie cost less depreciation to date
- funding method, such as cash, leasing or hire purchase
- disposal date

The details of the computer from the Case Study are shown in the fixed asset register. Note that there is no set layout for the register – a business will use whatever method suits it best: some will show each asset over its entire life on a separate page (as shown in the example); others will list several assets

EXTRACT FROM FIXED ASSET REGISTER

Description/serial no	Date acquired	Original cost £	Depreciation £	NBV £	Funding method	Disposal proceeds £	Disposal date
Office equipment							
Computer, Supra XL	4/1/01	2,000.00			Cash		
Year ended 31/12/01			500.00	1,500.00			
Year ended 31/12/02			500.00	1,000.00			
Year ended 31/12/03			500.00	500.00			
Year ended 31/12/04						400.00	12/7/04

on the same page for one year only, carrying forward fixed assets owned at the end of each year to a new page.

The fixed asset register enables a business to keep control of such assets; from time-to-time the accounting staff will ensure that the capital records are being kept up-to-date – in accordance with the organisation's policies and procedures – and will check the physical items of fixed assets listed in the register. Discrepancies may occur because:

- the fixed asset register has not been kept up-to-date
  - new assets have not been recorded
  - sold or scrapped assets have not been written out of the register
  - assets which have become obsolete or inadequate for the job have not been written down in value
- assets have been stolen and their theft has not been reported or recorded
- there are errors in recording details in the fixed asset register

Accounts assistants are often required to check the fixed asset register against the physical items. Any discrepancies that are identified, if they cannot be resolved, should be referred to the appropriate person – usually the accounts supervisor. It is for the management of a business, or the owners, to decide what action to take over discrepancies. If discrepancies prove to be occurring more frequently than is considered acceptable, it may be appropriate to review the way in which the capital records are maintained and to seek suggestions for improvements from the staff involved.

disposal of fixed assets

An important aspect of the control of fixed assets includes dealing with their disposal in an orderly way. In most cases old assets are replaced at the end of their useful lives with new assets, eg an old computer system is replaced with a new one. Sometimes, however, assets may become surplus to requirements part-way through their lives, eg a section of the business is closed. Whatever the circumstances, it is essential that disposal of assets is handled in such a way that the business receives the maximum amount of cash.

Old and surplus assets may be

- sold for their scrap value
- used as a part exchange value to help finance the acquisition of new assets
- sold on the secondhand market
- sold to employees

Before assets are disposed of, the approval of the appropriate person or department must be received. For example, the office manager in a small company may have authority to deal with disposals. In larger companies, a separate department may handle disposals and, for the closure of a section of the business, specialist staff may be brought in to ensure the orderly disposal of assets.

The sale proceeds, or part exchange value, must be accounted for correctly through disposals account (see pages 110 and 111). At the same time, the fixed asset register must be updated to record the disposal proceeds and date.

FRS 15 TANGIBLE FIXED ASSETS

In accounting for fixed assets, businesses should follow the requirements of FRS 15, the main points of which are:

- all fixed assets having a known useful economic life are to be depreciated (freehold land is not usually depreciated – unless it is a mine or a quarry)
- the objective of depreciation is to record in profit and loss account the cost of the use of fixed assets during the accounting period
- any acceptable depreciation method may be used to spread the cost of the fixed asset over its estimated useful economic life
- depreciation amounts are normally based on the cost of the fixed assets; (where assets are revalued, ie increased in value, depreciation is based on the revalued amount)
- where an asset is thought to have fallen below its net book value (eg the asset has been superseded by new technology), it should be written down to its estimated value and then depreciated over its remaining useful life
- a note to the accounts must show the depreciation method used for each class of fixed asset, and the useful economic life or depreciation rates used

LEASES AND HIRE PURCHASE CONTRACTS

Leasing and hire purchase contracts are means by which businesses obtain the right to use or purchase fixed assets, such as machinery and vehicles. The lessee (under a leasing contract), or the hirer (under a hire purchase contract), makes agreed payments for a period of time to a lessor or vendor (often a finance company). There is normally no provision in a leasing contract for legal ownership of the leased asset to pass to the lessee. By contrast, under a hire purchase contract, the hirer may acquire legal title by exercising an option to purchase the asset.

The accounting treatment for leases and hire purchase contracts varies according to how fixed assets are obtained for use by a business. The types of financing to consider are:

- an operating lease (a short-term lease)

- a finance lease (a long-term lease)

- a hire purchase agreement (a long-term agreement to pay by instalments)

A simple example illustrates the difference between these types of financing: hiring a van for the weekend to move some furniture is an operating lease; a business that leases a van under a four or five year contract does so under a finance lease; under a four or five year hire purchase contract, the business will own the van at the end of the period (subject to the terms of the contract).

hire purchase

A hire purchase (HP) agreement from a finance company enables a business (the hirer) to have the use of a fixed asset on payment of a deposit. Regular instalment payments – monthly, quarterly or half-yearly – are made which pay back the cost plus interest over a set period. At the end of the hire purchase period, ownership of the asset usually passes from the finance company to the business. HP is often used to finance fixed assets such as vehicles, machinery, computers and office equipment.

The accounting treatment in the final accounts of the hirer, is that an asset being bought under an HP agreement is shown as a fixed asset on the balance sheet of the hirer, despite that, in legal terms, the owner is the finance company. The reason for this is because the business has the use of the asset and, provided it keeps up with the HP payments, can treat the asset as though it owns it.

The asset being bought on hire purchase is treated as a capital cost (capitalised) so that the hirer's final accounts show:

- in the balance sheet, the cost of the fixed asset (excluding interest), less provision for depreciation

- in the profit and loss account, interest due for the year to the HP company, together with depreciation for the year

- in the balance sheet, a liability for future HP payments (excluding interest), divided between the current liabilities and long-term liabilities sections

leasing

Leasing arrangements are also used to finance fixed assets such as vehicles, machinery, computers and office equipment. With a leasing agreement, a business (the lessee) has the use of an asset bought by a finance company

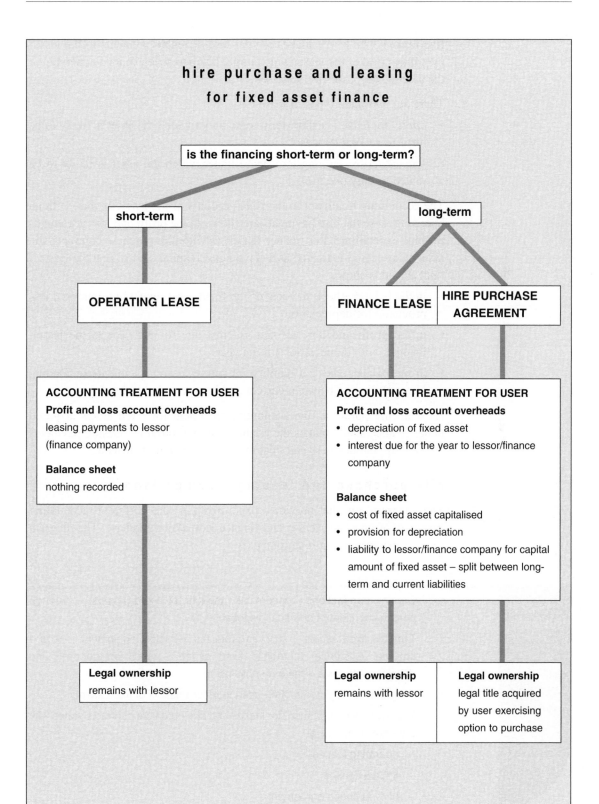

hire purchase and leasing
for fixed asset finance

is the financing short-term or long-term?

short-term

long-term

OPERATING LEASE

FINANCE LEASE | **HIRE PURCHASE AGREEMENT**

ACCOUNTING TREATMENT FOR USER
Profit and loss account overheads
leasing payments to lessor
(finance company)

Balance sheet
nothing recorded

ACCOUNTING TREATMENT FOR USER
Profit and loss account overheads
- depreciation of fixed asset
- interest due for the year to lessor/finance company

Balance sheet
- cost of fixed asset capitalised
- provision for depreciation
- liability to lessor/finance company for capital amount of fixed asset – split between long-term and current liabilities

Legal ownership
remains with lessor

Legal ownership
remains with lessor

Legal ownership
legal title acquired by user exercising option to purchase

(the lessor). The lessee makes regular hire or rental payments to the lessor over the period of the lease, which might be up to seven years. Ownership of the asset never passes to the lessee.

There are two main types of lease:

- *operating lease* – a short-term lease under which the asset is likely to be hired to several lessees
- *finance lease* – a long-term lease under which the asset is likely to be rented to only one lessee

The accounting treatment in the final accounts of the lessee is that, with an operating lease the hire payments are shown in the profit and loss account as revenue expenditure. For finance leases, as with hire purchase contracts, the asset being leased is treated as a capital cost (capitalised) so that the lessee's final accounts show:

- in the balance sheet, the cost of the fixed asset (excluding interest), less provision for depreciation
- in the profit and loss account, interest due for the year to the lessor, together with depreciation for the year
- in the balance sheet, a liability for future leasing payments (excluding interest) divided between current and long-term liabilities

As with hire purchase, the accounting treatment for fixed assets acquired under finance leases makes the assumption that, provided leasing payments are kept up, the business can treat the asset as though it owns it.

hire purchase and leasing – comparison

The diagram on the previous page explains the different accounting treatment of operating leases and finance leases/hire purchase. The diagram sets out the accounting requirements.

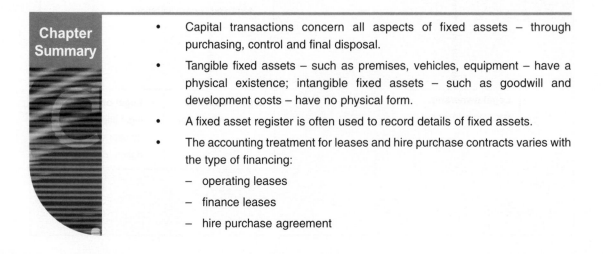

Chapter Summary

- Capital transactions concern all aspects of fixed assets – through purchasing, control and final disposal.
- Tangible fixed assets – such as premises, vehicles, equipment – have a physical existence; intangible fixed assets – such as goodwill and development costs – have no physical form.
- A fixed asset register is often used to record details of fixed assets.
- The accounting treatment for leases and hire purchase contracts varies with the type of financing:
  - operating leases
  - finance leases
  - hire purchase agreement

Key Terms		
	fixed assets	assets which "are held for use in the production or supply of goods or services . . . on a continuing basis in the reporting entity's activities" (FRS 15)
	goodwill	the purchase cost of the connections and reputations of a business being acquired
	fixed asset register	used for control purposes; records details of purchase, depreciation, disposal of all fixed assets owned by a business
	hire purchase	agreement between a finance company and a hirer which enables the hirer to have the use of a fixed asset against a deposit and regular instalment payments
	leasing	agreement between a finance company (lessor) and a business (lessee) which enables the lessee to have the use of a fixed asset against regular hire or rental payments
	operating lease	a short-term lease under which the asset is likely to be hired to several lessees
	finance lease	a long-term lease under which the asset is likely to be rented to only one lessee

Student Activities

10.1   Which one of the following is a tangible fixed asset?

(a)   premises

(b)   goodwill

(c)   debtors

(d)   bank loan

Answer (a) or (b) or (c) or (d)

10.2 A finance lease is

(a)   a short-term lease under which the asset is likely to be hired to several lessees

(b)   a long-term lease under which the asset is likely to be rented to only one lessee

(c)   a long-term lease over land

(d)   a type of hire purchase contract

Answer (a) or (b) or (c) or (d)

10.3 Wyvern Alarms Limited is considering leasing a photocopier for use in the business. The managing director, Jemima Tomkinson, understands that leases are classified as operating leases or finance leases and that the two types affect the accounts of a business in different ways. She asks you "Which type of lease would have to be treated as a capital cost in the company's accounts?"

(a)   finance lease

(b)   operating lease

(c)   both a finance lease and an operating lease

(d)   neither a finance lease nor an operating lease

Answer (a) or (b) or (c) or (d)

10.4 (a)   An extract from the fixed asset register of Wyvern Building Supplies is shown on the next page. You are to complete the register with depreciation on the fixed asset for the year ended 31 December 2003.

  (b)   The fixed asset is sold on 10 February 2004 for £500 (net of VAT); it is company policy not to charge depreciation in the year of sale. You are to complete the fixed asset register showing the asset's disposal.

10.5 QuickPrint Limited is a photographic processing company with a financial year end of 31 December. On 10 January 2001 it buys an automated machine to develop and print films; the cost is £32,000 (paid by cheque). The machine is expected to last for five years, after which its estimated value will be £2,500. Depreciation is charged at 40% each year, using the reducing balance method. It is company policy to charge a full year's depreciation in the year of purchase, but none in the year of sale.

The printing and developing machine works well but it is decided to replace it in 2004 by a more up-to-date model. The old machine is sold on 17 August 2004 for a part-exchange price of £5,000.

  (a)   You are to show the journal and accounting entries (cash book not required) to record the machine's:

   • acquisition

   • depreciation

   • disposal

   Note: VAT is to be ignored

  (b)   Draw up the page from the fixed asset register to show the machine's acquisition, depreciation and disposal. (A photocopiable register page is reproduced opposite).

EXTRACT FROM FIXED ASSET REGISTER							
Description/serial no	Date acquired	Original cost £	Depreciation £	NBV £	Funding method	Disposal proceeds £	Disposal date
Office equipment							
Computer, Supra ML	12/3/01	3,000.00			Cash		
Year ended 31/12/01			1,500.00	1,500.00			
Year ended 31/12/02			750.00	750.00			

10.6 John Aziz runs a taxi company called Silver Link Cabs. He started in business on 24 January 2001 when he bought two taxis, registration numbers W704 ZNP and W705 ZNP, at a cost of £15,000 each (paid by cheque).

John charges depreciation at the rate of 30 per cent each year, using the straight-line method. He charges a full year's depreciation in the year of purchase, but none in the year of sale.

On 17 February 2003 he buys another taxi, registration number Y81 ZUY, at a cost of £17,500 (paid by cheque). On 13 October 2003 he sells W704 ZNP for £6,500 (a cheque being received).

You are to show the accounting entries (journal and cash book not required) to record the acquisition, depreciation and disposal of his taxis for the years ended 31 December 2001, 2002 and 2003.

Notes:

- VAT is to be ignored

- use one fixed asset account for all three taxis, one depreciation account, and one provision for depreciation account

10.7 You are preparing the final accounts of Sharma Supplies. The business, which is owned by Sam Sharma, is buying a delivery van on hire purchase from Wyvern Finance plc.

Write notes to Sam which explain the accounting treatment you are using. In particular, respond to his comment that, until he makes the last hire purchase payment (which includes the option to purchase payment), he won't own the van and doesn't think it should be shown on his balance sheet.

11 Control accounts

Control accounts are 'master' accounts which record by means of totals the transactions passing through the accounts that they control. In this chapter we will look at:

- *the ledger system of accounts and the division of the ledger*
- *the concept of control accounts*
- *the layout of sales ledger and purchases ledger control accounts*
- *the use of control accounts as an aid to the management of a business*
- *control accounts and book-keeping*
- *the use of stock control account*

PERFORMANCE CRITERIA COVERED

unit 5: MAINTAINING FINANCIAL RECORDS AND PREPARING ACCOUNTS

element 5.2

collecting and collating information for the preparation of final accounts

A   *correctly prepare reconciliations for the preparation of final accounts*

B   *identify any discrepancies in the reconciliation process and either take steps to rectify them or refer them to the appropriate person*

G   *conduct investigations into business transactions with tact and courtesy*

TYPES OF ACCOUNT

Within a book-keeping system there are different types of accounts: a distinction is made between personal and impersonal accounts. Personal accounts are in the names of people or businesses, eg the accounts for debtors and creditors. Impersonal accounts are non-personal accounts; these are usually divided between real accounts, which represent things such as cash, bank balance, computers, motor vehicles, machinery, etc, and nominal accounts, which record income and expenses such as sales, purchases, wages, etc. The diagram below distinguishes between the different types of account.

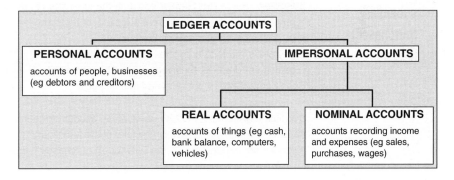

DIVISION OF THE LEDGER

The dual aspect concept (see page 142) of double-entry book-keeping involves making two entries in the ledger accounts for each business transaction. The traditional meaning of a ledger is a weighty leather-bound volume into which each account was entered on a separate page. With such a hand-written book-keeping system, as more and more accounts were opened, the point was reached where another ledger book was needed. Finally, in order to sort the accounts into a logical order, the accounting system was divided into four main sections, and this practice continues today:

- *subsidiary (sales) ledger*, containing the accounts of debtors
- *subsidiary (purchases) ledger*, containing the accounts of creditors
- *cash book*, containing bank and cash records of the receipts and payments of the business
- *main (or nominal) ledger*, containing all the other accounts

These four divisions comprise 'the ledger', and are illustrated on the next page. Note that sales and purchases ledgers are subsidiary ledgers, with control accounts (explained in this chapter) held in the main ledger.

DIVISION OF THE LEDGER

subsidiary (sales) ledger

Subsidiary (sales) ledger contains the accounts of debtors, and records:
- sales made on credit to customers of the business
- sales returns by customers
- payments received from debtors
- settlement discount allowed for prompt settlement

Cash sales are not recorded in this ledger.

Subsidiary (sales) ledger contains an account for each debtor and records the transactions with that debtor. The total of the subsidiary (sales) ledger account balances should agree with the balance of sales ledger control account in the main ledger.

subsidiary (purchases) ledger

Subsidiary (purchases) ledger contains the accounts of creditors, and records:
- purchases made on credit from suppliers of the business
- purchases returns made by the business
- payments made to creditors
- settlement discount received for prompt settlement

Cash purchases are not recorded in this ledger.

Subsidiary (purchases) ledger contains an account for each creditor and records the transactions with that creditor. The total of the subsidiary (purchases) ledger account balances should agree with the balance of purchases ledger control account in the main ledger.

cash books

The cash books comprise:
- Cash Book
  - records all transactions for bank account and cash account
  - cash book is also often used for listing the amounts of settlement (cash) discount received and allowed and for recording Value Added Tax

- Petty Cash Book
  - records low-value cash payments too small to be entered in the cash book

main ledger

The main ledger contains the other accounts of the business:
- Nominal Accounts
  - sales account (cash and credit sales)
  - purchases account (cash and credit purchases)
  - sales returns, purchases returns
  - expenses and income
  - loan
  - capital, drawings
  - Value Added Tax (where the business is VAT-registered)

- Real Accounts
  - fixed assets, eg premises, computers, motor vehicles
  - other assets, eg cash, bank balance, stock
  - control accounts, eg sales ledger, purchases ledger

THE CONCEPT OF CONTROL ACCOUNTS

Control accounts are 'master' accounts which control a number of subsidiary ledger accounts. Control accounts work in the following way:

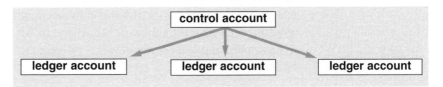

The control account (also known as a *totals account*) is used to record the totals of transactions passing through the subsidiary accounts. In this way, the balance of the control account will always be equal to the total balances of the subsidiary accounts, unless an error has occurred. Two commonly-used control accounts are:

- **sales ledger control account**, which controls the subsidiary (sales) ledger
- **purchases ledger control account**, which controls the subsidiary (purchases) ledger

In the illustration above we have seen how a control account acts as a master account for a number of subsidiary accounts. The principle is that, if the total of the opening balances for subsidiary accounts is known, together with the total of amounts increasing these balances, and the total of amounts decreasing these balances, then the total of the closing balances for the subsidiary accounts can be calculated.

For example:

	£
Total of opening balances	50,000
Add increases	10,000
	60,000
Less decreases	12,000
Total of closing balances	48,000

The total of the closing balances can now be checked against a separate listing of the balances of the subsidiary accounts to ensure that the two figures agree. If so, it proves that the ledgers within the section are correct (subject to any errors such as misposts and compensating errors – see Chapter 12). Let us now apply this concept to one of the divisions of the ledger – sales ledger.

The diagram on page 181 shows the personal accounts which form the entire sales ledger of a particular business – in practice there would, of course, be more than four accounts involved. The sales ledger control account acts as a totals account, which records totals of the transactions passing through the subsidiary accounts that it controls. Notice how transactions appear in the control account *on the same side* as they appear in the subsidiary accounts. The sales ledger control account can be reconciled with the balances of the subsidiary accounts which it controls (see below). Thus, control accounts act as an aid to locating errors: if the control account and subsidiary accounts agree, then the error is likely to lie elsewhere. In this way the control account acts as a checking and control device – proving the arithmetical accuracy of the ledger section.

Normally the whole of a ledger section is controlled by one control account, eg sales ledger control account or purchases ledger control account. However, it is also possible to have a number of separate control accounts for sections of the subsidiary ledgers, eg sales ledger control account A-K, purchases ledger control account S-Z, etc. It is for a business – the user of the accounting system – to decide what is most suitable, taking into account the number of accounts in the subsidiary ledgers, together with the type of book-keeping system – manual or computerised.

From the diagram on the next page the sales ledger control account and subsidiary (sales) ledger accounts are agreed at the beginning and end of the month, as follows:

Reconciliation of sales ledger control account		
	1 January 2004	31 January 2004
	£	£
A Ackroyd	100	150
B Barnes	200	200
C Cox	50	180
D Douglas	150	150
Sales ledger control account	500	680

The business will decide how often to reconcile (agree) the control account with the subsidiary accounts – weekly, monthly, quarterly or annually. Any discrepancy should be investigated immediately and the error(s) traced.

SALES LEDGER CONTROL ACCOUNT

The set-out of a sales ledger control account (also known as a debtors control account) is shown on page 182. Study the layout carefully and then read the text which explains the additional items.

Dr			Sales Ledger Control Account		Cr
2004		£	2004		£
1 Jan	Balance b/d	500	31 Jan	Bank	443
31 Jan	Sales	700	31 Jan	Discount allowed	7
			31 Jan	Sales returns	70
			31 Jan	Balance c/d	680
		1,200			1,200
1 Feb	Balance b/d	680			

Dr			A Ackroyd		Cr
2004		£	2004		£
1 Jan	Balance b/d	100	10 Jan	Bank	98
6 Jan	Sales	150	10 Jan	Discount allowed	2
			31 Jan	Balance c/d	150
		250			250
1 Feb	Balance b/d	150			

Dr			B Barnes		Cr
2004		£	2004		£
1 Jan	Balance b/d	200	13 Jan	Bank	195
6 Jan	Sales	250	13 Jan	Discount allowed	5
			27 Jan	Sales returns	50
			31 Jan	Balance c/d	200
		450			450
1 Feb	Balance b/d	200			

Dr			C Cox		Cr
2004		£	2004		£
1 Jan	Balance b/d	50	20 Jan	Bank	50
15 Jan	Sales	200	29 Jan	Sales returns	20
			31 Jan	Balance c/d	180
		250			250
1 Feb	Balance b/d	180			

Dr			D Douglas		Cr
2004		£	2004		£
1 Jan	Balance b/d	150	30 Jan	Bank	100
20 Jan	Sales	100	31 Jan	Balance c/d	150
		250			250
1 Feb	Balance b/d	150			

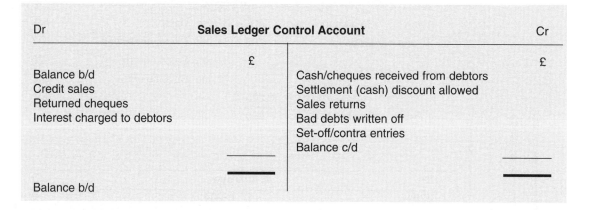

balance b/d

The figure for balance b/d on the debit side of the control account represents the total of the balances of the individual debtors' accounts in the sales ledger. This principle is illustrated in the diagram on page 181. Remember that, at the end of the month (or other period covered by the control account), the account must be balanced and carried down (on the credit side) on the last day of the month, and then brought down (on the debit side) on the first day of the next month.

Note that it is possible for a debtor's account to have a credit balance, instead of the usual debit balance. This may come about, for example, because the debtor has paid for goods and then returned them, or has overpaid in error: the business owes the amount due, ie the debtor has a credit balance for the time being. Most accounting systems 'net off' any such credit balances against the debit balances to give an overall figure for debtors.

credit sales

Only credit sales – and not cash sales – are entered in the control account because only credit sales are recorded in the debtors' accounts. The total sales of the business will comprise both credit and cash sales.

returned cheques

If a debtor's cheque is returned unpaid by the bank, ie the cheque has 'bounced', then authorisation for the entries to be made in the book-keeping system must be given by the accounts supervisor. These entries are:

– *debit* debtor's account

– *credit* cash book (bank columns)

As a transaction has been made in a debtor's account, then the amount must also be recorded in the sales ledger control account – on the debit side.

interest charged to debtors

Sometimes a business will charge a debtor for slow payment of an account. The accounting entries, which must be authorised by the supervisor, are:

– *debit* debtor's account

– *credit* interest received account

As a debit transaction has been made in the debtor's account, so a debit entry must be recorded in the control account. The documentation which shows how the interest has been calculated should be stored for future reference.

bad debts written off

The book-keeping entries for writing off a bad debt (see Chapter 8) are:

– *debit* bad debts written off account

– *credit* debtor's account

A credit transaction is entered in a debtor's account. This is because the control account 'masters' the subsidiary (sales) ledger and so the transaction must also be recorded as a credit transaction in the control account.

set-off/contra entries

See page 186.

PURCHASES LEDGER CONTROL ACCOUNT

The set-out of a purchases ledger control account (also known as a creditors control account) is shown below.

The layout is explained on the next page.

Dr	Purchases Ledger Control Account		Cr
	£		£
Cash/cheques paid to creditors		Balance b/d	
Settlement (cash) discount received		Credit purchases	
Purchases returns		Interest charged by creditors	
Set-off/contra entries			
Balance c/d			
	▬▬		▬▬
		Balance b/d	

balance b/d

The figure for balance b/d on the credit side of the control account represents the total of the balances of the individual creditors' accounts in the purchases ledger. This principle is illustrated in the diagram on the next page.

Note that it is possible for a creditor's account to have a debit balance, instead of the usual credit balance – for example, if the creditor has been overpaid. Most accounting systems 'net off' any such debit balances against the credit balances to give an overall figure for creditors.

credit purchases

Only credit purchases – and not cash purchases – are entered in the control account. However, the total purchases of the business will comprise both credit and cash purchases.

interest charged by creditors

If a creditor charges interest because of slow payment, this must be recorded on both the creditor's account and the control account. The supervisor might well enquire of the creditor why and how the interest has been calculated.

set-off/contra entries

See page 186.

reconciliation of purchases ledger control account

The diagram on page 185 shows how a purchases ledger control account acts as a totals account for the creditors of a business. Reconciliation (agreement) of the balances on the purchases ledger control account and subsidiary accounts is made as follows:

Reconciliation of purchases ledger control account		
	1 January 2004	31 January 2004
	£	£
F Francis	100	200
G Gold	200	350
H Harris	300	500
I Ingram	400	900
Purchases ledger control account	1,000	1,950

Any discrepancy should be investigated immediately and the error(s) traced.

Dr		Purchases Ledger Control Account			Cr
2004		£	2004		£
31 Jan	Purchases returns	150	1 Jan	Balance b/d	1,000
31 Jan	Bank	594	31 Jan	Purchases	1,700
31 Jan	Discount received	6			
31 Jan	Balance c/d	1,950			
		2,700			2,700
			1 Feb	Balance b/d	1,950

Dr		F Francis			Cr
2004		£	2004		£
17 Jan	Bank	98	1Jan	Balance b/d	100
17 Jan	Discount received	2	3 Jan	Purchases	200
31 Jan	Balance c/d	200			
		300			300
			1 Feb	Balance b/d	200

Dr		G Gold			Cr
2004		£	2004		£
15 Jan	Purchases returns	50	1 Jan	Balance b/d	200
28 Jan	Bank	100	9 Jan	Purchases	300
31 Jan	Balance c/d	350			
		500			500
			1 Feb	Balance b/d	350

Dr		H Harris			Cr
2004		£	2004		£
28 Jan	Purchases returns	100	1 Jan	Balance b/d	300
30 Jan	Bank	200	17 Jan	Purchases	500
31 Jan	Balance c/d	500			
		800			800
			1 Feb	Balance b/d	500

Dr		I Ingram			Cr
2004		£	2004		£
22 Jan	Bank	196	1 Jan	Balance b/d	400
22 Jan	Discount received	4	27 Jan	Purchases	700
31 Jan	Balance c/d	900			
		1,100			1,100
			1 Feb	Balance b/d	900

SET-OFF/CONTRA ENTRIES

These entries occur when the same person or business has an account in both subsidiary ledgers – sales ledger and purchases ledger – ie they are both buying from, and selling to, the business whose accounts we are preparing. For example, M Patel Limited has the following accounts in the subsidiary sales and purchases ledgers:

SUBSIDIARY (SALES) LEDGER

Dr		A Smith		Cr
	£			£
Balance b/d	200			

SUBSIDIARY (PURCHASES) LEDGER

Dr		A Smith		Cr
	£			£
		Balance b/d		300

From these accounts we can see that:

• A Smith owes M Patel Limited £200 (sales ledger)

• M Patel Limited owes A Smith £300 (purchases ledger)

To save each having to write out a cheque to send to the other, it is possible (with A Smith's agreement) to set-off one account against the other, so that they can settle their net indebtedness with one cheque. The book-keeping entries in M Patel's books will be:

– *debit* A Smith (purchases ledger) £200

– *credit* A Smith (sales ledger) £200

The accounts will now appear as:

SUBSIDIARY (SALES) LEDGER

Dr		A Smith		Cr
	£			£
Balance b/d	200	Set-off: purchases ledger		200

SUBSIDIARY (PURCHASES) LEDGER

Dr **A Smith** Cr

	£		£
Set-off: sales ledger	200	Balance b/d	300

The net result is that M Patel Limited owes A Smith £100. The important point to note is that, because transactions have been recorded in the subsidiary accounts, an entry needs to be made in the two control accounts:

– *debit* purchases ledger control account

– *credit* sales ledger control account

Set-off transactions should be appropriately documented with a journal entry (see Chapter 12) authorised by the accounts supervisor.

SOURCES OF INFORMATION FOR CONTROL ACCOUNTS

Control accounts use totals (remember that their other name is 'totals accounts') for the week, month, quarter or year – depending on what time period is decided upon by the business. The totals come from a number of sources in the accounting system:

sales ledger control account
- total credit sales (including VAT) – from the 'total' column of the sales day book
- total sales returns (including VAT) – from the 'total' column of the sales returns day book
- total cash/cheques received from debtors – from the cash book
- total settlement discount allowed – from the discount allowed column of the cash book, or from discount allowed account
- bad debts – from the journal, or bad debts written off account

purchases ledger control account
- total credit purchases (including VAT) – from the 'total' column of the purchases day book
- total purchases returns (including VAT) – from the 'total' column of the purchases returns day book
- total cash/cheques paid to creditors – from the cash book
- total settlement discount received – from the discount received column of the cash book, or from discount received account

CONTROL ACCOUNTS AS AN AID TO MANAGEMENT

When the manager of a business needs to know the figure for debtors or creditors the balance of the appropriate control account will give the information immediately: there is no need to add up the balances of all the individual debtors' or creditors' accounts. With a computer accounting system, control accounts can be printed at any time.

The use of control accounts makes fraud more difficult – particularly in a manual accounting system. If a fraudulent transaction is to be recorded on a subsidiary account, the transaction must also be entered in the control account. As the control account will be either maintained by a supervisor, or checked regularly by the manager, the control accounts add another level of security within the accounting system.

We have already seen in this chapter how control accounts can help in locating errors. Remember, though, that a control account only proves the arithmetical accuracy of the accounts which it controls – there could still be errors, such as misposts and compensating errors (see Chapter 12), within the ledger section.

A further use of control accounts is to help with the construction of final accounts when a business has not kept double-entry accounts and a trial balance cannot be extracted – see Chapter 13, which deals with *incomplete records*.

CONTROL ACCOUNTS AND BOOK-KEEPING

A business must decide how to use control accounts in its book-keeping system. The usual way of doing this is to incorporate the control accounts into double-entry book-keeping.

The control accounts form part of the double-entry system in the main ledger. The balances of the sales ledger control account and the purchases ledger control account are recorded in the trial balance as the figures for debtors and creditors respectively. This means that the individual accounts of debtors and creditors are not part of double-entry, but are *subsidiary accounts* which record how much each debtor owes, and how much is owed to each creditor. From time-to-time, the balances of the subsidiary accounts are agreed with the balance of the appropriate control account.

The diagrams on the next two pages show how the sales ledger control account and the purchases ledger control account are incorporated in the main ledger of the double-entry book-keeping system, with the individual debtors' and creditors' accounts kept in the form of subsidiary accounts.

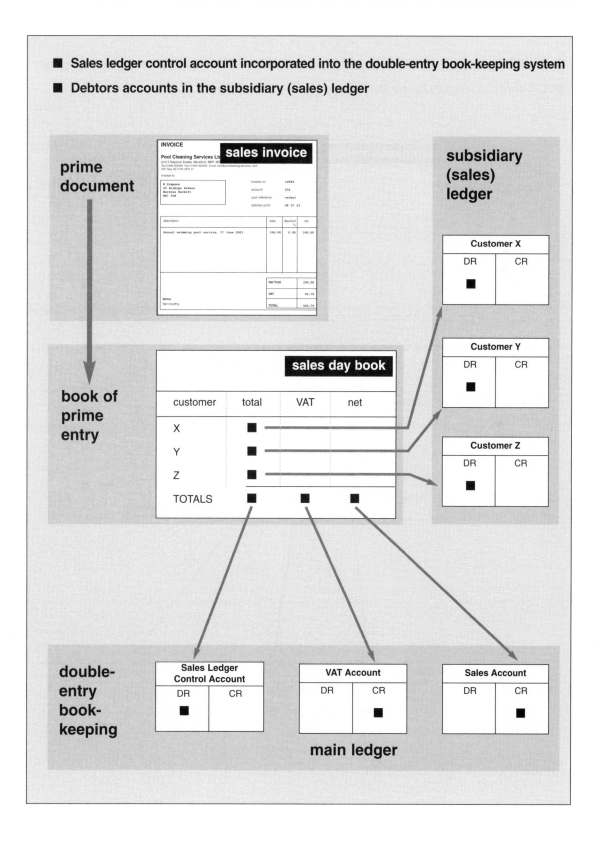

- Sales ledger control account incorporated into the double-entry book-keeping system
- Debtors accounts in the subsidiary (sales) ledger

prime document

INVOICE

Pool Cleaning Services Ltd

sales invoice

subsidiary (sales) ledger

Customer X

DR	CR
■	

Customer Y

DR	CR
■	

book of prime entry

sales day book

customer	total	VAT	net
X	■		
Y	■		
Z	■		
TOTALS	■	■	■

Customer Z

DR	CR
■	

double-entry book-keeping

Sales Ledger Control Account

DR	CR
■	

VAT Account

DR	CR
	■

Sales Account

DR	CR
	■

main ledger

- Purchases ledger control account incorporated into the double-entry book-keeping system
- Creditors' accounts in the subsidiary (purchases) ledger

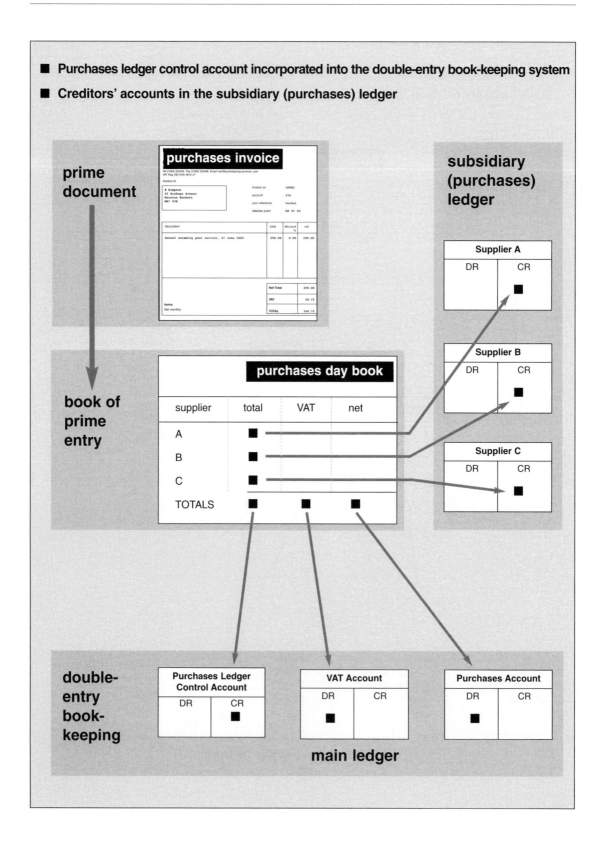

STOCK CONTROL ACCOUNT

This control account is used to record the value of stock of goods that a business holds for resale. As a part of the double-entry system, stock control account acts as the master account for the subsidiary records of each stock item or stock line held by the business. This relationship is illustrated in the following way:

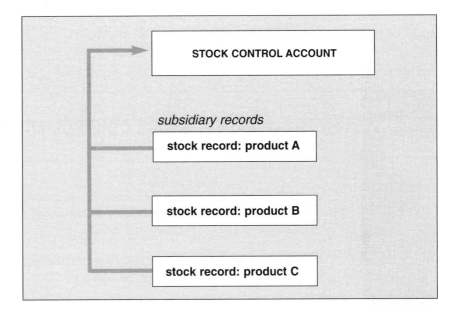

The stock records are based on receipts and issues of stock – often a computer accounting system is used to keep these records. As we have seen earlier (page 149) three commonly-used methods of calculating stock volumes are:

- FIFO (first in, first out), where the first stocks received are assumed to be the first to be used

- LIFO (last in, first out), where the last stocks received are assumed to be the first to be used

- AVCO (average cost), where a weighted average cost is calculated as new stocks are received

A business will choose a suitable stock valuation method from the above; this then gives a cost price of the stock. However, in accordance with SSAP 9 (page 147), this cost price must be compared with selling price so that the stock valuation is *at the lower of cost and net realisable value.*

When a business stock takes, a physical count of the stock is carried out which may reveal discrepancies between the stock records and the actual stock held. A stock take may also show items of stock where the selling price is lower than cost price. Thus the stock take may reveal discrepancies in the form of:

- differences between the physical stock and the stock records
- selling price being lower than cost price

Any discrepancies should be identified and either rectified, or referred to the accounts supervisor or other appropriate person.

GOLF SALES: STOCK CONTROL ACCOUNT

situation

Golf Sales trades in two types of golf ball: the 'Superspeed' and the 'Titanium'. Each ball is sold in packs of fifteen balls which sell to golf shops at £10 per pack for 'Superspeed' and £15 per pack for 'Titanium'.

At 31 December 2004 – the end of the firm's financial year – the computerised stock records for the two products show the following:

STOCK RECORD			
Product Superspeed			
Stock units packs of 15 balls			
Date	Received	Issued	Balance
2004			
12 Jun	2,000		2,000
5 Jul		500	1,500
9 Aug		1,000	500
28 Sep	1,000		1,500
19 Oct		400	1,100
5 Dec		250	850

STOCK RECORD			
Product Titanium			
Stock units packs of 15 balls			
Date	Received	Issued	Balance
2004			
12 Sep	1,000		1,000
29 Sep		400	600
17 Oct	1,000		1,600
7 Nov		500	1,100
28 Nov		200	900
13 Dec		400	500

From these records, the following stock valuations have been entered into the double-entry accounts:

			£
'Superspeed'	850 packs at cost price of £10 per pack	=	8,500
'Titanium'	500 packs at cost price of £15 per pack	=	7,500
			16,000

The total valuation has been recorded in stock control account – and transferred to the trading and profit and loss account – as follows:

Dr	**Stock Control Account**		Cr
2004	£	2004	£
31 Dec Profit and loss account 16,000			

A stock take was carried out on 31 December 2004 and the following discrepancies were discovered:

- the physical stock of 'Superspeed' balls was 840 packs
- ten packs of 'Titanium' balls were found to have damaged packaging – they are to be offered for sale at £7.50 per pack

All other stocks have a selling price which is above cost price.

solution

The physical stock shows that there is a difference when compared with the stock records. A process of stock reconciliation needs to be carried out so that small discrepancies can be adjusted and significant discrepancies can be investigated.

As the stock records of Golf Sales show small discrepancies, they can be adjusted by reducing the stock valuation to a revised figure of:

	£
'Superspeed'	
840 packs at cost price of £10 per pack	= 8,400
'Titanium'	
490 packs at cost price of £15 per pack	= 7,350
10 packs at net realisable value of £7.50 per pack	= 75
	15,825

This reduction in valuation of £16,000 − £15,825 = £175 is recorded by means of a journal entry (see Chapter 12).

Date	Details	Folio	Dr	Cr
2004			£	£
31 Dec	Profit and loss	ML	175	
	Stock control	ML		175
	Adjustment of stock valuation *following physical stock take*			

This adjustment is recorded in stock control account as follows:

Dr			Stock Control Account		Cr
2004		£	2004		£
31 Dec	Profit and loss account	16,000	31 Dec	Profit and loss account	175
			31 Dec	Balance c/d	15,825
		16,000			16,000
2005			2005		
1 Jan	Balance b/d	15,825			

As can be seen, stock control account now reconciles with the revised stock valuation. A debit entry for £175 will be recorded in trading and profit and loss account.

The stock record of 'Superspeed' is corrected by means of a stock adjustment (ADJ) as follows:

SUPERSPEED

Date	Received	Issued	Balance
2004			
31 Dec		ADJ 10	840

Larger discrepancies will need to be investigated as they could have been caused by:

- an error in the stock record, such as a failure to record a receipt, an issue, or a return of stock
- theft of stock
- damaged stock being disposed of without any record having been made

If discrepancies cannot be resolved, they should be referred to the accounts supervisor or other appropriate person.

Chapter Summary

- Accounts are either personal (eg accounts of debtors and creditors) or impersonal ('real' items such as assets or 'nominal' items such as income).

- The ledger is divided for convenience into four sections: subsidiary (sales) ledger, subsidiary (purchases) ledger, cash book and main (or nominal) ledger

- Control accounts (or totals accounts) are 'master' accounts, which control a number of subsidiary accounts within the ledger.

- Two commonly used control accounts are:
    - sales ledger control account
    - purchases ledger control account

- Transactions are recorded on the same side of the control account as on the subsidiary accounts.

- Set-off/contra entries occur when one person has an account in both subsidiary ledgers – sales and purchases ledger – and it is agreed to set-off one balance against the other to leave a net balance. This usually results in the following control account entries:
    - debit purchases ledger control account
    - credit sales ledger control account

- Control accounts are an aid to management:
    - they give up-to-date information on the total of debtors or creditors
    - by making fraud more difficult
    - in helping to locate errors
    - in assisting with the preparation of accounts from incomplete records

- Control accounts are usually incorporated into the main ledger of the double-entry book-keeping system. The individual accounts of debtors and creditors are set up as separate subsidiary accounts.

- Stock control account is used to record the value of stock held.

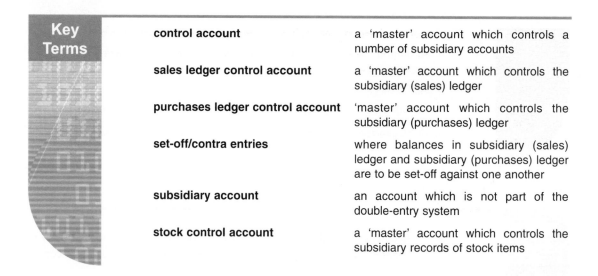

Key Terms	control account	a 'master' account which controls a number of subsidiary accounts
	sales ledger control account	a 'master' account which controls the subsidiary (sales) ledger
	purchases ledger control account	'master' account which controls the subsidiary (purchases) ledger
	set-off/contra entries	where balances in subsidiary (sales) ledger and subsidiary (purchases) ledger are to be set-off against one another
	subsidiary account	an account which is not part of the double-entry system
	stock control account	a 'master' account which controls the subsidiary records of stock items

Student Activities

11.1 You have the following information:

- opening creditor balances at start of month   £18,600
- cash/cheques paid to creditors during month   £9,400
- credit purchases for month   £9,100
- purchases returns for month   £800

What is the figure for closing creditor balances at the end of the month?

(a)   £18,100

(b)   £19,100

(c)   £36,300

(d)   £17,500

Answer (a) or (b) or (c) or (d)

11.2   Which one of the following does not appear in sales ledger control account?

(a)   bad debts written off

(b)   settlement discount received

(c)   sales returns

(d)   cash/cheques received from debtors

Answer (a) or (b) or (c) or (d)

11.3   Prepare a sales ledger control account for the month of June 2004 from the following information:

2004		£
1 Jun	Sales ledger balances	17,491
30 Jun	Credit sales for month	42,591
	Sales returns	1,045
	Payments received from debtors	39,024
	Settlement discount allowed	593
	Bad debts written off	296

The debtors figure at 30 June is to be entered as the balancing figure.

11.4   Prepare a purchases ledger control account for the month of April 2004 from the following information:

2004		£
1 Apr	Purchases ledger balances	14,275
30 Apr	Credit purchases for month	36,592
	Purchases returns	653
	Payments made to creditors	31,074
	Settlement discount received	1,048
	Transfer of credit balances to sales ledger	597

The creditors figure at 30 April is to be entered as the balancing figure.

11.5   The subsidiary (sales) ledger of Rowcester Traders contains the following accounts on 1 February 2004:

Arrow Valley Retailers, balance £826.40 debit

B Brick (Builders) Limited, balance £59.28 debit

Mereford Manufacturing Company, balance £293.49 debit

Redgrove Restorations, balance £724.86 debit

Wyvern Warehouse Limited, balance £108.40 debit

The following transactions took place during February:

3 Feb	Sold goods on credit to Arrow Valley Retailers £338.59, and to Mereford Manufacturing Company £127.48
7 Feb	Redgrove Restorations returned goods £165.38
15 Feb	Received a cheque from Wyvern Warehouse Limited for the balance of the account after deduction of 2.5% settlement discount
17 Feb	Sold goods on credit to Redgrove Restorations £394.78, and to Wyvern Warehouse Limited £427.91
20 Feb	Arrow Valley Retailers settled an invoice for £826.40 by cheque after deducting 2.5% settlement discount
24 Feb	Mereford Manufacturing Company returned goods £56.29
29 Feb	Transferred the balance of Mereford Manufacturing Company's account to the company's account in the subsidiary (purchases) ledger
29 Feb	Wrote off the account of B Brick (Builders) Limited as a bad debt

You are to:

(a)   write up the accounts in the subsidiary (sales) ledger of Rowcester Traders for February 2004, balancing them at the end of the month

(b)   prepare a sales ledger control account for February 2004, balancing it at the end of the month

(c)   reconcile the control account balance with the subsidiary accounts at 1 February and 29 February 2004.

Note: VAT is to be ignored on all transactions and day books are not required.

11.6   You work as an accounts assistant for The Stationery Box, a retailer of office stationery and supplies.

One of the items stocked by The Stationery Box is photocopying paper – this is packed in boxes each containing five reams (a ream = 500 sheets of paper). The accounts supervisor gives you the stock record (shown on the next page) and tells you that the stock valuation of £3,520 has been entered already into the computer accounting system and is included in the debit balance of £28,350 on stock control account (which has been posted by the computer to the trading and profit and loss account for the year ended 30 June 2004).

You carry out a physical stock take of the photocopying paper. This shows that there are 350 boxes in stock at a cost of £10 each, together with two damaged boxes which are unsaleable and are to be thrown away.

Photocopying paper is sold by The Stationery Box at a price of £3.50 per ream.

STOCK RECORD					
Product: photocopying paper					
Stock units: boxes of five reams					
Date	Details	Received	Issued	Balance	Value at £10 per box
2004					£
1 Jun	Opening balance			300	3,000
4 Jun	Receipt	100		400	4,000
5 Jun	Issued		30	370	3,700
6 Jun	Issued		20	350	3,500
8 Jun	Issued		25	325	3,250
11 Jun	Issued		40	285	2,850
13 Jun	Receipt	100		385	3,850
15 Jun	Issued		35	350	3,500
18 Jun	Issued		24	326	3,260
19 Jun	Receipt	100		426	4,260
20 Jun	Issued		32	394	3,940
22 Jun	Issued		28	366	3,660
25 Jun	Issued		42	324	3,240
27 Jun	Issued		35	289	2,890
28 Jun	Receipt	100		389	3,890
29 Jun	Issued		37	352	3,520

You are to:

(a) make adjustments which reconcile the stock take and stock record as at 30 June 2004

(b) prepare a journal entry for authorisation by the accounts supervisor which will correct the discrepancy you have discovered

(c) show how the authorised adjustment will be recorded in stock control account

this chapter covers . . .

The journal is the book of prime (or original) entry for non-regular transactions, eg purchase and sale of fixed assets on credit, correction of errors, end-of-year transfers (such as depreciation and provision for doubtful debts), and other transfers.

As a book of prime entry, the journal is not part of double-entry book-keeping; instead the journal is used to list transactions before they are entered into the accounts. In this way, the journal completes the accounting system by providing the book of prime entry for non-regular transactions.

PERFORMANCE CRITERIA COVERED

unit 5: MAINTAINING FINANCIAL RECORDS AND PREPARING ACCOUNTS

element 5.2

collecting and collating information for the preparation of final accounts

C   accurately prepare a trial balance and open a suspense account to record any imbalance

D   establish the reasons for any imbalance and clear the suspense account by correcting the errors, or reduce them and resolve outstanding items to the appropriate person

E   correctly identify, calculate and record appropriate adjustments

F   make the relevant journal entries to close off the revenue accounts in preparation for the transfer of balances to the final accounts

G   conduct investigations into business transactions with trust and courtesy

H   ensure that the organisation's policies, regulations, procedures and timescales relating to preparing final accounts are observed

USES OF THE JOURNAL

The journal completes the accounting system by providing the book of prime entry for non-regular transactions, which are not recorded in any other book of prime entry. The categories of such non-regular transactions include:

- opening entries
- purchase and sale of fixed assets on credit
- correction of errors
- year end transfers

The reasons for using a journal are:

- to provide a book of prime entry for non-regular transactions
- to eliminate the need for remembering why non-regular transactions were put through the accounts – the journal acts as a notebook
- to reduce the risk of fraud, by making it difficult for unauthorised transactions to be entered in the accounting system
- to reduce the risk of errors, by listing the transactions that are to be put into the double-entry accounts
- to ensure that entries can be traced back to a prime document, thus providing an audit trail for non-regular transactions

THE JOURNAL – A BOOK OF PRIME ENTRY

The journal is a book of prime (or original) entry; it is not, therefore, part of the double-entry book-keeping system. The journal is used to list the transactions that are then to be put through the accounts. The accounting system for non-regular transactions is as follows:

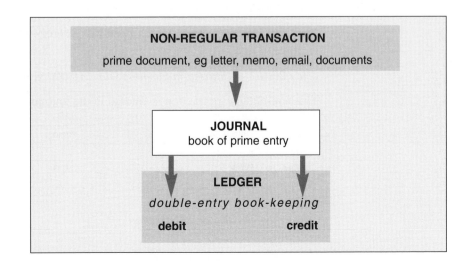

Look at the way the journal is set out, and then read the notes that follow.

Date	Details	Folio	Dr	Cr
			£	£

- the names of the accounts to be debited and credited in the book-keeping system are written in the details column; it is customary to show the debit transaction first
- the money amount of each debit and credit is stated in the appropriate columns
- the folio column cross-references to the division of the ledger where each account will be found, eg ML = main ledger, CB = cash book; the cross reference can also include an account number
- a journal entry always balances, ie debit and credit entries are for the same amount or total
- it is usual to include a brief narrative explaining why the transaction is being carried out, and making reference to the prime document whenever possible (in Skills Tests and Examinations you should always include a narrative unless specifically told otherwise)
- each journal entry is complete in itself and is ruled off to separate it from the next entry

These principles are applied in the examples which follow. Note that, in these examples, the book-keeping system in use has control accounts in the main ledger for sales ledger and purchases ledger – the individual accounts for each debtor and creditor are held in subsidiary ledgers.

OPENING ENTRIES

These are the transactions which open the accounts of a new business. For example, a first business transaction is:

1 Jan 2004   Started in business with £10,000 in the bank

This non-regular transaction is entered in the journal as follows:

Date	Details	Folio	Dr	Cr
2004			£	£
1 Jan	Bank	CB	10,000	
	Capital	ML		10,000
	Opening capital introduced			

After the journal entry has been made, the transaction can be recorded in the double-entry accounts.

Here is another opening entries transaction to be recorded in the journal:

2 Feb 2004   *Started in business with cash £100, bank £5,000, stock £1,000, machinery £2,500, creditors £850*

The journal entry is:

Date	Details	Folio	Dr	Cr
2004			£	£
2 Feb	Cash	CB	100	
	Bank	CB	5,000	
	Stock	ML	1,000	
	Machinery	ML	2,500	
	Purchase ledger control	ML		850
	Capital	ML		7,750
			8,600	8,600
	Assets and liabilities			
	at the start of business			

Notes:

- Capital is the balancing figure, ie assets minus liabilities.

- The journal is the book of prime entry for all opening entries, including cash and bank; however the normal book of prime entry for other cash/bank transactions is the cash book.

- The amounts from the journal entry will now need to be recorded in the double-entry accounts.

PURCHASE AND SALE OF FIXED ASSETS ON CREDIT

The purchase and sale of fixed assets are non-regular business transactions which are recorded in the journal as the book of prime entry. Only *credit* transactions are entered in the journal (because cash/bank transactions are recorded in the cash book as the book of prime entry). However, a business (or Skills Test or an Examination) may choose to journalise cash entries: strictly, though, this is incorrect as two books of prime entry are being used.

15 Apr 2004   *Bought a machine for £1,000 plus VAT (at 17.5%) on credit from Machinery Supplies Limited, purchase order no 2341.*

Date	Details	Folio	Dr	Cr
2004			£	£
15 Apr	Machinery	ML	1,000	
	VAT	ML	175	
	Purchases ledger control*	ML		1,175
			1,175	1,175
	Purchase of machine from creditor, Machinery Supplies Limited: purchase order 2341			

20 May 2004   Car sold for £2,500 on credit to Wyvern Motors Limited (no VAT chargeable).

Date	Details	Folio	Dr	Cr
2004			£	£
20 May	Sales ledger control*	ML	2,500	
	Disposals	ML		2,500
	Sale of car, registration no Q201 HAB to debtor, Wyvern Motors Limited			

* Instead of entering these transactions in the subsidiary purchases and sales ledgers, an alternative treatment would be to open main ledger accounts for the creditor (Machinery Supplies Limited) and the debtor (Wyvern Motors Limited). This would avoid confusion with trade creditors – in the subsidiary (purchases) ledger – and trade debtors in the subsidiary (sales) ledger.

CORRECTION OF ERRORS

In any book-keeping system there is always the possibility of an error. Ways to avoid errors, or ways to reveal them sooner, include:

- division of the accounting function between a number of people, so that no one person is responsible for both the debit and credit entries of a business transaction
- regular circulation of statements to debtors, who will check the transactions on their accounts and advise any discrepancies
- checking of statements received from creditors
- extraction of a trial balance at regular intervals
- the preparation of bank reconciliation statements
- checking cash and petty cash balances against cash held
- the use of control accounts
- the use of a computer accounting program

Despite all of these, errors will still occur from time-to-time and, in this section, we will look at:

* correction of errors not shown by a trial balance

* correction of errors shown by a trial balance, using a suspense account

errors not shown by a trial balance

In Chapter 3 we have already seen that some types of errors in a book-keeping system are not revealed by a trial balance. These are:

* error of omission

* reversal of entries

* mispost/error of commission

* error of principle

* error of original entry (or transcription)

* compensating error

Although these errors are not shown by a trial balance, they are likely to come to light if the procedures suggested on the previous page are followed. For example, a debtor will soon let you know if her account has been debited with goods she did not buy. When an error is found, it needs to be corrected by means of a journal entry which shows the book-keeping entries that have been made.

We will now look at an example of each of the errors not shown by a trial balance, and will see how it is corrected by means of a journal entry. (A practical hint which may help in correcting errors is to write out the 'T' accounts as they appear with the error. Then write in the correcting entries and see if the result has achieved what was intended.)

ERROR OF OMISSION

Credit sale of goods, £200 plus VAT (at 17.5%) on invoice 4967 to H Jarvis completely omitted from the accounting system; the error is corrected on 12 May 2004

Date	Details	Folio	Dr	Cr
2004			£	£
12 May	Sales ledger control	ML	235	
	Sales	ML		200
	VAT	ML		35
			235	235
	Invoice 4967 omitted from accounts:			
	in the subsidiary (sales) ledger –			
	debit H Jarvis £235			

This type of error can happen in a very small business – often where the book-keeping is done by one person. For example, an invoice, when typed out, is 'lost' down the back of a filing cabinet. In a large business, particularly one using a computer accounting system, it should be impossible for this error to occur. Also, if documents are numbered serially, then none should be mislaid.

REVERSAL OF ENTRIES

A payment, on 5 May 2004 by cheque of £50 to a creditor, S Wright (receipt no 93459) has been debited in the cash book and credited to purchases ledger control and Wright's account; the error is corrected on 14 May 2004

Date	Details	Folio	Dr	Cr
2004			£	£
14 May	Purchases ledger control	ML	50	
	Bank	CB		50
	Purchases ledger control	ML	50	
	Bank	CB		50
			100	100
	Correction of £50 reversal of entries: receipt 93459: in the subsidiary (purchases) ledger *– debit S Wright £50* *– debit S Wright £50*			

To correct this type of error it is best to reverse the entries that have been made incorrectly (the first two journal entries), and then to put through the correct entries. This is preferable to debiting £100 to purchases ledger control account and crediting £100 to bank account: there was never a transaction for this amount – the original transaction was for £50.

As noted earlier, it is often an idea to write out the 'T' accounts, complete with the error, and then to write in the correcting entries. As an example, the two accounts involved in this last error are shown with the error made on 5 May, and the corrections made on 14 May indicated by the shading:

Dr		**Purchases Ledger Control Account**		Cr
2004		£	2004	£
14 May	Bank	50	5 May Bank	50
14 May	Bank	50		

Dr	Bank Account		Cr
2004	£	2004	£
5 May Purchases ledger control 50		14 May Purchases ledger control 50	
		14 May Purchases ledger control 50	

The accounts now show a net debit transaction of £50 on the purchases ledger control account, and a net credit transaction of £50 on bank account, which is how this payment to a creditor should have been recorded in the first place.

MISPOST/ERROR OF COMMISSION

Credit sales of £47, including VAT (at 17.5%), on invoice no 321 have been debited to the account of J Adams, instead of the account of J Adams Limited; the error is corrected on 15 May 2004

Date	Details	Folio	Dr	Cr
2004			£	£
15 May	Sales ledger control	ML	47	
	Sales ledger control	ML		47
	Correction of mispost (invoice 321):			
	in the subsidiary (sales) ledger			
	– debit J Adams Limited £47			
	– credit J Adams £47			

This type of error can be avoided, to some extent, by the use of account numbers, and by persuading the customer to quote the account number or reference on each transaction.

ERROR OF PRINCIPLE

The cost of petrol, £30 (excluding VAT) on receipt no 34535 has been debited to vehicles account; the error is corrected on 20 May 2004

Date	Details	Folio	Dr	Cr
2004			£	£
20 May	Vehicle running expenses	ML	30	
	Vehicles	ML		30
	Correction of error: receipt 34535			

This type of error is similar to a mispost except that, instead of the wrong person's account being used, it is the wrong class of account. In this example, the vehicle running costs must be kept separate from the cost of the asset (the vehicle), otherwise the expense and asset accounts will be incorrect, leading to profit for the year being overstated and the fixed asset being shown in the balance sheet at too high a figure.

ERROR OF ORIGINAL ENTRY

Postages of £45 paid by cheque entered in the accounts as £54; the error is corrected on 27 May 2004

Date	Details	Folio	Dr	Cr
2004			£	£
27 May	Bank	CB	54	
	Postages	ML		54
	Postages	ML	45	
	Bank	CB		45
			99	99
	Correction of error: postages of £45			
	entered into the accounts as £54			

This error could have been corrected by debiting bank and crediting postages with £9, being the difference between the two amounts. However, there was no original transaction for this amount, and it is better to reverse the wrong transaction and put through the correct one. A reversal of figures either has a difference of nine (as above), or an amount divisible by nine. An error of original entry can also be a 'bad' figure on a cheque or an invoice, which is entered wrongly into both accounts.

COMPENSATING ERROR

Rates account is added up by £100 more than it should be (ie it is overadded, or overcast); sales account is also overcast by the same amount; the error is corrected on 29 May 2004

Date	Details	Folio	Dr	Cr
2004			£	£
29 May	Sales	ML	100	
	Rates	ML		100
	Correction of overcast on rates			
	account and sales account			

Here, an account with a debit balance – rates – has been overcast; this is compensated by an overcast on an account with a credit balance – sales. There are several permutations on this theme, eg two debit balances, one overcast, one undercast (ie underadded); a debit balance undercast, a credit balance undercast. Note the following important points:

- The journal is the book of prime entry for non-regular transactions. The journal entries must then be recorded in the book-keeping system.

- In the journal entries shown above, the book-keeping system in use has control accounts in the main ledger for sales ledger and purchases ledger; remember that transactions which involve the individual accounts of each debtor and creditor must also be recorded in the subsidiary (sales) ledger and subsidiary (purchases) ledger respectively.

TRIAL BALANCE ERRORS: USE OF SUSPENSE ACCOUNT

There are many types of errors revealed by a trial balance. Included amongst these are:

- omission of one part of the double-entry transaction

- recording two debits or two credits for a transaction

- recording a different amount for a transaction on the debit side from the credit side

- errors in the calculation of balances (not compensated by other errors)

- error in transferring the balance of an account to the trial balance

- error of addition in the trial balance

When errors are shown, the trial balance is 'balanced' by recording the difference in a suspense account, as shown in the Case Study below.

Case Study

TEMESIDE TRADERS: SUSPENSE ACCOUNT

The book-keeper of Temeside Traders is unable to balance the trial balance on 30 June 2004. As the error or errors cannot be found quickly the trial balance is balanced by recording the difference in a suspense account, as follows:

	Dr £	Cr £
Trial balance totals	100,000	99,850
Suspense account		150
	100,000	100,00

A suspense account is opened in the main ledger with, in this case, a credit balance of £150 – see next page.

Dr	Suspense Account				Cr
2004		£	2004		£
			30 Jun Trial balance difference		150

A detailed examination of the book-keeping system is now made in order to find the errors. As errors are found, they are corrected by means of a journal entry. The journal entries will balance, with one part of the entry being either a debit or credit to suspense account. In this way, the balance on suspense account is eliminated by book-keeping transactions. Using the above suspense account, the following errors are found and corrected on 15 July 2004:

- sales account is undercast by £100

- a payment to a creditor, A Wilson, for £65, has been recorded in the bank as £56

- telephone expenses of £55 have not been entered in the expenses account

- stationery expenses £48 have been debited to both the stationery account and the bank account

These errors are corrected by the journal entries shown below. Note that the journal narrative includes details of cheque numbers and dates taken from the records of the business.

Date	Details	Folio	Dr	Cr
2004			£	£
15 Jul	Suspense	ML	100	
	Sales	ML		100
	Undercast on 27/5/04 now corrected			
15 Jul	Bank	CB	56	
	Suspense	ML		56
	Suspense	ML	65	
	Bank	CB		65
	Payment to A Wilson for £65 (cheque no. 783726) on 30/5/04 entered in bank as £56 in error		121	121
15 Jul	Telephone expenses	ML	55	
	Suspense	ML		55
	Omission of entry in expenses account paid by cheque no. 783734			
15 Jul	Suspense	ML	48	
	Bank	CB		48
	Suspense	ML	48	
	Bank	CB		48
	Correction of error: payment by cheque 783736 debited in error to bank account		96	96

After these journal entries have been posted in the accounts, suspense account appears:

Dr			Suspense Account		Cr
2004		£	2004		£
15 Jul	Sales	100	30 Jun	Trial balance difference	150
15 Jul	Bank	65	15 Jul	Bank	56
15 Jul	Bank	48	15 Jul	Telephone expenses	55
15 Jul	Bank	48			
		261			261

Thus all the errors have now been found, and suspense account has a nil balance.

EFFECT ON PROFIT AND BALANCE SHEET

The correction of errors, whether shown by a trial balance or not, often has an effect on the profit figure calculated before the errors were found. For example, an undercast of sales account, when corrected, will increase profit and, of course, the profit figure shown in the balance sheet. Some errors, however, only affect the balance sheet, eg errors involving debtors' and creditors' accounts. The diagram below shows the effect of errors when corrected on the profit figure and the balance sheet.

	correction of error	profit	balance sheet
trading and profit and loss account	sales undercast/understated	increase	profit increase
	sales overcast/overstated	decrease	profit decrease
	purchases undercast/understated	decrease	profit decrease
	purchases overcast/overstated	increase	profit increase
	opening stock undervalued	decrease	profit decrease
	opening stock overvalued	increase	profit increase
	closing stock undervalued	increase	profit increase /stock increase
	closing stock overvalued	decrease	profit decrease/stock decrease
	expense undercast/understated	decrease	decrease in profit
	expense overcast/overstated	increase	increase in profit
	income undercast/understated	increase	increase in profit
	income overcast/overstated	decrease	decrease in profit
balance sheet	asset undercast/understated	–	increase asset
	asset overcast/overstated	–	decrease asset
	liability undercast/understated	–	increase liability
	liability overcast/overstated	–	decrease liability

YEAR END TRANSFERS

All other non-regular transactions need to be recorded in the journal. Many of these take place at the end of a firm's financial year and are concerned with:

- transfers to profit and loss account
- accruals and prepayments
- expenses charged to the owner's drawings
- goods for the owner's use
- depreciation
- disposal of fixed assets
- bad debts written off
- provision for doubtful debts

transfers to profit and loss account

As we have seen earlier (Chapter 4), the profit and loss account forms part of double-entry book-keeping. Therefore, each amount recorded in profit and loss account must have an opposite entry in another account: such transfers are recorded in the journal as the book of prime entry, as shown by the entries which follow.

31 Dec 2004   *Balance of sales account at the year end, £155,000, transferred to trading and profit and loss account (debit sales account; credit profit and loss account)*

Date	Details	Folio	Dr	Cr
2004			£	£
31 Dec	Sales	ML	155,000	
	Profit and loss	ML		155,000
	Transfer to trading and profit and			
	loss account of sales for the year			

31 Dec 2004   *Balance of purchases account at the year end, £105,000, transferred to trading and profit and loss account (debit profit and loss account; credit purchases account)*

Date	Details	Folio	Dr	Cr
2004			£	£
31 Dec	Profit and loss	ML	105,000	
	Purchases	ML		105,000
	Transfer to trading and profit and loss			
	account of purchases for the year			

31 Dec 2004   *Closing stock has been valued at £12,500 and is to be entered into the accounts*

Date	Details	Folio	Dr	Cr
2004			£	£
31 Dec	Stock	ML	12,500	
	Profit and loss	ML		12,500
	Stock valuation at 31 December 2004 transferred to trading and profit and loss account			

Remember that the closing stock valuation for the year is recorded in stock account as an asset (*debit* stock account; *credit* profit and loss account).

31 Dec 2004   *Balance of wages account, £23,500, transferred to profit and loss account (debit profit and loss account; credit wages account)*

Date	Details	Folio	Dr	Cr
2004			£	£
31 Dec	Profit and loss	ML	23,500	
	Wages	ML		23,500
	Transfer to profit and loss account of expenditure for the year			

accruals and prepayments

The amounts of accruals and prepayments (see Chapter 6) are recorded in the accounts: such transfers are recorded in the journal as the book of prime entry.

31 Dec 2004   *The balance of telephone account at the year end is £500. A telephone bill for £100 is received on 4 January 2005 and relates to costs incurred in 2004.*

Date	Details	Folio	Dr	Cr
2004			£	£
31 Dec	Profit and loss	ML	600	
	Telephone	ML		500
	Accruals	ML		100
			600	600
	Transfer to profit and loss account of expenditure for the year			

The above transaction leaves a credit balance on accruals account, being the amount due at 31 December 2004.

31 Dec 2004   The balance of rent paid account at the year end is £750. Of this, £675 relates to 2004, while £75 is a prepayment for 2005

Date	Details	Folio	Dr	Cr
2004			£	£
31 Dec	Profit and loss	ML	675	
	Prepayments	ML	75	
	Rent paid	ML		750
			750	750
	Transfer to profit and loss account			
	of expenditure for the year			

The above transaction leaves a debit balance on prepayments account, being the amount prepaid at 31 December 2004.

expenses charged to owner's drawings

Sometimes the owner of a business uses business facilities for private use, eg telephone, or car. The owner will agree that part of the expense shall be charged to him or her as drawings, while the other part represents a business expense. The book-keeping entry to record the adjustment is:

– *debit* drawings account

– *credit* expense account, eg telephone

31 Dec 2004   The balance of telephone account at the year end is £600; of this, one-quarter is the estimated cost of the owner's private usage

The journal entry is:

Date	Details	Folio	Dr	Cr
2004			£	£
31 Dec	Drawings	ML	150	
	Telephone	ML		150
	Transfer of private use to			
	drawings account			

goods for the owner's use

When the owner of a business takes some of the goods in which the business trades for his or her own use, the double-entry book-keeping is:

– *debit* drawings account

– *credit* purchases account

15 Oct 2004   *Owner of the business takes goods for own use, £105 (no VAT)*

The journal entry is:

Date	Details	Folio	Dr	Cr
2004			£	£
15 Oct	Drawings	ML	105	
	Purchases	ML		105
	Goods taken for own use			
	by the owner			

Notes:

• Where a business is VAT-registered, VAT must be accounted for on goods taken by the owner

• An alternative method of accounting for goods for own use is:

– *debit* drawings account

– *credit* sales account

This method is favoured by HM Revenue & Customs for taxation purposes; however, either is acceptable for the purpose of financial records and accounts – which method is used will depend on the custom and practice of the business.

depreciation

As we have seen in Chapter 7, the amount of depreciation on fixed assets is recorded in the profit and loss account:

– *debit* profit and loss account

– *credit* depreciation account

31 Dec 2004   Depreciation on a machine is calculated at £400 for the year

The journal entry is:

Date	Details	Folio	Dr	Cr
2004			£	£
31 Dec	Profit and loss	ML	400	
	Depreciation	ML		400
	Depreciation charge for year			
	on machine			

As already seen in Chapter 7, the amount credited to depreciation account (the annual charge for depreciation) is then transferred to provision for depreciation account (which records the accumulated total of depreciation for each class of asset):

– *debit* depreciation account

– *credit* provision for depreciation account

The journal entry for depreciation on the machine is:

Date	Details	Folio	Dr	Cr
2004			£	£
31 Dec	Depreciation	ML	400	
	Provision for depreciation account	ML		400
	– machinery			
	Transfer of depreciation charge for year			
	to provision for depreciation account			

disposal of fixed assets

When a fixed asset is sold or disposed, the book-keeping entries (see page 110) bring together:

• the original cost of the asset

• depreciation provided over the life of the asset

• sale proceeds

31 Dec 2006   A machine had been bought on 1 January 2004 (ie three years ago) for £2,000 (net of VAT). Provision for depreciation (including the current year) totals £1,200. On 31 December 2006 the machine is sold for £600 plus VAT (cheque received)

The journal entry is:

Date	Details	Folio	Dr	Cr
2006			£	£
31 Dec	Disposals	ML	2,000	
	Machinery	ML		2,000
	Provision for depreciation account			
	– machinery	ML	1,200	
	Disposals	ML		1,200
	Bank	CB	705	
	Disposals	ML		600
	VAT	ML		105
	Profit and loss	ML	200	
	Disposals	ML		200
			4,105	4,105
	Sale of machine no. 123456; loss on			
	sale £200 transferred to profit and loss			
	account			

(If you wish to check the book-keeping entries for this transaction, they are set out in full on pages 111-112.)

bad debts written off

We have already seen, in Chapter 8, the double-entry book-keeping entries to write off a debtor's account as bad:

– *debit* bad debts written off account

– *credit* debtor's account

15 Dec 2004   Write off the account of T Hughes, which has a balance of £25, as a bad debt

The journal entry is:

Date	Details	Folio	Dr	Cr
2004			£	£
15 Dec	Bad debts written off	ML	25	
	Sales ledger control	ML		25
	Account of T Hughes in the			
	subsidiary (sales) ledger written off			
	as a bad debt – see memo			
	dated 14 December 2004			

provision for doubtful debts

In Chapter 8 we saw that the creation of a provision for doubtful debts is recorded in the profit and loss account:

- *debit* profit and loss account
- *credit* provision for doubtful debts: adjustment account

31 Dec 2004   A provision for doubtful debts of £500 is to be created

The journal entry is:

Date	Details	Folio	Dr	Cr
2004			£	£
31 Dec	Profit and loss	ML	500	
	Provision for doubtful debts:			
	adjustment	ML		500
	Creation of a provision for doubtful			
	debts			

As already seen in Chapter 8, the amount credited to provision for doubtful debts: adjustment account (the annual change in the provision) is then transferred to provision for doubtful debts account (which records the accumulated total of the provision):

- *debit* provision for doubtful debts: adjustment account
- *credit* provision for doubtful debts account

The journal entry to record this transfer is:

Date	Details	Folio	Dr	Cr
2004			£	£
31 Dec	Provision for doubtful debts:			
	adjustment	ML	500	
	Provision for doubtful debts	ML		500
	Transfer of charge for year to			
	provision for doubtful debts account			

An existing provision for doubtful debts will usually be increased or decreased as the level of debtors changes. The book-keeping entries (see Chapter 8) are:

increasing the provision

- *debit* profit and loss account
- *credit* provision for doubtful debts: adjustment account

decreasing the provision

- *debit* provision for doubtful debts: adjustment account

- *credit* profit and loss account

31 Dec 2005   The existing provision for doubtful debts is to be increased by £250

The journal entry is:

Date	Details	Folio	Dr	Cr
2005			£	£
31 Dec	Profit and loss	ML	250	
	Provision for doubtful debts:			
	adjustment	ML		250
	Increase in provision for doubtful			
	debts			

This is then transferred to provision for doubtful debts account as follows:

Date	Details	Folio	Dr	Cr
2005			£	£
31 Dec	Provision for doubtful debts:			
	adjustment	ML	250	
	Provision for doubtful debts	ML		250
	Transfer of charge for year to			
	provision for doubtful debts account			

MAKING JOURNAL ENTRIES

As we have seen in this chapter, the journal is the book of prime entry for non-regular transactions. Because of the irregular nature of journal transactions, it is important that they are correctly authorised by the appropriate person – such as the accounts supervisor, the manager of the organisation, the owner of the business. The authorisation will, ideally, be a prime document – eg letter, memo, email or other document – but may well be verbal – eg "make the year end transfers to profit and loss account", or "find the errors and put them right".

A great deal of tact and courtesy is needed when investigating business transactions. For example, when investigating errors, it is likely that the person who made the errors will be the one who can be of most assistance to you in correcting them – that person invariably knows the book-keeping system better than you do, and his or her co-operation is needed, firstly, to put the errors right and, secondly, to see that they do not happen again.

It might well be that not all errors can be corrected without the assistance of other people, eg the accounts supervisor. Under such circumstances you, as an accounts assistant, should make the corrections that you are able to do – which may go some way to reducing the imbalance shown by suspense account – and then seek assistance from the appropriate person for help in resolving any outstanding items.

At another level, the investigation of errors may reveal that fraudulent transactions have been entered into the accounts. Tact and courtesy are needed to ensure that such transactions are investigated thoroughly, and the appropriate person in the organisation advised of the findings so that further action can be taken.

With journal entries for year end transfers it is essential to ensure that the organisation's policies, regulations, procedures and timescales are observed in relation to the preparation of final accounts. Thus journal entries are needed for profit and loss account transfers, accruals and prepayments, depreciation, bad debts and provision for bad debts – all of these must be made at the correct time for the organisation and for the correct amounts.

It is good practice in an organisation to ensure that journal entries are checked by an appropriate person before they are entered into the double-entry book-keeping system. It is all too easy to get a journal entry the wrong way round resulting in an error becoming twice as much as it was in the first place!

Chapter Summary

- The journal is used to list non-regular transactions.

- The journal is a book of prime (or original) entry – it is not a double-entry account.

- The journal is used for:
  - opening entries
  - purchase and sale of fixed assets on credit
  - correction of errors
  - year end transfers

- Correction of errors is always a difficult topic to put into practice: it tests knowledge of book-keeping procedures and it is all too easy to make the error worse than it was in the first place! The secret of dealing with this topic well is to write down – in account format – what has gone wrong. It should then be relatively easy to see what has to be done to put the error right.

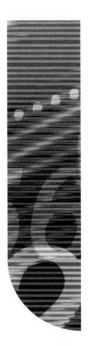

- Errors not shown by a trial balance: error of omission, reversal of entries, mispost/error of commission, error of principle, error of original entry (or transcription), compensating error.

- Errors shown by a trial balance include: omission of one part of the book-keeping transaction, recording two debits/credits for a transaction, recording different amounts in the two accounts, calculating balances incorrectly, transferring wrong balances to the trial balance.

- All errors are non-regular transactions and need to be corrected by means of a journal entry: the book-keeper then records the correcting transactions in the accounts.

- When error(s) are shown by a trial balance, the amount of the error is placed in a suspense account. As the errors are found, journal entries are made which 'clear out' the suspense account.

- Correction of errors may have an effect on profit calculated before the errors were found, and on the balance sheet.

Key Terms

journal	the book of prime entry for non-regular transactions
opening entries	the transactions which open the accounts of a new business
suspense account	account in which to place an error in the trial balance, pending further investigation

Student Activities

12.1 Which one of the following will *not* be recorded in the journal?

(a)　credit purchase of a fixed asset

(b)　cash sale of goods to a customer

(c)　write-off of a bad debt

(d)　correction of an error not shown by the trial balance

Answer (a) or (b) or (c) or (d)

12.2 A trial balance fails to agree by £75 and the difference is placed to a suspense account. Later it is found that a credit sale for this amount has not been entered in the sales account. Which one of the following journal entries is correct?

(a)   debit suspense account £75; credit sales account £75

(b)   debit suspense account £150; credit sales account £150

(c)   debit sales account £75; credit suspense account £75

(d)   credit sales account £75

Answer (a) or (b) or (c) or (d)

12.3 Lucy Wallis started in business on 1 May 2004 with the following assets and liabilities:

	£
Motor vehicle	6,500
Fixtures and fittings	2,800
Opening stock	4,100
Cash	150
Loan from husband	5,000

You are to prepare Lucy's opening journal entry, showing clearly her capital at 1 May 2004.

12.4 The trial balance of Thomas Wilson balanced. However, a number of errors have been found in the book-keeping system:

(a)   Credit sale of £150 to J Rigby has not been entered in the accounts.

(b)   A payment by cheque for £125 to H Price Limited, a creditor, has been recorded in the account of H Prince.

(c)   The cost of a new delivery van, £10,000, has been entered to vehicle expenses account.

(d)   Postages of £55, paid by cheque, have been entered on the wrong sides of both accounts.

(e)   Both purchases account and purchases returns account have been undercast by £100.

(f)   A payment for £89 from L Johnson, a debtor, has been entered in the accounts as £98.

You are to take each error in turn and:
* state the type of error
* show the correcting journal entry

Note: VAT is to be ignored

12.5   Jeremy Johnson extracts a trial balance from his book-keeping records on 30 September 2004. Unfortunately the trial balance fails to balance and the difference, £19 debit, is placed to a suspense account in the main ledger pending further investigation.

The following errors are later found:

(a)   A cheque payment of £85 for office expenses has been entered in the cash book but no entry has been made in the office expenses account.

(b)   A payment for photocopying of £87 by cheque has been correctly entered in the cash book, but is shown as £78 in the photocopying account.

(c)   Sales returns account has been overcast by £100.

(d)   Commission received of £25 has been entered twice in the account.

You are to:

•   make journal entries to correct the errors

•   show the suspense account after the errors have been corrected

12.6   Show the journal entries for the following transfers which relate to Trish Hall's business for the year ended 31 December 2004:

(a)   Closing stock is to be recorded in the accounts at a valuation of £22,600.

(b)   Telephone expenses for the year, amounting to £890, are to be transferred to profit and loss account.

(c)   Salaries account shows a balance of £22,950, but £980 is owing; the amount due for the year is to be transferred to profit and loss account.

(d)   Photocopying expenses account shows a balance of £1,240, but this includes copier rental of £80 in respect of January and February 2005; the amount due for the year is to be transferred to profit and loss account.

(e)   Motoring expenses account shows a balance of £800; one-quarter of this relates to Trish Hall's private motoring.

(f)   Trish has taken goods for her own use of £175 (no VAT).

(g)   Depreciation on fixtures and fittings for the year is calculated at £500.

(h)   A machine had been bought on 1 January 2002 for £5,000 (net of VAT). Provision for depreciation (including the current year) totals £3,750. On 31 December 2004 the machine is sold for £2,000 plus VAT, a cheque being received.

(i)   The following accounts in the subsidiary (sales) ledger are to be written off as bad (bad debt relief is not available): Nick Marshall, £55; Crabbe & Company, £30; A Hunt, £40.

These are the only bad debts written off during the year; the total is to be transferred to profit and loss account.

(j)   The provision for doubtful debts is £550; the amount is to be reduced to £450.

13 Incomplete records

So far our studies of financial records and accounts have concentrated on the double-entry system and, from this, we have extracted a trial balance and prepared for the production of final accounts. However, many smaller businesses do not use the double-entry system, and no trial balance is available. Such businesses keep some records – incomplete records – and, at the end of the year, it is the task of the accountant to construct the final accounts from these.

This chapter looks at

- the information available when constructing final accounts from incomplete records
- how information that is required can be calculated
- preparing final accounts from incomplete records
- the use of gross profit mark-up and margin in incomplete records accounting

PERFORMANCE CRITERIA COVERED

unit 5: MAINTAINING FINANCIAL RECORDS AND PREPARING ACCOUNTS

KNOWLEDGE AND UNDERSTANDING – ACCOUNTING PRINCIPLES AND THEORY

18   the methods of restructuring accounts from incomplete evidence

element 5.2

collecting and collating information for the preparation of final accounts

G   conduct investigations into business transactions with trust and courtesy

H   ensure that the organisation's policies, regulations, procedures and timescales relating to preparing final accounts are observed

element 5.3

preparing the final accounts of sole traders and partnerships

C   observe the organisation's policies, regulations, procedures and timescales in relation to preparing final accounts of sole traders and partnerships

D   identify and resolve or refer to the appropriate person discrepancies, unusual features or queries

WHAT ARE INCOMPLETE RECORDS?

Incomplete records is the term used where the book-keeping system does not use double-entry principles and no trial balance is available. Some records are kept and the accountant will construct final accounts by

- using the information available (see below)
- seeing what information may not be available, and how 'missing' figures can be calculated

information available to the accountant

The basic financial record kept by most businesses is a cash book, often operated as a *single-entry* system. In practice, even if a cash book has not been kept, it is usually possible to reconstruct it from banking records, although this task can prove to be time-consuming. Other financial information will be available so that, in all, the accountant has the following to work from:

- cash book – the basic record for any single entry system
- banking details – statements, paying-in books, cheque counterfoils
- invoices – both received (for purchases) and sent (for sales) during the year
- expenses – during the year
- assets and liabilities – fixed and current assets, long-term and current liabilities, both at the beginning and end of the year
- fixed assets – bought or sold during the year

Information which may not be available, and will need to be calculated includes:

- capital at the beginning of the financial year
- purchases and sales for the year
- cash book summary
- profit for the year

the tools of accounting

In the two Case Studies which follow (pages 226 and 232) we shall see how to take the financial information that is available and, using the *tools of accounting*, to construct the accounts that are required. The tools of accounting that may be needed are:

- the use of an opening trial balance, or statement of assets and liabilities
- the construction of a cash account and/or bank account

- the use of control accounts – sales ledger control account and purchases ledger control account
- the preparation of final accounts – profit and loss account and balance sheet

In addition, the following may be of use:

- the accounting equation (assets – liabilities = capital)
- gross profit mark-up and margin (see page 238)

The two Case Studies make use of these tools of accounting, although it should be emphasised that no two incomplete records situations are the same; however practice will help to develop your skills in this aspect of financial accounting.

Case Study

JAYNE PERRY – STATIONERY SUPPLIES

The following information has been taken from the incomplete records of Jayne Perry, who runs a small stationery supplies business.

LIST OF ASSETS AND LIABILITIES

	1 Jan 2004	31 Dec 2004
	£	£
Shop fittings	8,000	8,000
Stock	25,600	29,800
Debtors	29,200	20,400
Bank balance	5,000	not known
Creditors	20,800	16,000
Expenses owing	200	300

BANK SUMMARY FOR 2004

	£
Receipts from debtors	127,800
Payments to creditors	82,600
Drawings	12,500
Business expenses	30,600

In the text which follows we shall see how Jayne Perry's accountant will construct the final accounts for 2004 from incomplete records. The information to be calculated is:

- opening capital, at the beginning of the financial year
- cash book summary for the year
- purchases and sales for the year
- profit for the year, and a year end balance sheet in proper form

Note: for the sake of simplicity we will ignore VAT on all transactions

OPENING CAPITAL

Opening capital is needed in Jayne Perry's case because a year-end statement of assets, liabilities and capital is to be prepared. In other situations with incomplete records, opening capital may be stated, being the difference between assets and liabilities. To calculate the capital at the beginning of the financial year, we use the formula *assets − liabilities = capital.*

This is presented as a *statement of assets and liabilities* as follows:

	£	£
JAYNE PERRY		
STATEMENT OF ASSETS AND LIABILITIES		
as at 1 January 2004		
Assets		
Shop fittings		8,000
Stock		25,600
Debtors		29,200
Bank balance		5,000
		67,800
Less Liabilities		
Creditors	20,800	
Expenses owing	200	
		21,000
Capital at 1 January 2004		46,800

Notes:

- Here, the bank balance is an asset, ie money in the bank; if it was marked as an overdraft, it would be included amongst the liabilities.

- Look out for the opening bank balance or overdraft being stated elsewhere in the information; for example, a bank summary may be given which starts with the bank figure at the beginning of the year – this figure must be included in the statement of assets and liabilities, which is used to calculate opening capital.

CASH BOOK SUMMARY

A cash book summary enables us to find out the cash and bank balances at the year-end. (Sometimes this is not necessary, as a cash book may have been prepared already by the owner of the business.) In practice, the entries on the firm's bank statement can be used to produce a summary of receipts and payments for the year. In the case of Jayne Perry's business, the cash book (bank columns) are:

Dr		Cash Book (bank columns)		Cr
2004		£	2004	£
1 Jan	Balance b/d	5,000	Payments to creditors	82,600
	Receipts from debtors	127,800	Drawings	12,500
			Expenses	30,600
			31 Dec Balance c/d	7,100
		132,800	missing figure	132,800
2005			2005	
1 Jan	Balance b/d	7,100		

The bank balance of £7,100 on 31 December 2004 is calculated by filling in the missing figure.

Notes:

- When preparing a cash book summary, look out for an opening bank balance that is *overdrawn*; this is entered on the credit side.

- At the end of the cash book summary, a credit balance brought down is an overdraft.

PURCHASES AND SALES

In calculating purchases and sales, we need to take note of the creditors and debtors at both the beginning and the end of the year. The important point to note is that payments to creditors are *not* the same as purchases for the year (because of the change in the level of creditors). Likewise, receipts from debtors are not the same as sales (because of the change in debtors). Only in a business which trades solely on cash terms and has no debtors/creditors would the receipts and payments be the figures for sales and purchases.

calculating purchases and sales

The method of calculating the purchases and sales figures is:

- **purchases for year** = payments to creditors in year, *less* creditors at the beginning of the year, *plus* creditors at the end of the year

- **sales for year** = receipts from debtors in year, *less* debtors at the beginning of the year, *plus* debtors at the end of the year

When calculating purchases and sales, also take note of any cash discounts received and allowed, and – for sales – bad debts written off.

The figures from Jayne Perry's business are:

purchases   = £82,600 - £20,800 + £16,000   = £77,800

sales   = £127,800 - £29,200 + £20,400   = £119,000

use of control accounts

The use of control accounts is recommended for calculating purchases and sales in incomplete records questions. We can use the information for purchases given in the Case Study as follows:

Dr		Purchases Ledger Control Account			Cr
2004		£	**2004**		£
	Payments to creditors	82,600	1 Jan	Balance b/d	20,800
31 Dec	Balance c/d	16,000		Purchases *(missing figure)*	?
		98,600			98,600
2005			**2005**		
			1 Jan	Balance b/d	16,000

The missing figure of purchases for the year is calculated as:

£98,600 – £20,800 = **£77,800**

In a similar way, the sales figure can be calculated:

Dr		Sales Ledger Control Account			Cr
2004		£	**2004**		£
1 Jan	Balance b/d	29,200		Receipts from debtors	127,800
	Sales (missing figure)	?	31 Dec	Balance c/d	20,400
		148,200			148,200
2005			**2005**		
1 Jan	Balance b/d	20,400			

The missing figure of sales for the year is £148,200 – £29,200 = **£119,000**

The control account method, although its use is not essential in incomplete records questions, does bring a discipline to calculating the two important figures of purchases and sales. Do not forget that the control accounts give the figures for *credit* purchases and sales: cash purchases and sales need to be added, where applicable, to obtain total purchases and sales for the year.

purchases and sales – summary

Whichever method of calculating purchases or sales is used – calculation, or a control account – four pieces of information are usually required:

- opening balance
- closing balance
- payments or receipts for the year
- purchases or sales for the year

Provided that any three are known, the fourth can be calculated – the figure for purchases and sales was the missing figure in the examples above. However if, for example, we know the opening and closing debtors totals, together with sales for the year, then it is a simple matter to calculate the missing figure for receipts from debtors.

Remember that, if they are applicable, cash discounts allowed and received, and – for sales – bad debts written off, should also be incorporated into the control accounts.

PREPARATION OF THE FINAL ACCOUNTS

trading and profit and loss account

Having calculated the figures for purchases and sales, we can now prepare the trading and profit and loss account. The section as far as gross profit is:

	£	£
JAYNE PERRY		
TRADING AND PROFIT AND LOSS ACCOUNT		
for the year ended 31 December 2004		
Sales		119,000
Opening stock	25,600	
Purchases	77,800	
	103,400	
Less Closing stock	29,800	
Cost of sales		73,600
Gross profit		45,400

The overheads section of the profit and loss account follows but, before we are able to complete this, we need to know the figure for expenses for the year. The relevant information from the Case Study is:

- bank payments for expenses during year, £30,600
- expenses owing at 1 January 2004, £200
- expenses owing at 31 December 2004, £300

Like the calculation of purchases and sales, we cannot simply use the bank payments figure for expenses; we must take note of cash payments, together with accruals (and prepayments). The calculation is:

expenses for year = bank and cash payments less accruals at the beginning of the year (or plus prepayments), plus accruals at the end of the year (or less prepayments)

Thus the figure for Jayne Perry's business expenses is:

£30,600 – £200 + £300 = £30,700.

Alternatively, expenses can be calculated by means of a control account:

Dr			**Expenses Control Account**		Cr
2004		£	2004		£
	Cash/bank	30,600	1 Jan	Balance b/d	200
31 Dec	Balance c/d	300	31 Dec	Profit and loss account *(missing figure)*	?
		30,900			30,900
2005			2005		
			1 Jan	Balance b/d	300

The missing figure is £30,900 – £200 = £30,700

Jayne Perry's profit and loss account concludes as follows:

	£
Gross profit	45,400
Less overheads:	
Expenses	30,700
Net profit	14,700

balance sheet

The balance sheet can now be prepared using the assets and liabilities from the Case Study.

JAYNE PERRY
BALANCE SHEET
as at 31 December 2004

	£	£	£
Fixed assets			
Shop fittings			8,000
Current assets			
Stock		29,800	
Debtors		20,400	
Bank		7,100	
		57,300	
Less Current liabilities			
Creditors	16,000		
Accruals	300		
		16,300	
Working capital			41,000
NET ASSETS			49,000
FINANCED BY			
Capital			
Opening capital			46,800
Add net profit			14,700
			61,500
Less drawings			12,500
Closing capital			49,000

ELECTROPARTS

We will now look at a more comprehensive example of incomplete records accounting. This incorporates points on depreciation and the sale of a fixed asset and concludes with the production of final accounts. You may like to work through the Case Study before comparing your solution with the one shown.

situation

John Anstey owns a small business, Electroparts, which supplies spare parts for a wide range of electrical goods – cookers, fridges, freezers, kettles, dishwashers, etc. Most of his customers are self-employed repairers who buy parts for specific jobs from his trade counter – John allows them credit terms; some sales are made to members of the public carrying out 'do-it-yourself' repairs – these customers pay in cash at the time of sale. All purchases from suppliers are made on credit.

John does not keep a full set of accounting records; however, the following information has been produced for the year ended 31 December 2004:

Assets and Liabilities of Electroparts at 1 January 2004

		£	£
ASSETS	Buildings at cost	100,000	
	Less provision for depreciation	10,000	
			90,000
	Fixtures and fittings at cost	15,000	
	Less provision for depreciation	7,500	
			7,500
			97,500
	Stock	24,400	
	Debtors	21,650	
	Prepayment: general expenses	140	
	Cash	250	
			46,440
	TOTAL ASSETS		143,940
LIABILITIES	Creditors	15,950	
	Bank overdraft	12,850	
	TOTAL LIABILITIES		28,800
CAPITAL			115,140

Summary of the bank account (year ended 31 December 2004)

	£		£
Cash sales	45,280	Balance b/d	12,850
Receipts from debtors	177,410	Payments to creditors	149,620
Sale proceeds of fixtures		General expenses	17,340
and fittings	1,950	Wages	18,280
		Drawings	25,390
		Balance c/d	1,160
	224,640		224,640

other information:

- On 31 December 2004, stock was valued at £28,400
- Depreciation is calculated at the rate of 2% on the cost of buildings and 10% on the cost of fixtures and fittings held at the end of the financial year. No depreciation is calculated in the year of sale/disposal
- Fixtures and fittings purchased on 1 January 2002 for £2,500 were sold on 30 September 2004, the purchaser paying by cheque

– The proceeds from cash sales are placed in the till and paid into the bank account at the end of the day, apart from a cash float which is retained in the till; the amount of the cash float was £250 until October, when it was increased to £500

– On 31 December 2004, creditors were £18,210, debtors were £23,840 and £210 was owing for general expenses

– During the year, bad debts of £870 have been written off

John Anstey asks you to:

1   Calculate the amount of credit sales during the year

2   Calculate the total sales during the year

3   Calculate the amount of purchases during the year

4   Calculate the profit or loss on the sale of fixtures and fittings

5   Calculate the figure for general expenses to be shown in the profit and loss account for the year ended 31 December 2004

6   Prepare the trading and profit and loss account for the year ended 31 December 2004

7   Prepare the balance sheet at 31 December 2004

Note: for the sake of simplicity we will ignore VAT

solution

1

Dr		Sales Ledger Control Account			Cr
2004		£	2004		£
1 Jan	Balance b/d	21,650		Receipts from debtors	177,410
	Credit sales			Bad debts written off	870
	(missing figure)	180,470	31 Dec	Balance c/d	23,840
		202,120			202,120

2

Dr		Sales Account			Cr
2004		£	2004		£
31 Dec	Trading account			Credit sales (see above)	180,470
	(sales for year)	226,000		Cash sales	45,280
				Increase in cash float	250
		226,000			226,000

3

Dr		Purchases Ledger Control Account			Cr
2004			£	2004		£
	Payments to creditors	149,620	1 Jan	Balance b/d	15,950
31 Dec	Balance c/d	18,210		Purchases *(missing figure)*	151,880
		167,830			167,830

4

Profit or loss on disposal of fixtures and fittings

Depreciation per year	£250
Number of years' depreciation	2 (2002, 2003; no depreciation in year of sale)
Provision for depreciation	£500

Dr		Disposals Account			Cr
2004			£	2004		£
30 Sep	Fixtures and fittings	2,500	30 Sep	Provision for depreciation	500
			30 Sep	Bank (sale proceeds)	1,950
			31 Dec	Profit and loss account	
				(loss on sale)	50
		2,500			2,500

5

Dr		General Expenses Control Account			Cr
2004			£	2004		£
1 Jan	Balance b/d	140	31 Dec	Profit and loss account	
	Bank	17,340		*(missing figure)*	17,690
31 Dec	Balance c/d	210			
		17,690			17,690

6

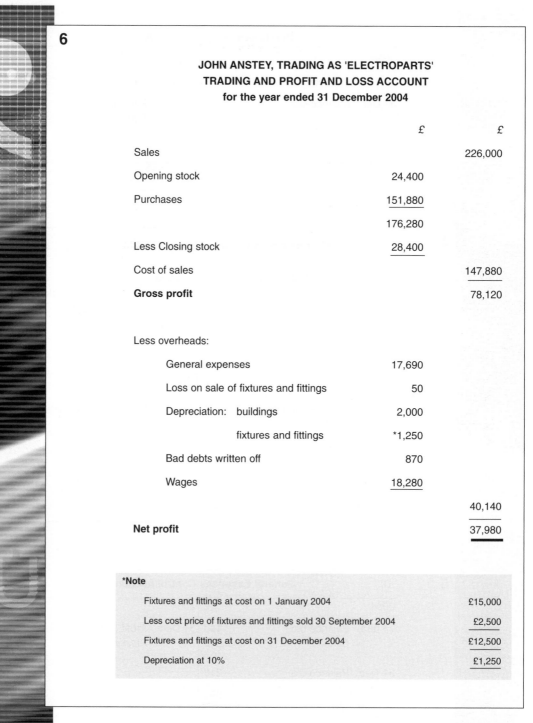

JOHN ANSTEY, TRADING AS 'ELECTROPARTS'
TRADING AND PROFIT AND LOSS ACCOUNT
for the year ended 31 December 2004

	£	£
Sales		226,000
Opening stock	24,400	
Purchases	151,880	
	176,280	
Less Closing stock	28,400	
Cost of sales		147,880
Gross profit		78,120
Less overheads:		
General expenses	17,690	
Loss on sale of fixtures and fittings	50	
Depreciation: buildings	2,000	
fixtures and fittings	*1,250	
Bad debts written off	870	
Wages	18,280	
		40,140
Net profit		37,980

*Note

Fixtures and fittings at cost on 1 January 2004	£15,000
Less cost price of fixtures and fittings sold 30 September 2004	£2,500
Fixtures and fittings at cost on 31 December 2004	£12,500
Depreciation at 10%	£1,250

7

JOHN ANSTEY, TRADING AS 'ELECTROPARTS'
BALANCE SHEET
as at 31 December 2004

Fixed assets	£ Cost	£ Provision for depreciation	£ Net
Buildings	100,000	12,000	88,000
Fixtures and fittings	12,500	*8,250	4,250
	112,500	20,250	92,250

Current assets

Stock		28,400
Debtors		23,840
Bank		1,160
Cash		500
		53,900

Less Current liabilities

Creditors	18,210	
Accrual: general expenses	210	
		18,420
Working capital		35,480
NET ASSETS		127,730

FINANCED BY
Capital

Opening capital (from assets and liabilities at 1 January 2004)	115,140
Add net profit	37,980
	153,120
Less drawings	25,390
Closing capital	127,730

*Note	
Provision for depreciation of fixtures and fittings at 1 January 2004	7,500
Less provision for depreciation on asset sold	500
	7,000
Depreciation for year (see profit and loss account)	1,250
Provision for depreciation of fixtures and fittings at 31 December 2004	8,250

THE USE OF GROSS PROFIT MARK-UP AND MARGIN

It is often necessary to use accounting ratios and percentages in the preparation of final accounts from incomplete records.

The two main percentages used for incomplete records accounting are:

*   gross profit mark-up
*   gross profit margin

It is quite common for a business to establish its selling price by reference to either a mark-up or a margin. The difference between the two is that:

*   mark-up is a profit percentage added to *buying* or *cost* price
*   margin is a percentage profit based on the *selling* price

For example, a product is bought by a retailer at a cost of £100; the retailer sells it for £125, ie

$$\text{cost price} + \text{gross profit} = \text{selling price}$$

$$£100 \quad + \quad £25 \quad = \quad £125$$

The **mark-up** is:

$$\frac{\text{gross profit}}{\text{cost price}} \times \frac{100}{1} = \frac{£25}{£100} \times \frac{100}{1} = \mathbf{25\%}$$

The **margin** is:

$$\frac{\text{gross profit}}{\text{selling price}} \times \frac{100}{1} = \frac{£25}{£125} \times \frac{100}{1} = \mathbf{20\%}$$

In incomplete records accounting, mark-up or the margin percentages can be used to calculate either cost of sales (which, if opening stock and closing stock are known, will enable the calculation of purchases) or sales. We will now study two examples.

WORKED EXAMPLES

example 1 – calculation of sales

*   Cost of sales is £150,000
*   Mark-up is 40%
*   What are sales?

$$\text{Gross profit} = £150,000 \times \frac{40}{100} = £60,000$$

Sales = cost of sales + gross profit, ie £150,000 + £60,000 = **£210,000**

example 2 – calculation of purchases

*   Sales are £450,000

*   Margin is 20%

*   Opening stock is £40,000; closing stock is £50,000

*   What are purchases?

Gross profit = £450,000 x $\dfrac{20}{100}$ = £90,000

Cost of sales = sales – gross profit, ie £450,000 – £90,000 = £360,000

The purchases calculation is:

Opening stock		£40,000
+	Purchases (missing figure)	?
–	Closing stock	£50,000
=	Cost of sales	£360,000
Therefore purchases =		**£370,000**

STOCK LOSSES

A loss of stock may occur as a result of an event such as a fire, a flood or a theft. When such a loss occurs, an estimate of the value of the stock lost needs to be made in order for the business to make an insurance claim (always assuming that the stock was adequately insured). The value is calculated by preparing an accounting summary to the date of the event, and often making use of margins and mark-ups. The calculations are best carried out in three steps:

1	Opening stock	
	+	Purchases
	=	Cost of stock available for sale
2	Sales	
	–	Gross profit (using normal gross profit margin)
	=	Cost of sales
3	Cost of stock available for sale (from 1, above)	
	–	Cost of sales (2, above)
	=	Estimated closing stock
	–	Value of stock remaining or salvaged
	=	Value of stock lost through fire, flood or theft

CLOTHING SUPPLIES: THEFT OF STOCK

situation

Peter Kamara runs Clothing Supplies, a small clothing wholesalers. Peter is convinced that various items of clothing have been stolen during the year and he asks you to calculate, from the accounting details, the value of stock stolen. The following information is available:

- sales for the year, £500,000
- opening stock at the beginning of the year, £15,000
- purchases for the year, £310,000
- closing stock at the end of the year, £22,000
- the gross profit margin achieved on all sales is 40 per cent

solution

CALCULATION OF STOCK LOSS FOR THE YEAR		
	£	£
Opening stock		15,000
Purchases		310,000
Cost of stock available for sale		325,000
Sales	500,000	
Less Normal gross profit margin (40%)	200,000	
Cost of sales		300,000
Estimated closing stock		25,000
Less Actual closing stock		22,000
Value of stock loss		3,000

- Incomplete records is the term used where the book-keeping system does not use double-entry principles.

- In order to prepare final accounts, the accountant may well have to calculate:
  - capital at the beginning of the financial year
  - purchases and sales for the year
  - cash book summary
  - profit for the year

- On the basis of these calculations, the accountant can then construct the final accounts without recourse to a trial balance.

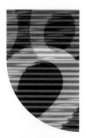

- Two ratios and percentages used in incomplete records accounting are:
  - gross profit mark-up
  - gross profit margin

- The value of stock losses caused by fire, flood or theft is calculated using margins and mark-ups.

Key Terms

incomplete records	a book-keeping system in which double-entry principles are not used
gross profit mark-up	profit percentage added to the buying price
gross profit margin	profit percentage based on the selling price
stock loss	loss of stock caused by fire, flood or theft

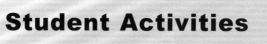

Student Activities

13.1
- Cost of sales for the year is £200,000.
- Mark-up is 30%.

What are sales for the year?

13.2
- Sales for the year are £100,000.
- Gross profit margin is 25%.
- Opening stock is £10,000; closing stock is £12,000.

What are purchases for the year?

13.3 You are preparing accounts from incomplete records. Debtors at the start of the year were £2,500, and at the end were £3,250. Cheques received from debtors total £17,850; cash sales total £2,500. What is the sales figure for the year?

13.4 Jane Price owns a fashion shop called 'Trendsetters'. She has been in business for one year and, although she does not keep a full set of accounting records, the following information has been produced for the first year of trading, which ended on 31 December 2004:

Summary of the business bank account for the year ended 31 December 2004:

	£
Capital introduced	60,000
Receipts from sales	153,500
Payments to suppliers	95,000
Advertising	4,830
Wages	15,000
Rent and rates	8,750
General expenses	5,000
Shop fittings	50,000
Drawings	15,020

Summary of assets and liabilities as at 31 December 2004:

	£
Shop fittings at cost	50,000
Stock	73,900
Debtors	2,500
Creditors	65,000

Other information:

• Jane wishes to depreciate the shop fittings at 20% per year using the straight-line method

• At 31 December 2004, rent is prepaid by £250, and wages of £550 are owing

You are to:

(a) Calculate the amount of sales during the year.

(b) Calculate the amount of purchases during the year.

(c) Calculate the figures for
   • rent and rates
   • wages
   to be shown in the profit and loss account for the year ended 31 December 2004

(d) Prepare Jane Price's trading and profit and loss account for the year ended 31 December 2004.

(e) Prepare Jane Price's balance sheet at 31 December 2004.

Note: VAT is to be ignored on all transactions

13.5 James Harvey runs a stationery supplies shop. He is convinced that one of his employees is stealing stationery. He asks you to calculate from the accounting records the value of stock stolen. The following information is available:

• sales for the year, £180,000

• opening stock at the beginning of the year, £21,500

• purchases for the year, £132,000

• closing stock at the end of the year, £26,000

• the gross profit margin achieved on all sales is 30 per cent

You are to calculate the value of stock stolen (if any) during the year.

13.6 Colin Smith owns a business which sells specialist central heating parts to trade customers. He has been in business for a number of years. Although he does not keep a full set of accounting records, the following information is available in respect of the year ended 30 June 2005:

Summary of assets and liabilities:

	1 July 2004	30 June 2005
	£	£
Assets		
Stock	25,000	27,500
Fixtures and fittings (cost £50,000)	40,000	35,000
Debtors	36,000	35,000
Bank	1,500	1,210
Liabilities		
Creditors	32,500	30,000
Accrual: business expenses	500	700

Summary of the business bank account for the year ended 30 June 2005:

	£
Business expenses	30,000
Drawings	28,790
Receipts from debtors	121,000
Payments to suppliers	62,500

Other information:

- Fixtures and fittings are being depreciated at 10% per year using the straight line method
- Bad debts of £550 have been written off during the year

You are to:

(a) Calculate the amount of sales during the year ended 30 June 2005

(b) Calculate the amount of purchases during the year ended 30 June 2005

(c) Calculate the figure for business expenses to be shown in the profit and loss account for the year ended 30 June 2005

(d) Prepare Colin Smith's trading and profit and loss account for the year ended 30 June 2005

(e) Prepare Colin Smith's balance sheet at 30 June 2005

Note: VAT is to be ignored on all transactions

So far, when discussing final accounts, we have considered the accounts of a sole trader, ie one person in business. However, a partnership is a common form of business unit, and can be found in the form of:

- *sole traders who have joined together with others in order to raise finance and expand the business*

- *family businesses, such as builders, car repairers, gardeners*

- *professional firms such as solicitors, accountants, doctors, dentists*

In this chapter we look at

- *the definition of a partnership*

- *the accounting requirements of the Partnership Act 1890*

- *the accounting requirements which may be incorporated into a partnership agreement*

- *the use of capital accounts and current accounts*

- *the appropriation of profits*

- *the layout of the capital section of the balance sheet*

- *partnership final accounts, using the extended trial balance method and the conventional format*

PERFORMANCE CRITERIA COVERED

unit 5: MAINTAINING FINANCIAL RECORDS AND PREPARING ACCOUNTS

element 5.2

collecting and collating information for the preparation of final accounts

E   correctly identify, calculate and record appropriate adjustments

element 5.3

preparing the final accounts of sole traders and partnerships

B   *prepare final accounts of partnerships in proper form and in compliance with the partnership agreement, from the trial balance*

C   *observe the organisation's policies, regulations, procedures and timescales in relation to preparing final accounts of sole traders and partnerships*

D   *identify and resolve or refer to the appropriate person discrepancies, unusual features or queries*

WHAT DOES A PARTNERSHIP INVOLVE?

The Partnership Act of 1890 defines a partnership as:

the relation which subsists between persons carrying on a business in common with a view of profit

Normally, partnerships consist of between two and twenty partners (exceptions being large professional firms, eg solicitors and accountants). Partnerships are often larger businesses than sole traders because, as there is more than one owner, there is likely to be more capital. A partnership may be formed to set up a new business or it may be the logical growth of a sole trader taking in partners to increase the capital.

advantages and disadvantages

Partnerships are cheap and easy to set up; their **advantages** are:

- there is the possibility of increased capital
- individual partners may be able to specialise in particular areas of the business
- with more people running the business, there is cover for illness and holidays

The **disadvantages** are:

- as there is more than one owner, decisions may take longer because other partners may need to be consulted
- there may be disagreements amongst the partners
- each partner is liable in law for the dealings and business debts of the *whole* firm (unless it is a 'limited liability partnership' set up under the Limited Liability Partnerships Act, 2000)

- the retirement or death of one partner may adversely affect the running of the business

accounting requirements of a partnership

The accounting requirements of a partnership are:

- either to follow the rules set out in the Partnership Act 1890

- or – and more likely – for the partners to agree amongst themselves, by means of a partnership agreement (see next page), to follow different accounting rules

Unless the partners agree otherwise, the Partnership Act 1890 states the following accounting rules:

- profits and losses are to be shared equally between the partners

- no partner is entitled to a salary

- partners are not entitled to receive interest on their capital

- interest is not to be charged on partners' drawings

- when a partner contributes more capital than agreed, he or she is entitled to receive interest at five per cent per annum on the excess

As noted above, the partners may well decide to follow different accounting rules – these will be set out in a partnership agreement (see the next page).

YEAR END ACCOUNTS OF A PARTNERSHIP

A partnership prepares the same type of year end accounts as a sole trader business:

- trading and profit and loss account

- balance sheet

The main difference is that, immediately after the profit and loss account, follows an **appropriation section** (often described as an appropriation account). This shows how the net profit from profit and loss account is shared amongst the partners.

example of sharing profits

Jan, Kay and Lil are partners sharing profits and losses equally; their profit and loss account for 2004 shows a net profit of £60,000. The appropriation of profits appears as:

```
JAN, KAY AND LIL
PROFIT AND LOSS APPROPRIATION ACCOUNT
for the year ended 31 December 2004
                                        £
Net profit                          60,000
Share of profits:
      Jan                           20,000
      Kay                           20,000
      Lil                           20,000
                                    60,000
```

The above is a simple appropriation of profits. A more complex appropriation account (see Case Study on page 249) deals with other accounting points from the partnership agreement.

PARTNERSHIP AGREEMENT

The accounting rules from the Partnership Act are often varied with the agreement of all partners, by means of a partnership agreement. In particular, a partnership agreement will usually cover the following main points:

*   division of profits and losses between partners

*   partners' salaries

*   whether interest is to be allowed on capital and at what rate

The money amounts involved for each of these points (where allowed by the partnership agreement) are shown in the partnership appropriation account (see Case Study on page 249).

division of profits and losses between partners

The Partnership Act states that, in the absence of an agreement to the contrary, profits and losses are to be shared equally. A partner's share of the profits is normally taken out of the business in the form of drawings. Clearly, if one partner has contributed much more capital than the other partner(s), it would be unfair to apply this clause from the Act. Consequently, many partnerships agree to share profits and losses on a different basis – often in the same proportions as they have contributed capital. Note that, in Skills Tests and Examinations, you will normally be told the agreed division of profits; however, if there is no mention of this, you should assume that the partners receive an equal share.

partners' salaries

Although the Act says that no partner is entitled to a salary, it is quite usual in the partnership agreement for one or more partners to be paid a salary. The reason for doing this is that often in a partnership, one of the partners spends more time working in the partnership than the other(s). The agreement to pay a salary is in recognition of the work done. Note that partners' salaries are not shown as an expense in profit and loss account; instead they appear in the partnership appropriation account (see Case Study on the next page).

Many professional partnerships, such as solicitors and accountants, have junior partners who receive a partnership salary because they work full-time in the business, but have not yet contributed any capital. In a partnership, there may not be a requirement to contribute capital, unless the partnership agreement states otherwise; however, most partners will eventually do so.

interest allowed on capital

Many partnerships include a clause in their partnership agreement which allows interest to be paid on capital; the rate of interest will be stated also. This clause is used to compensate partners for the loss of use of their capital, ie it is not available to invest elsewhere. Often, interest is allowed on capital in partnerships where profits and losses are shared equally – it is one way of partly adjusting for different capital balances. As noted earlier, the Partnership Act does not permit interest to be paid on capital, so reference to it must be made in the partnership agreement.

When calculating interest on capital, it may be necessary to allow for part years. For example:

1 January 2004 capital balance	£20,000
1 July 2004 additional capital contributed	£4,000
the rate of interest allowed on capital	10% per annum
the partnership's financial year end	31 December 2004

Interest allowed on capital is calculated as:

1 January - 30 June £20,000 x 10% (for 6 months)	£1,000
1 July - 31 December £24,000 x 10% (for 6 months)	£1,200
Interest allowed on capital for year	£2,200

CAPITAL ACCOUNTS AND CURRENT ACCOUNTS

The important book-keeping difference between a sole trader and a partnership is that each partner usually has a capital account *and* a current account. The capital account is normally *fixed,* and only alters if a permanent increase or decrease in capital contributed by the partner takes place. The current account is *fluctuating* and it is to this account that:

- share of profit is credited
- share of loss is debited
- salary (if any) is credited
- interest allowed on partners' capital is credited
- drawings and goods for own use are debited

Thus, the current account is treated as a *working* account, while capital account remains fixed, except for capital introduced or withdrawn.

A partner's current account has the following layout:

Dr	**Partner Aye: Current Account**		Cr
	£		£
Drawings/goods for own use		Balance b/d	
		Salary*	
		Interest on capital*	
Balance c/d		Share of profit	

* if these items are allowed by the partnership agreement

Note that whilst the normal balance on a partner's current account is credit, when the partner has drawn out more than his or her share of the profits, then the balance will be debit.

Case Study

ALI AND BOB:
APPROPRIATION OF PARTNERSHIP PROFITS

As we have seen earlier in this chapter, the appropriation section (often described as the appropriation account) follows the profit and loss account and shows how net profit has been divided amongst the partners. This Case Study shows a partnership salary (which is not shown in profit and loss account) and interest allowed on partners' capital.

situation

Ali and Bob are in partnership sharing profits and losses 60 per cent and 40 per cent respectively. Net profit for the year ended 31 March 2004 is £42,000.

At 1 April 2003 (the start of the year), the partners have the following balances:

	Capital account	Current account
	£	£
Ali	40,000	2,000 Cr
Bob	30,000	400 Cr

- There have been no changes to the capital accounts during the year; interest is allowed on partners' capitals at the rate of eight per cent per year.
- Bob is entitled to a salary of £16,000 per year.
- During the year partners' drawings were: Ali £18,000, Bob £24,000.

solution

The appropriation of profits will be made as follows:

ALI AND BOB, IN PARTNERSHIP
PROFIT AND LOSS APPROPRIATION ACCOUNT
for the year ended 31 March 2004

	£	£
Net profit		42,000
Less appropriation of profit:		
Salary: Bob		16,000
Interest allowed on partners' capitals:		
Ali £40,000 x 8%	3,200	
Bob £30,000 x 8%	2,400	
		5,600
		20,400
Share of remaining profit:		
Ali (60%)	12,240	
Bob (40%)	8,160	
		20,400

Note that all of the available profit – after allowing for any salary, and interest on capital – is shared amongst the partners, in the ratio in which they share profits and losses.

The partners' current accounts for the year are shown on the next page. Note that the layout for the partners' current accounts uses a normal 'T' account but in a side-by-side format with a column for each partner on both the debit and credit sides. As an alternative, separate current accounts can be produced for each partner.

Dr				Partners' Current Accounts			Cr	
		Ali	Bob				Ali	Bob
2003/4		£	£	2003/4			£	£
31 Mar	Drawings	18,000	24,000	1 Apr	Balances b/d		2,000	400
31 Mar	Balance c/d	–	2,960		Salary		–	16,000
				31 Mar	Interest on capital		3,200	2,400
				31 Mar	Share of profit		12,240	8,160
				31 Mar	Balance c/d		560	–
		18,000	26,900				18,000	26,960
2004/5				2004/5				
1 Apr	Balance b/d	560	–	1 Apr	Balance b/d		–	2,960

From the current accounts we can see that Ali has drawn more out than the balance of the account; accordingly, at the end of the year, Ali has a debit balance of £560 on current account. By contrast, Bob has a credit balance of £2,960 on current account.

BALANCE SHEET

The balance sheet of a partnership must show the year end balances on each partner's capital and current account. However, the transactions that have taken place on each account can be shown in summary form – in the same way that, in a sole trader's balance sheet, net profit for the year is added and drawings for the year are deducted.

The other sections of the balance sheet – fixed assets, current assets, current and long-term liabilities – are presented in the same way as for a sole trader.

The following is an example balance sheet layout for the 'financed by' section (the other sections of the balance sheet are not shown). It details the capital and current accounts of the partnership of Ali and Bob (see Case Study above).

ALI AND BOB, IN PARTNERSHIP
BALANCE SHEET (EXTRACT) as at 31 March 2004

FINANCED BY	£	£
Capital Accounts		
Ali	40,000	
Bob	30,000	
		70,000
Current Accounts		
Ali	(560)	
Bob	2,960	
		2,400
		72,400

PARTNERSHIP FINAL ACCOUNTS FROM THE TRIAL BALANCE

Final accounts for a partnership can be prepared using the extended trial balance method and can then be set out in proper form, using the conventional format. The procedures are exactly the same as for sole traders. The only differences to note are that partners' capital and current accounts are shown in the balance sheet. Transactions affecting the partners' current accounts – such as share of profits, partners' salaries, drawings, etc – can be shown either in the form of a double-entry 'T' account (see page 251 for an example), or directly on the face of the balance sheet (see the following Case Study). Whichever is done, it is the closing balances of the current accounts that are added in to the 'financed by' section of the balance sheet.

Case Study

RAMJIT SINGH AND VETA BIX: PARTNERSHIP FINAL ACCOUNTS

situation

The extended trial balance for the partnership of Ramjit Singh and Veta Bix, trading as 'RaVe Music', at 31 December 2005 is shown on the next page. All columns of the ETB have been completed ready for the completion of final accounts in the conventional format.

Note that the ETB includes the following points:

- there are both accruals and prepayments
- fixed assets have been depreciated
- during the year the partners have taken goods for their own use – purchases has been reduced and the goods charged to each partner (note that the amounts of goods for own use have been shown separately on the ETB to show clearly the accounting treatment; they can be incorporated into the figure for drawings)
- one partner, Veta Bix, receives a salary* – this is shown in the profit and loss columns and the balance sheet columns
- interest has been allowed on partners' capital accounts* at a rate of 10 per cent per year – the amounts are shown in the profit and loss and the balance sheet columns
- the partners share remaining profits* equally – shown in the profit and loss columns and the balance sheet columns

* in conventional format accounts these items are shown in the appropriation section of the profit and loss account, ie *after* net profit has been calculated – see page 254

solution

The final accounts of the partnership of Ramjit Singh and Veta Bix, trading as 'RaVe Music', are shown in ETB format on the next page and in the conventional format on pages 254 and 255.

EXTENDED TRIAL BALANCE   RAMJIT SINGH AND VETA BIX, IN PARTNERSHIP, TRADING AS 'RAVE MUSIC'   31 DECEMBER 2005

Account name	Ledger balances		Adjustments		Profit and loss		Balance sheet	
	Dr £	Cr £	Dr £	Cr £	Dr £	Cr £	Dr £	Cr £
Opening stock	20,000				20,000			
Sales		250,000				250,000		
Purchases	120,000			900	119,100			
Premises	200,000						200,000	
Provision for depreciation: premises		9,000		3,000				12,000
Fixtures and fittings	20,000						20,000	
Provision for depreciation: fixtures & fittings		8,000		2,000				10,000
Wages and salaries	35,000		1,700		36,700			
Shop expenses	20,000			800	19,200			
Debtors	3,000						3,000	
Creditors		7,000						7,000
Value Added Tax		4,000						4,000
Bank		2,000						2,000
Bank loan		80,000						80,000
Capital account: Ramjit Singh		50,000						50,000
Capital account: Veta Bix		45,000						45,000
Current account: Ramjit Singh		4,000						4,000
Current account: Veta Bix		1,000						1,000
Drawings: Ramjit Singh	24,000						24,000	
Drawings: Veta Bix	18,000						18,000	
Goods for own use: Ramjit Singh			500				500	
Goods for own use: Veta Bix			400				400	
Closing stock: Profit and loss				30,000		30,000		
Closing stock: Balance sheet			30,000				30,000	
Accruals				1,700				1,700
Prepayments			800				800	
Depreciation			5,000		5,000			
Partnership salary: Veta Bix					10,000			10,000
Interest on capital: Ramjit Singh					5,000			5,000
Interest on capital: Veta Bix					4,500			4,500
Net profit/loss: Ramjit Singh					30,250			30,250
Net profit/loss: Veta Bix					30,250			30,250
	460,000	460,000	38,400	38,400	280,000	280,000	296,700	296,700

**RAMJIT SINGH AND VETA BIX IN PARTNERSHIP,
TRADING AS 'RAVE MUSIC'**

**TRADING AND PROFIT AND LOSS ACCOUNT
for the year ended 31 December 2005**

	£	£	£
Sales			250,000
Opening stock		20,000	
Purchases	120,000		
Less Goods for own use	900		
		119,100	
		139,100	
Less Closing stock		30,000	
Cost of sales			109,100
Gross profit			140,900
Less overheads:			
Wages and salaries		36,700	
Shop expenses		19,200	
Depreciation:			
freehold buildings		3,000	
fixtures and fittings		2,000	
			60,900
Net profit			80,000
Less appropriation of profit:			
Salary: Veta Bix			10,000
Interest allowed on partners' capitals:			
Ramjit Singh	£50,000 x 10%	5,000	
Veta Bix	£45,000 x 10%	4,500	
			9,500
			60,500
Share of remaining profit:			
Ramjit Singh (50%)			30,250
Veta Bix (50%)			30,250
			60,500

**RAMJIT SINGH AND VETA BIX IN PARTNERSHIP,
TRADING AS 'RAVE MUSIC'
BALANCE SHEET as at 31 December 2005**

	£ Cost	£ Provision for dep'n	£ Net
Fixed assets			
Premises	200,000	12,000	188,000
Fixtures and fittings	20,000	10,000	10,000
	220,000	22,000	198,000
Current assets			
Stock (closing)		30,000	
Debtors		3,000	
Prepayments		800	
		33,800	
Less Current liabilities			
Creditors	7,000		
Accruals	1,700		
Value Added Tax	4,000		
Bank	2,000		
		14,700	
Working capital			19,100
			217,100
Less Long-term liabilities			
Bank loan			80,000
NET ASSETS			137,100
FINANCED BY			
Capital Accounts			
Ramjit Singh		50,000	
Veta Bix		45,000	
			95,000

Current Accounts	R. Singh	V. Bix	
Opening Balance	4,000	1,000	
Add: salary	–	10,000	
interest on capital	5,000	4,500	
share of profit	30,250	30,250	
	39,250	45,750	
Less: drawings	24,000	18,000	
goods for own use*	500	400	
	14,750	27,350	
			42,100
			137,100

* goods for own use can be incorporated into the amount for drawings – shown here separately so that the accounting treatment can be seen clearly.

PREPARING PARTNERSHIP FINAL ACCOUNTS

When partnership final accounts are being prepared, the accounts assistant must take note of:

- the terms of the partnership agreement
- the policies, regulations, procedures and timescales of the partnership

If there are any discrepancies, unusual features or queries, they should be identified and, where possible, resolved by the accounts assistant. Any outstanding issues will need to be referred to the appropriate person – such as the accounts supervisor, the manager of the partnership, one or more of the partners.

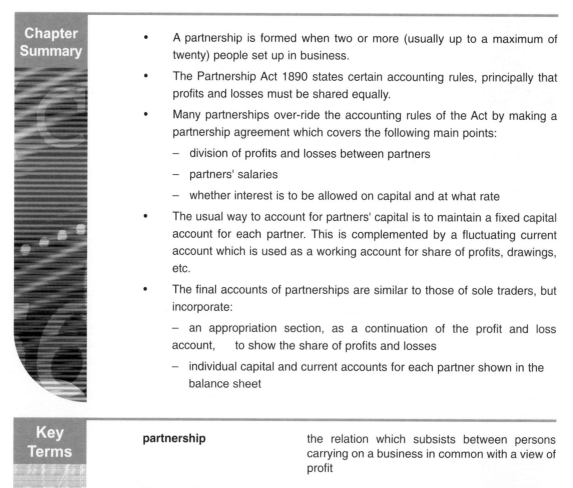

Chapter Summary

- A partnership is formed when two or more (usually up to a maximum of twenty) people set up in business.

- The Partnership Act 1890 states certain accounting rules, principally that profits and losses must be shared equally.

- Many partnerships over-ride the accounting rules of the Act by making a partnership agreement which covers the following main points:
  - division of profits and losses between partners
  - partners' salaries
  - whether interest is to be allowed on capital and at what rate

- The usual way to account for partners' capital is to maintain a fixed capital account for each partner. This is complemented by a fluctuating current account which is used as a working account for share of profits, drawings, etc.

- The final accounts of partnerships are similar to those of sole traders, but incorporate:
  - an appropriation section, as a continuation of the profit and loss account,   to show the share of profits and losses
  - individual capital and current accounts for each partner shown in the balance sheet

Key Terms

partnership	the relation which subsists between persons carrying on a business in common with a view of profit
Partnership Act 1890	legislation which includes the accounting rules of partnerships

partnership agreement	agreement between the partners which, amongst other things, often varies the accounting rules of the Partnership Act 1890
appropriation section	part of the profit and loss account which shows how the net profit is shared amongst the partners
capital account	account which records the amount of capital contributed by a partner; usually for a fixed amount, which only alters where a permanent increase or decrease takes place
current account	a fluctuating account to which is credited: share of profits, salary (if any), interest allowed on capital, and to which is debited: share of losses and drawings

Student Activities

14.1 In the absence of a partnership agreement, which one of the following contravenes the provisions of the Partnership Act 1890?

(a) no partner is entitled to a salary

(b) profits and losses are to be shared in proportion to capital

(c) partners are not entitled to receive interest on their capital

(d) interest is not to be charged on partners' drawings

Answer (a) or (b) or (c) or (d)

14.2 The current account of a partner, Tara Shah, has a balance at the beginning of the financial year of £550 debit. During the year, the following transactions pass through her current account:

- interest on capital account, £900

- salary, £10,000

- drawings, £14,000

- share of profits, £4,230

What is the balance of Tara Shah's current account at the end of the financial year?

(a) £580 Cr

(b) £1,220 Dr

(c) £1,680 Dr

(d) £120 Cr

Answer (a) or (b) or (c) or (d)

14.3 Lysa and Mark are in partnership and own a shop, 'Trends', which sells fashionable teenage clothes. The following figures are extracted from their accounts for the year ended 31 December 2004:

	£	
Capital accounts at 1 January 2004:		
Lysa	50,000	Cr
Mark	40,000	Cr
Current accounts at 1 January 2004:		
Lysa	420	Cr
Mark	1,780	Cr
Drawings for the year:		
Lysa	13,000	
Mark	12,250	
Interest on capital for the year:		
Lysa	2,500	
Mark	2,000	
Share of profits for the year:		
Lysa	9,300	
Mark	9,300	

Note: neither partner is entitled to receive a salary

You are to show the partners' capital and current accounts for the year ended 31 December 2004.

14.4 John James and Steven Hill are in partnership and own a wine shop called 'Grapes'. The following trial balance has been taken from their accounts for the year ended 31 December 2004, after the calculation of gross profit:

	Dr £	Cr £
Capital accounts:		
James		38,000
Hill		32,000
Current accounts:		
James	3,000	
Hill		1,000
Drawings:		
James	10,000	
Hill	22,000	
Gross profit		89,000
Rent and rates	7,500	
Advertising	12,000	
Heat and light	3,500	
Wages and salaries	18,000	
Sundry expenses	4,000	
Shop fittings at cost	20,000	
*Closing stock – balance sheet	35,000	
Bank	29,000	
Debtors	6,000	
Creditors		8,000
Value Added Tax		2,000
	170,000	170,000

* Only the closing stock is included in the trial balance because gross profit for the year has already been calculated.

Notes at 31 December 2004:
- depreciation is to be charged on the shop fittings at 10 per cent per year
- Steven Hill is to receive a partnership salary of £15,000
- interest is to be allowed on partners' capital accounts at 10 per cent per year
- remaining profits and losses are to be shared equally

Task 1

Prepare the partnership final accounts for the year ended 31 December 2004, using the extended trial balance method.

Task 2

Show the partners' capital and current accounts for the year ended 31 December 2004.

Task 3

Prepare the partnership final accounts for the year ended 31 December 2004 in proper form, using the conventional format.

Task 4

On receiving the accounts, John James asks a question about the partners' current accounts. He wants to know why the balances brought down at the start of the year for the two partners are on opposite sides.

Draft a note to John James explaining:

- what the balance on a partner's current account represents

- what a debit balance on a partner's current account means

- what a credit balance on a partner's current account means

15 Changes in partnerships

In this chapter we continue our study of partnerships by looking at the principles involved and the accounting entries, for:

- admission of a new partner
- retirement of a partner
- death of a partner
- changes in profit-sharing ratios
- partnership changes when there are split years

Before we look at each of these, we need to consider the goodwill of the business, which features in all of the changes listed above.

PERFORMANCE CRITERIA COVERED

unit 5: MAINTAINING FINANCIAL RECORDS AND PREPARING ACCOUNTS
element 5.2
collecting and collating information for the preparation of final accounts

E   correctly identify, calculate and record appropriate adjustments

element 5.3
preparing the final accounts of sole traders and partnerships

B   prepare final accounts of partnerships in proper form and in compliance with the partnership agreement, from the trial balance

C   observe the organisation's policies, regulations, procedures and timescales in relation to preparing final accounts of sole traders and partnerships

D   identify and resolve or refer to the appropriate person discrepancies, unusual features or queries

GOODWILL

The balance sheet of a partnership, like that of many businesses, rarely indicates the true 'going concern' value of the business: usually the recorded figures underestimate the worth of a business. There are two main reasons for this:

- **Prudence** – if there is any doubt about the value of assets, they are stated at the lowest possible figure.
- **Goodwill** – a going concern business will often have a value of goodwill, because of various factors, eg the trade that has been built up, the reputation of the business, the location of the business, the skill of the workforce, and the success at developing new products.

definition of goodwill

Goodwill can be defined formally in accounting terms as:

the difference between the value of a business as a whole, and the net value of its separate assets and liabilities.

For example, an existing business is bought for £500,000, with the separate assets and liabilities being worth £450,000 net; goodwill is, therefore, £50,000.

Thus goodwill has a value as an intangible fixed asset to the owner or owners of a going concern business, whether or not it is recorded on the balance sheet. As you will see in the sections which follow, a valuation has to be placed on goodwill when changes take place in a partnership.

valuation of goodwill

The valuation of goodwill is always subject to negotiation between the people concerned if, for instance, a partnership business is to be sold. It is, most commonly, based on the profits of the business – eg the average net profit over the last, say, three years and multiplied by an agreed figure, perhaps six times.

We will now see how goodwill is created when changes are made to partnerships, such as the admission of a new partner or retirement of an existing partner. For these changes, a value for goodwill is agreed and this amount is temporarily debited to goodwill account, and credited to the partners' capital accounts in their profit-sharing ratio. After the change in the partnership, it is usual practice for the goodwill to be written off – the partners' capital accounts are debited and goodwill account is credited. Thus a 'nil' balance remains on goodwill account and, therefore, it is not recorded on the partnership balance sheet. This follows the prudence concept, and is the method commonly followed when changes are made to partnerships.

ADMISSION OF A NEW PARTNER

A new partner – who can only be admitted with the consent of all existing partners – is normally charged a premium for goodwill. This is because the new partner will start to share in the profits of the business immediately and will benefit from the goodwill established by the existing partners. If the business was to be sold shortly after the admission of a new partner, a price will again be agreed for goodwill and this will be shared amongst all the partners (including the new partner).

To make allowance for this benefit it is necessary to make book-keeping adjustments in the partners' capital accounts. The most common way of doing this is to use a goodwill account which is opened by the old partners with the agreed valuation of goodwill and, immediately after the admission of the new partner, is closed by transfer to the partners' capital accounts, including that of the new partner.

The procedures on admission of a new partner are:

- **agree a valuation for goodwill**

- **old partners: goodwill created**
    - debit goodwill account with the amount of goodwill
    - credit partners' capital accounts (in their old profit-sharing ratio) with the amount of goodwill

- **old partners + new partner: goodwill written off**
    - debit partners' capital accounts (in their new profit-sharing ratio) with the amount of goodwill
    - credit goodwill account with the amount of goodwill

The effect of this is to charge the new partner with a premium for goodwill.

Case Study

AL AND BEN:
ADMISSION OF A NEW PARTNER

situation

Al and Ben are in partnership sharing profits and losses equally. Their balance sheet as at 31 December 2004 is as follows:

```
BALANCE SHEET OF AL AND BEN as at 31 December 2004
                                                    £
Net assets                                      80,000
Capital accounts:
    Al                                          45,000
    Ben                                         35,000
                                                80,000
```

On 1 January 2005 the partners agree to admit Col into the partnership, with a new profit-sharing ratio of Al (2), Ben (2) and Col (1). Goodwill has been agreed at a valuation of £25,000. Col will bring £20,000 of cash into the business as his capital, part of which represents a premium for goodwill.

solution

The accounting procedures on the admission of Col into the partnership are as follows:

* goodwill has been valued at £25,000

* old partners: goodwill created
  - debit goodwill account   £25,000
  - credit capital accounts (in their old profit-sharing ratio)
      Al   £12,500
      Ben   £12,500

* old partners + new partner: goodwill written off

  - debit capital accounts (in their new profit-sharing ratio)
      Al   £10,000
      Ben   £10,000
      Col   £5,000
  - credit goodwill account   £25,000

The capital accounts of the partners, after the above transactions have been recorded, appear as:

Dr	Al £	Ben £	Col £	**Partners' Capital Accounts**	Al £	Ben £	Col £	Cr
Goodwill written off	10,000	10,000	5,000	Balances b/d	45,000	35,000	-	
Balances c/d	47,500	37,500	15,000	Goodwill created	12,500	12,500	-	
				Bank	-	-	20,000	
	57,500	47,500	20,000		57,500	47,500	20,000	
				Balances b/d	47,500	37,500	15,000	

The balance sheet, following the admission of Col, appears as:

BALANCE SHEET OF AL, BEN AND COL as at 1 January 2005

	£
Net assets (£80,000 + £20,000)	100,000
Capital accounts:	
Al (£45,000 + £12,500 – £10,000)	47,500
Ben (£35,000 + £12,500 – £10,000)	37,500
Col (£20,000 – £5,000)	15,000
	100,000

In this way, the new partner has paid the existing partners a premium of £5,000 for a one-fifth share of the profits of a business with a goodwill value of £25,000.

Although a goodwill account has been used, it has been fully utilised with adjusting entries made in the capital accounts of the partners, as follows:

Dr			**Goodwill Account**			Cr
		£				£
Al	goodwill	12,500	Al	goodwill		10,000
Ben	created	12,500	Ben	written off		10,000
			Col			5,000
		25,000				25,000

RETIREMENT OF A PARTNER

When a partner retires it is necessary to calculate how much is due to the partner in respect of capital and profits. The partnership agreement normally details the procedures to be followed when a partner retires. The most common procedure requires goodwill to be valued and this operates in a similar way to the admission of a new partner, as follows:

- **agree a valuation for goodwill**
- **old partners: goodwill created**
  - debit goodwill account with the amount of goodwill
  - credit partners' capital accounts (in their old profit-sharing ratio) with the amount of goodwill
- **remaining partners: goodwill written off**
  - debit partners' capital accounts (in their new profit-sharing ratio) with the amount of goodwill
  - credit goodwill account with the amount of goodwill

The effect of this is to credit the retiring partner with the amount of the goodwill built up whilst he or she was a partner. This amount, plus the retiring partner's capital and current account balances can then be paid out of the partnership bank account. (If there is insufficient money for this, it is quite usual for a retiring partner to leave some of the capital in the business as a loan, which is repaid over a period of time.)

Case Study

JAN, KAY AND LIL: RETIREMENT OF A PARTNER

situation

Jan, Kay and Lil are in partnership sharing profit and losses in the ratio of 2:2:1 respectively. Partner Jan decides to retire on 31 December 2004 when the partnership balance sheet is as follows:

BALANCE SHEET OF JAN, KAY AND LIL as at 31 December 2004	
	£
Net assets	100,000
Capital accounts:	
Jan	35,000
Kay	45,000
Lil	20,000
	100,000

Goodwill is agreed at a valuation of £30,000. Kay and Lil are to continue in partnership and will share profits and losses in the ratio of 2:1 respectively. Jan agrees to leave £20,000 of the amount due to her as a loan to the new partnership.

solution

The accounting procedures on the retirement of Jan from the partnership are as follows:

- goodwill has been valued at £30,000

- old partners: goodwill created

  - debit goodwill account   £30,000

  - credit capital accounts (in their old profit-sharing ratio of 2:2:1)

Jan	£12,000
Kay	£12,000
Lil	£6,000

- remaining partners: goodwill written off
    - debit capital accounts (in their new profit-sharing ratio of 2:1)

        Kay   £20,000

        Lil   £10,000

    - credit goodwill account   £30,000

The capital accounts of the partners, after the above transactions have been recorded, appear as:

Dr	Jan	Kay	Lil	**Partners' Capital Accounts**	Jan	Kay	Lil	Cr
	£	£	£		£	£	£	
Goodwill written off	–	20,000	10,000	Balances b/d	35,000	45,000	20,000	
Loan account	20,000			Goodwill created	12,000	12,000	6,000	
Bank	27,000							
Balances c/d	–	37,000	16,000					
	47,000	57,000	26,000		47,000	57,000	26,000	
				Balances b/d	–	37,000	16,000	

Note: After recording goodwill, the balance of Jan's capital account is £47,000 (ie £35,000 + £12,000, being her share of the goodwill). Of this, £20,000 will be retained in the business as a loan, and £27,000 will be paid to her from the partnership bank account.

The balance sheet, after the retirement of Jan, appears as follows:

BALANCE SHEET OF KAY AND LIL as at 1 January 2005

	£
Net assets (£100,000 – £27,000 paid to Jan)	73,000
Less Loan account of Jan	20,000
	53,000
Capital accounts:	
Kay (£45,000 + £12,000 – £20,000)	37,000
Lil (£20,000 + £6,000 – £10,000)	16,000
	53,000

The effect of this is that the remaining partners have bought out Jan's £12,000 share of the goodwill of the business, ie it has cost Kay £8,000, and Lil £4,000. If the business was to be sold later, Kay and Lil would share the goodwill obtained from the sale in their new profit-sharing ratio.

DEATH OF A PARTNER

The accounting procedures on the death of a partner are very similar to those for a partner's retirement. The only difference is that the amount due to the deceased partner is placed in an account called 'Executors (or Administrators) of X deceased' pending payment.

CHANGES IN PROFIT-SHARING RATIOS

It may be necessary, from time-to-time, to change the profit-sharing ratios of partners. A partner's share of profits might be increased because of an increase in capital in relation to the other partners, or because of a more active role in running the business. Equally, a share of profits may be decreased if a partner withdraws capital or spends less time in the business. Clearly, the agreement of all partners is needed to make changes, and the guidance of the partnership agreement should be followed.

Generally, a change in profit-sharing ratios involves establishing a figure for goodwill, even if the partnership is to continue with the same partners; this is to establish how much goodwill was built up while they shared profits in their old ratios. Each partner will, therefore, receive a value for the goodwill based on the old profit-sharing ratio.

Case Study

DES AND EVE: CHANGES IN PROFIT-SHARING RATIOS

situation
Des and Eve are in partnership sharing profits and losses equally. The balance sheet at 31 December 2004 is as follows:

BALANCE SHEET OF DES AND EVE as at 31 December 2004	
	£
Net assets	60,000
Capital accounts:	
Des	35,000
Eve	25,000
	60,000

The partners agree that, as from 1 January 2005, Des will take a two-thirds share of the profits and losses, with Eve taking one-third. It is agreed that goodwill shall be valued at £30,000.

solution

The accounting procedures on the change in the profit-sharing ratio are as follows:

- goodwill has been valued at £30,000
- old profit-sharing ratio: goodwill created
  - debit goodwill account £30,000
  - credit capital accounts (in their old profit-sharing ratio of 1:1)

Des	£15,000
Eve	£15,000

- new profit-sharing ratio: goodwill written off
  - debit capital accounts (in their new profit-sharing ratio of 2:1)

Des	£20,000
Eve	£10,000

  - credit goodwill account £30,000

The capital accounts of the partners, after the above transactions have been recorded, appear as:

Dr			Partners' Capital Accounts			Cr
	Des	Eve		Des	Eve	
	£	£		£	£	
Goodwill written off	20,000	10,000	Balances b/d	35,000	25,000	
Balances c/d	30,000	30,000	Goodwill created	15,000	15,000	
	50,000	40,000		50,000	40,000	
			Balances b/d	30,000	30,000	

The balance sheet at 1 January 2005 appears as:

BALANCE SHEET OF DES AND EVE as at 1 January 2005

	£
Net assets	60,000
Capital accounts:	
Des (£35,000 + £15,000 − £20,000)	30,000
Eve (£25,000 + £15,000 − £10,000)	30,000
	60,000

The effect is that Des has 'paid' Eve £5,000 to increase his share of the profits from half to two-thirds. This may seem unfair but neither partner is worse off in the event of the business being sold, assuming that the business is sold for £90,000 (£60,000 assets + £30,000 goodwill). Before the change in the profit-sharing ratio they would have received:

Des £35,000 capital + £15,000 half-share of goodwill = £50,000

Eve £25,000 capital + £15,000 half-share of goodwill = £40,000

After the change, they will receive:

Des £30,000 capital + £20,000 two-thirds share of goodwill = £50,000

Eve £30,000 capital + £10,000 one-third share of goodwill = £40,000

As far as the realisation amounts are concerned, the position remains unchanged: it is only the profit-sharing ratios that will be different as from 1 January 2005. Also, any increase in goodwill above the £30,000 figure will be shared in the new ratio.

PARTNERSHIP CHANGES: SPLIT YEARS

Any of the changes in partnerships that we have looked at so far in this chapter may occur during the course of an accounting year, rather than at the end of it.

For example, part-way through the year:

- the partners may decide to admit a new partner
- a partner might retire, or die
- the partners may decide to change their profit-sharing ratios

To avoid having to prepare final accounts at the date of the change, it is usual to continue the accounts until the normal year-end. Then, when profit for the year has been calculated, it is necessary to apportion the profit between the two parts of the financial year, ie to split the year into the period before the change, and the period after the change. This is often done by assuming that the profit for the year has been earned at an equal rate throughout the year.

The apportionment is done by dividing the appropriation account between the two time periods.

RAJ AND SAM: SPLIT YEARS

situation

Raj and Sam are in partnership; their partnership agreement states:

* interest is allowed on partners' capital accounts at the rate of ten per cent per annum

* Sam receives a partnership salary of £18,000 per annum

* the balance of partnership profits and losses are shared between Raj and Sam in the ratio 2:1 respectively

At the beginning of the financial year, on 1 January 2004, the balances of the partners' capital accounts were:

Raj	£70,000
Sam	£50,000

During the year ended 31 December 2004, the net profit of the partnership was £50,500 before appropriations. The profit arose uniformly throughout the year.

On 1 October 2004, Raj and Sam admitted Tom as a partner. Tom introduced £40,000 of cash into the business as his capital.

The partnership agreement was amended on 1 October 2004 as follows:

* interest is allowed on partners' capital accounts at the rate of ten per cent per annum

* Sam and Tom are each to receive a partnership salary of £12,000 per annum

* the balance of partnership profits and losses are to be shared between Raj, Sam and Tom in the ratio of 2:2:1 respectively

Note: no accounting entries for goodwill are to be recorded.

solution

The appropriation account of the partnership for the year is shown on the next page.

PROFIT AND LOSS APPROPRIATION ACCOUNT OF RAJ, SAM AND TOM
for the year ended 31 December 2004

	9 months to 30 September £	3 months to 31 December £	Total for year £
Net profit	37,875	12,625	50,500
Less appropriation of profit:			
Salaries:			
Sam £18,000 pa x 9 months	13,500	–	
£12,000 pa x 3 months		3,000	16,500
Tom £12,000 pa x 3 months		3,000	3,000
Interest on partners' capitals:			
Raj £70,000 @ 10% pa x 9 months	5,250	–	
£70,000 @ 10% pa x 3 months	–	1,750	7,000
Sam £50,000 @ 10% pa x 9 months	3,750	–	
£50,000 @ 10% pa x 3 months	–	1,250	5,000
Tom £40,000 @ 10% pa x 3 months	–	1,000	1,000
	*15,375	**2,625	18,000
Share of remaining profit:			
Raj	(2/3) 10,250	(2/5) 1,050	11,300
Sam	(1/3) 5,125	(2/5) 1,050	6,175
Tom	–	(1/5) 525	525
	15,375	2,625	18,000

*   Raj and Sam shared profits 2:1 respectively
** Raj, Sam and Tom shared profits 2:2:1 respectively

RECORDING PARTNERSHIP CHANGES

The accounting effects of partnership changes usually have a significant impact upon partners' capital accounts and the ratio in which they share profits and losses. Before implementing changes, the accounts assistant must check that the correct actions are being taken. This may mean referring issues to the appropriate person – such as the accounts supervisor, the manager of the partnership, one or more of the partners.

The accounts assistant must take note of:

• the terms of the partnership agreement

• the policies, regulations, procedures and timescales of the partnership

If there are any discrepancies, unusual features or queries they should be identified and, where possible, resolved – any outstanding issues will need to be referred to the appropriate person.

CONFIDENTIALITY PROCEDURES

The financial details of changes to partnerships should always be treated with confidentiality. In particular:

• details of the amount of goodwill should be discussed only with existing or new partners; as it normally does not appear on the balance sheet, the valuation of goodwill is confidential

• new partners will expect details of the amount of capital they are bringing in to an existing partnership to be kept confidential, and also the premium paid for goodwill

• all partners, existing or new, will expect details of changes made to the ratios in which they share profits and losses to be kept confidential

Very few details of partnerships need be revealed to other people; HM Revenue & Customs, lenders, and solicitors involved with the legal aspects are the only professionals outside the partnership who may need to have details of changes being made. Any disclosures should only be made with the prior approval of the partners.

Chapter Summary

- Goodwill is an intangible fixed asset.
- With partnerships, goodwill is normally valued for transactions involving changes in the structure of the business to cover:
  – admission of a new partner
  – retirement of a partner
  – death of a partner
  – changes in profit-sharing ratios

  A goodwill account is normally created just before the change, and then written off immediately after the change, ie it does not appear on the partnership balance sheet.

- When partnership changes take place part-way through the financial year, it is necessary to apportion the profit between the two parts of the financial year, usually by assuming that the profit has been earned at a uniform rate throughout the year.

Key Terms

goodwill — the difference between the value of a business as a whole, and the net value of its separate assets and liabilities

goodwill account — an account to which goodwill, an intangible fixed asset, is debited

premium for goodwill — amount charged to a new partner who joins an existing partnership

Student Activities

15.1 Where changes in partnerships take place, a goodwill account is opened, usually temporarily. After the change has taken place, goodwill account is usually written off. This follows the accounting concept of:

(a) prudence

(b) accruals

(c) going concern

(d) consistency

Answer (a) or (b) or (c) or (d)

15.2 Andrew and Barry are in partnership sharing profits equally. Colin is admitted to the partnership and the profit sharing ratios now become Andrew (2), Barry (2) and Colin (1). Goodwill at the time of Colin joining is valued at £50,000. What will be the goodwill adjustments to Andrew's capital account?

(a)   debit £25,000, credit £25,000

(b)   debit £20,000, credit £25,000

(c)   debit £20,000, credit £20,000

(d)   debit £25,000, credit £20,000

Answer (a) or (b) or (c) or (d)

15.3 Jim and Maisie are in partnership sharing profits and losses in the ratio 3:2 respectively. At 31 December 2004 the balances of their capital accounts are £60,000 and £40,000 respectively. Current accounts are not used by the partnership.

On 1 January 2005, Matt is admitted into the partnership, with a new profit-sharing ratio of Jim (3), Maisie (2) and Matt (1). Goodwill has been agreed at a valuation of £48,000. Matt will bring £28,000 of cash into the business as his capital and premium for goodwill. Goodwill is to be eliminated from the accounts.

For the year ended 31 December 2005, the partnership profits amount to £60,000, and the partners' drawings were:

	£
Jim	12,000
Maisie	12,000
Matt	8,000

You are to show the partners' capital accounts for the period from 31 December 2004 to 1 January 2006.

15.4 Reena, Sam and Tamara are in partnership sharing profits in the ratio 4:2:2 respectively. Sam is to retire on 31 August 2004 and is to be paid the amount due to him by cheque.

The balance sheet drawn up immediately before Sam's retirement was as follows:

		£
Fixed assets		50,000
Current assets		10,000
Bank		25,000
		85,000
Creditors		(10,000)
		75,000
Capital Accounts:		
Reena		33,000
Sam		12,000
Tamara		30,000
		75,000

Goodwill is to be valued at £16,000. No goodwill is to remain in the accounts after Sam's retirement.

In the new partnership Reena and Tamara are to share profits equally.

Note that current accounts are not used by the partnership.

Task 1

Prepare the partners' capital accounts, showing the amount Sam is to be paid upon retirement.

Task 2

Show the balance sheet immediately after Sam's retirement from the partnership.

15.5 Dave and Elsa are in partnership sharing profits and losses equally. Their balance sheet at 30 September 2004 is as follows:

BALANCE SHEET OF DAVE AND ELSA as at 30 September 2004

	£
Net assets	130,000
Capital Accounts:	
Dave	80,000
Elsa	50,000
	130,000

The partners agree that, as from 1 October 2004, Dave will take a two-thirds share of the profits and losses, with Elsa taking one-third. It is agreed that goodwill should be valued at £45,000. No goodwill is to remain in the accounts following the change.

Note that current accounts are not used by the partnership.

Task 1

Show the journal entries to record the creation of goodwill and its subsequent write-off for the change in the profit-sharing ratio.

Task 2

Show the partners' capital accounts with the entries to record the change in the profit-sharing ratio.

Task 3

Show the balance sheet of Dave and Elsa after the change in the profit-sharing ratio.

15.6 Jean and David are in partnership. Net profit for the year ended 31 December 2004 is £32,700 before appropriation of profit. Their capital account balances at 31 December 2004 are Jean £10,000, David £12,000. Their partnership agreement allows for the following:

- partnership salaries

  – Jean £12,000

  – David £10,000

- interest is allowed on capital at 5 per cent per year on the balance at the year end

- profit share, effective until 30 June 2004

  – Jean two-thirds

  – David one-third

- profit share, effective from 1 July 2004

  – Jean one-half

  – David one-half

Notes:

- no accounting entries for goodwill are to be recorded

- profits accrued evenly during the year

- drawings for the year were: Jean £18,600, David £14,200

Task 1

Prepare the appropriation account for the partnership of Jean and David for the year ended 31 December 2004

Task 2

Update the current accounts for the partnership for the year ended 31 December 2004. Show clearly the balances carried down.

Dr				**Partners' Current Accounts**				Cr
2004		Jean	David	2004		Jean	David
		£	£			£	£
1 Jan	Balance b/d	–	1,250	1 Jan	Balance b/d	2,400	–

ANSWERS TO STUDENT ACTIVITIES

CHAPTER 1: THE ACCOUNTING SYSTEM

1.1 (a) ledger (b) debtor (c) creditor (d) sales day book
(e) cash book (f) main (or nominal) ledger (g) assets minus liabilities equals capital

1.2 (a) assets – items owned by a business; liabilities – items owed by a business
(b) debtors – individuals or businesses who owe money in respect of goods or services supplied by the business; creditors – individuals or businesses to whom money is owed by the business
(c) purchases – goods bought, either on credit or for cash, which are intended to be resold later; sales – the sale of goods, whether on credit or for cash, in which the business trades
(d) credit purchases – goods bought, with payment to be made at a later date; cash purchases – goods bought and paid for immediately

1.3 (a) asset of bank increases by £8,000
capital increases by £8,000
asset £8,000 – liability £0 = capital £8,000

(b) asset of computer increases by £4,000
asset of bank decreases by £4,000
asset £8,000 – liability £0 = capital £8,000

(c) asset of bank increases by £3,000
liability of loan increases by £3,000
asset £11,000 – liability £3,000 = capital £8,000

(d) asset of van increases by £6,000
asset of bank decreases by £6,000
asset £11,000 – liability £3,000 = capital £8,000

1.4 (a) capital £20,000
(b) capital £10,000
(c) liabilities £7,550
(d) assets £14,100
(e) liabilities £18,430
(f) assets £21,160

1.5 (a) owner started in business with capital of £10,000 in the bank
(b) bought office equipment for £2,000, paying by cheque
(c) received a loan of £6,000 by cheque
(d) bought a van for £10,000, paying by cheque
(e) owner introduces £2,000 additional capital by cheque
(f) loan repayment of £3,000 made by cheque

CHAPTER 2: DOUBLE-ENTRY BOOK-KEEPING

2.1 (d) **2.2** (b) **2.3** (d)

2.4   **JAMES ANDERSON (summary of transactions)**

			Dr			Cr
Account	2004		£	2004	£	
Capital				2 Feb	Bank	7,500
Computer	6 Feb	Bank	2,000			
Rent Paid	9 Feb	Bank	750			
Wages	12 Feb	Bank	425			
	25 Feb	Bank	380			
Bank Loan				13 Feb	Bank	2,500
Commission Rec'd				20 Feb	Bank	145
Drawings	23 Feb	Bank	200			
Van	27 Feb	Bank	6,000			

CHAPTER 3: BALANCING ACCOUNTS AND THE TRIAL BALANCE

3.1   (c)   **3.2**   (b)   **3.3**   (c)

3.4   (a) and (c)   **ANDREW JOHNSTONE**

Dr		**Bank Account**				Cr
2004		£	2004			£
1 Jan	Capital	10,000	4 Jan	Rent paid		500
11 Jan	Sales	1,000	5 Jan	Shop fittings		1,500
12 Jan	Sales	1,250	20 Jan	Comp Supplies Ltd		5,000
22 Jan	Sales	1,450	31 Jan	Balance c/d		6,700
		13,700				13,700
1 Feb	Balance b/d	6,700	2 Feb	Rent paid		500
4 Feb	Sales	1,550	15 Feb	Shop fittings		850
10 Feb	Sales	1,300	27 Feb	Comp Supplies Ltd		6,350
12 Feb	Rowcester College	750	29 Feb	Balance c/d		5,300
19 Feb	Sales	1,600				
25 Feb	Sales	1,100				
		13,000				13,000
1 Mar	Balance b/d	5,300				

Dr		**Capital Account**			Cr
2004		£	2004		£
			1 Jan	Bank	10,000

Dr		**Rent Paid Account**			Cr
2004		£	2004		£
4 Jan	Bank	500	29 Feb	Balance c/d	1,000
2 Feb	Bank	500			
		1,000			1,000
1 Mar	Balance b/d	1,000			

Dr			Shop Fittings Account				Cr
2004			£	2004			£
5 Jan	Bank		1,500	29 Feb	Balance c/d		2,350
15 Feb	Bank		850				
			2,350				2,350
1 Mar	Balance b/d		2,350				

Dr			Purchases Account				Cr
2004			£	2004			£
7 Jan	Comp Supplies Ltd		5,000	31 Jan	Balance c/d		11,500
25 Jan	Comp Supplies Ltd		6,500				
			11,500				11,500
1 Feb	Balance b/d		11,500	29 Feb	Balance c/d		17,000
24 Feb	Comp Supplies Ltd		5,500				
			17,000				17,000
1 Mar	Balance b/d		17,000				

Dr			Comp Supplies Limited				Cr
2004			£	2004			£
20 Jan	Bank		5,000	7 Jan	Purchases		5,000
31 Jan	Balance c/d		6,500	25 Jan	Purchases		6,500
			11,500				11,500
5 Feb	Purchases returns		150	1 Feb	Balance b/d		6,500
27 Feb	Bank		6,350	24 Feb	Purchases		5,500
29 Feb	Balance c/d		5,500				
			12,000				12,000
				1 Mar	Balance b/d		5,500

Dr			Sales Account				Cr
2004			£	2004			£
31 Jan	Balance c/d		4,550	11 Jan	Bank		1,000
				12 Jan	Bank		1,250
				16 Jan	Rowcester College		850
				22 Jan	Bank		1,450
			4,550				4,550
29 Feb	Balance c/d		11,150	1 Feb	Balance b/d		4,550
				4 Feb	Bank		1,550
				10 Feb	Bank		1,300
				19 Feb	Bank		1,600
				25 Feb	Bank		1,100
				26 Feb	Rowcester College		1,050
			11,150				11,150
				1 Mar	Balance b/d		11,150

Dr		**Rowcester College**			Cr
2004		£	2004		£
16 Jan	Sales	850	27 Jan	Sales returns	100
			31 Jan	Balance c/d	750
		850			850
1 Feb	Balance b/d	750	12 Feb	Bank	750
26 Feb	Sales	1,050	29 Feb	Balance c/d	1,050
		1,800			1,800
1 Mar	Balance b/d	1,050			

Dr		**Sales Returns Account**		Cr
2004		£	2004	£
27 Jan	Rowcester College	100		

Dr	**Purchases Returns Account**			Cr
2004	£	2004		£
		5 Feb	Comp Supplies Ltd	150

(b)

Trial balance as at 31 January 2004

	Dr	Cr
	£	£
Bank	6,700	
Capital		10,000
Rent paid	500	
Shop fittings	1,500	
Purchases	11,500	
Comp Supplies Limited		6,500
Sales		4,550
Rowcester College	750	
Sales returns	100	
	21,050	21,050

(d)

Trial balance as at 29 February 2004

	Dr	Cr
	£	£
Bank	5,300	
Capital		10,000
Rent paid	1,000	
Shop fittings	2,350	
Purchases	17,000	
Comp Supplies Limited		5,500
Sales		11,150
Rowcester College	1,050	
Sales returns	100	
Purchases returns		150
	26,800	26,800

CHAPTER 4: FINAL ACCOUNTS – THE EXTENDED TRIAL BALANCE

4.1   (b)   **4.2**   (d)

4.3   Business A: net profit £40,000; capital £100,000
Business B: expenses £70,000; liabilities £100,000
Business C: income £70,000; assets £90,000
Business D: expenses £75,000; liabilities £60,000
Business E: net loss £10,000; assets £100,000

4.4

| | | TRIAL BALANCE | | FINAL ACCOUNTS | | | |
| | | | | PROFIT & LOSS | | BALANCE SHEET | |
		Debit	Credit	Debit	Credit	Debit	Credit
(a)	Salaries	✓		✓			
(b)	Purchases	✓		✓			
(c)	Debtors	✓				✓	
(d)	Sales returns	✓		✓			
(e)	Discount received		✓		✓		
(f)	Motor vehicle	✓				✓	
(g)	Capital		✓				✓

4.5   Extended trial balance – see next page

4.6   Extended trial balance – see page 284

4.5   EXTENDED TRIAL BALANCE

NICK JOHNSON   **31 DECEMBER 2004**

Account name	Ledger balances Dr £	Ledger balances Cr £	Adjustments Dr £	Adjustments Cr £	Profit and loss Dr £	Profit and loss Cr £	Balance sheet Dr £	Balance sheet Cr £
Opening stock	25,000				25,000			
Purchases	210,000				210,000			
Sales		310,000				310,000		
Administration expenses	12,400				12,400			
Wages	41,000				41,000			
Rent paid	7,500				7,500			
Telephone	1,000				1,000			
Interest paid	9,000				9,000			
Travel expenses	1,100				1,100			
Premises	200,000						200,000	
Machinery	40,000						40,000	
Debtors	31,000						31,000	
Bank	900						900	
Cash	100						100	
Capital		150,000						150,000
Drawings	14,000						14,000	
Loan from bank		100,000						100,000
Creditors		29,000						29,000
Value Added Tax		4,000						4,000
Closing stock: Profit & loss				21,000		21,000		
Closing stock: Balance sheet			21,000				21,000	
Net profit/loss					24,000			24,000
	593,000	593,000	21,000	21,000	331,000	331,000	307,000	307,000

4.6   EXTENDED TRIAL BALANCE

ALAN HARRIS   **30 JUNE 2004**

Account name	Ledger balances		Adjustments		Profit and loss		Balance sheet	
	Dr £	Cr £	Dr £	Cr £	Dr £	Cr £	Dr £	Cr £
Opening stock	13,250				13,250			
Capital		70,000						70,000
Premises	65,000						65,000	
Motor vehicle	5,250						5,250	
Purchases	55,000				55,000			
Sales		85,500				85,500		
Administration expenses	850				850			
Wages	9,220				9,220			
Rent paid	1,200				1,200			
Telephone	680				680			
Interest paid	120				120			
Travel expenses	330				330			
Debtors	1,350						1,350	
Creditors		6,400						6,400
Value Added Tax		1,150						1,150
Bank	2,100						2,100	
Cash	600						600	
Drawings	8,100						8,100	
Closing stock: Profit & loss		18,100				18,100		
Closing stock: Balance sheet	18,100						18,100	
Net profit/loss					22,950			22,950
	181,150	181,150			103,600	103,600	100,500	100,500

CHAPTER 5: SOLE TRADER FINAL ACCOUNTS

5.1

NICK JOHNSON

TRADING AND PROFIT AND LOSS ACCOUNT
for the year ended 31 December 2004

	£	£
Sales		310,000
Opening stock	25,000	
Purchases	210,000	
	235,000	
Less Closing stock	21,000	
Cost of sales		214,000
Gross profit		96,000
Less overheads:		
Administration expenses	12,400	
Wages	41,000	
Rent paid	7,500	
Telephone	1,000	
Interest paid	9,000	
Travel expenses	1,100	
		72,000
Net profit		24,000

BALANCE SHEET as at 31 December 2004

	£	£	£
Fixed assets			
Premises			200,000
Machinery			40,000
			240,000
Current assets			
Stock (closing)		21,000	
Debtors		31,000	
Bank		900	
Cash		100	
		53,000	
Less Current liabilities			
Creditors	29,000		
Value Added Tax	4,000		
		33,000	
Working capital			20,000
			260,000
Less Long-term liabilities			
Loan from bank			100,000
NET ASSETS			160,000

continued on next page

FINANCED BY
Capital

Opening capital	150,000
Add net profit	24,000
	174,000
Less drawings	14,000
Closing capital	160,000

5.2

ALAN HARRIS

TRADING AND PROFIT AND LOSS ACCOUNT
for the year ended 30 JUNE 2004

	£	£
Sales		85,500
Opening stock	13,250	
Purchases	55,000	
	68,250	
Less Closing stock	18,100	
Cost of sales		50,150
Gross profit		35,350
Less overheads:		
Administration expenses	850	
Wages	9,220	
Rent paid	1,200	
Telephone	680	
Interest paid	120	
Travel expenses	330	
		12,400
Net profit		22,950

BALANCE SHEET
as at 30 June 2004

	£	£	£
Fixed assets			
Premises			65,000
Motor vehicle			5,250
			70,250
Current assets			
Stock (closing)		18,100	
Debtors		1,350	
Bank		2,100	
Cash		600	
		22,150	
Less Current liabilities			
Creditors	6,400		
Value Added Tax	1,150		
		7,550	
Working capital			14,600
NET ASSETS			84,850
FINANCED BY			
Capital			
Opening capital			70,000
Add net profit			22,950
			92,950
Less drawings			8,100
Closing capital			84,850

CHAPTER 6: ACCRUALS AND PREPAYMENTS

6.1 (d)   **6.2** (c)

6.3

Dr			Vehicle Expenses Account		Cr
2004		£	2004		£
31 Dec	Balance b/d	1,680	31 Dec	Drawings	420
			31 Dec	Profit and loss account	1,260
		1,680			1,680

6.4

Dr			Insurance Claims Account		Cr
2004		£	2004		£
17 Dec	Purchases	845			

Dr			Purchases		Cr
2004		£	2004		£
			17 Dec Insurance claims		845

If the amount is not paid by 31 December 2004, the balance sheet will show the amount of insurance claims account as a current asset.

6.5 (a) Overhead in profit and loss account of £56,760; balance sheet shows accruals account (current liability) of £1,120.

(b) Overhead in profit and loss account of £2,852 (ie £3,565 – £713); balance sheet shows prepayments account (current asset) of £713.

(c) Overhead in profit and loss account of £1,800; balance sheet shows prepayments account (current asset) of £150.

6.6 Extended trial balance – see next page

6.6 EXTENDED TRIAL BALANCE

DON SMITH **31 DECEMBER 2004**

Account name	Ledger balances		Adjustments		Profit and loss		Balance sheet	
	Dr £	Cr £	Dr £	Cr £	Dr £	Cr £	Dr £	Cr £
Debtors	24,325						24,325	
Creditors		15,408						15,408
Value Added Tax		4,276						4,276
Capital		30,000						30,000
Bank		1,083						1,083
Rent and rates	10,862			250	10,612			
Electricity	2,054		110		2,164			
Telephone	1,695				1,695			
Salaries	55,891		365		56,256			
Motor vehicles	22,250						22,250	
Office equipment	7,500						7,500	
Motor vehicle expenses	10,855				10,855			
Drawings	15,275						15,275	
Discount allowed	478				478			
Discount received		591				591		
Purchases	138,960				138,960			
Sales		257,258				257,258		
Opening stock	18,471				18,471			
Closing stock: Profit & loss				14,075		14,075		
Closing stock: Balance sheet			14,075				14,075	
Accruals				475				475
Prepayments			250				250	
Net profit/loss					32,433			32,433
	308,616	308,616	14,800	14,800	271,924	271,924	83,675	83,675

DON SMITH

TRADING AND PROFIT AND LOSS ACCOUNT
for the year ended 31 December 2004

	£	£
Sales		257,258
Opening stock	18,471	
Purchases	138,960	
	157,431	
Less Closing stock	14,075	
Cost of sales		143,356
Gross profit		113,902
Add income: Discount received		591
		114,493
Less overheads:		
Rent and rates 10,862 – 250	10,612	
Electricity 2,054 + 110	2,164	
Telephone	1,695	
Salaries 55,891 + 365	56,256	
Motor vehicle expenses	10,855	
Discount allowed	478	
		82,060
Net profit		32,433

For balance sheet – see next page

DON SMITH

BALANCE SHEET as at 31 December 2004

	£	£	£
Fixed assets			
Motor vehicles			22,250
Office equipment			7,500
			29,750
Current assets			
Stock (closing)		14,075	
Debtors		24,325	
Prepayment		250	
		38,650	
Less Current liabilities			
Creditors	15,408		
Accrual	475		
Value Added Tax	4,276		
Bank	1,083		
		21,242	
Working capital			17,408
NET ASSETS			47,158
FINANCED BY			
Capital			
Opening capital			30,000
Add net profit			32,433
			62,433
Less drawings			15,275
Closing capital			47,158

6.7   Extended trial balance – see next page

6.7 EXTENDED TRIAL BALANCE

JOHN BARCLAY

30 JUNE 2004

Account name	Ledger balances		Adjustments		Profit and loss		Balance sheet	
	Dr £	Cr £	Dr £	Cr £	Dr £	Cr £	Dr £	Cr £
Sales		864,321				864,321		
Purchases	600,128				599,878			
Sales returns	2,746			250	2,746			
Purchases returns		3,894				3,894		
Office expenses	33,947			346	33,601			
Salaries	122,611				122,611			
Motor vehicle expenses	36,894		1,250		38,144			
Discount allowed	3,187				3,187			
Discount received		4,951				4,951		
Debtors and creditors	74,328	52,919					74,328	52,919
Value Added Tax		10,497						10,497
Opening stock	63,084				63,084			
Motor vehicles	83,500						83,500	
Office equipment	23,250						23,250	
Land and buildings	100,000						100,000	
Bank loan		75,000						75,000
Bank	1,197						1,197	
Capital		155,000						155,000
Drawings	21,710		250				21,960	
Closing stock: Profit & loss				66,941		66,941		
Closing stock: Balance sheet			66,941				66,941	
Accruals				1,250				1,250
Prepayments			346				346	
Net profit/loss					76,856			76,856
	1,166,582	1,166,582	68,787	68,787	940,107	940,107	371,522	371,522

JOHN BARCLAY

TRADING AND PROFIT AND LOSS ACCOUNT
for the year ended 30 June 2004

	£	£	£
Sales			864,321
Less Sales returns			2,746
			861,575
Opening stock		63,084	
Purchases 600,128 – 250*	599,878		
Less Purchases returns	3,894	595,984	
		659,068	
Less Closing stock		66,941	
Cost of sales			592,127
Gross profit			269,448
Add income: Discount received			4,951
			274,399
Less overheads:			
Office expenses 33,947 – 346		33,601	
Salaries		122,611	
Motor vehicle expenses 36,894 + 1,250		38,144	
Discount allowed		3,187	
			197,543
Net profit			76,856

* goods for own use

BALANCE SHEET as at 30 June 2004

	£	£	£
Fixed assets			
Land and buildings			100,000
Motor vehicles			83,500
Office equipment			23,250
			206,750
Current assets			
Stock (closing)		66,941	
Debtors		74,328	
Prepayment		346	
Bank		1,197	
		142,812	
Less Current liabilities			
Creditors	52,919		
Accrual	1,250		
Value Added Tax	10,497	64,666	
Working capital			78,146
			284,896
Less Long-term liabilities			
Bank loan			75,000
NET ASSETS			209,896

continued on next page

FINANCED BY
Capital

Opening capital		155,000
Add net profit		76,856
		231,856
Less drawings 21,710 + 250*		21,960
Closing capital		209,896

* goods for own use

CHAPTER 7: DEPRECIATION OF FIXED ASSETS

7.1 (a)

7.2
- With reducing balance depreciation a fixed percentage is written off the reduced balance of the asset each year.
- When compared with straight-line depreciation, reducing balance needs a much higher percentage to be written off each year to achieve the same residual value.
- Thus the money amounts for reducing balance are greater in the early years and smaller in the later years when compared with straight-line depreciation.
- As delivery vans depreciate more in the early years and are unlikely to be kept for the whole of their expected lives, reducing balance depreciation is a more accurate reflection of their worth than is straight-line depreciation.
- The depreciation charge will be high in the early years but smaller in the later years; by contrast repair costs are likely to be low early on but will increase in later years. By using reducing balance depreciation, the total charge to profit and loss account for both depreciation and repair costs is likely to be similar throughout the assets' lives.

7.3 (a)

Dr	Provision for Depreciation Account – Car				Cr
2004		£	2004		£
31 Dec	Balance c/d	3,000	31 Dec	Depreciation account	3,000
2005			2005		
31 Dec	Balance c/d	5,250	1 Jan	Balance b/d	3,000
			31 Dec	Depreciation account	2,250
		5,250			5,250
2006			2006		
31 Dec	Disposals account	6,937	1 Jan	Balance b/d	5,250
			31 Dec	Depreciation account	1,687
		6,937			6,937

(b)

MARTIN JACKSON
Balance sheet (extract) as at 31 December 2004

	£ Cost	£ Provision for dep'n	£ Net
Fixed assets			
Car	12,000	3,000	9,000

Balance sheet (extract) as at 31 December 2005

	£ Cost	£ Provision for dep'n	£ Net
Fixed assets			
Car	12,000	5,250	6,750

(c)

Dr			**Disposals Account**			Cr
2006		£	2006			£
31 Dec	Car account	12,000	31 Dec	Prov for dep'n account	6,937
31 Dec	Profit and loss account		31 Dec	Bank	5,500
	(profit on sale)	437			
		12,437			12,437

7.4   Extended trial balance – see next page

7.4 EXTENDED TRIAL BALANCE

JOHN HENSON

31 DECEMBER 2004

Account name	Ledger balances Dr £	Ledger balances Cr £	Adjustments Dr £	Adjustments Cr £	Profit and loss Dr £	Profit and loss Cr £	Balance sheet Dr £	Balance sheet Cr £
Purchases	71,600				71,600			
Sales		122,000				122,000		
Opening stock	6,250				6,250			
Vehicle running expenses	1,480				1,480			
Rent and rates	5,650				5,650			
Office expenses	2,220				2,220			
Discount received		285				285		
Wages and salaries	18,950				18,950			
Office equipment	10,000						10,000	
Prov for dep'n: office equip				1,000				1,000
Vehicle	12,000						12,000	
Prov for dep'n: vehicle				3,000				3,000
Debtors	5,225						5,225	
Creditors		3,190						3,190
Value Added Tax		1,720						1,720
Capital		20,000						20,000
Drawings	13,095						13,095	
Bank	725						725	
Closing stock: Profit & loss				8,500		8,500		
Closing stock: Balance sheet			8,500				8,500	
Depreciation			4,000		4,000			
Net profit/loss					20,635			20,635
	147,195	147,195	12,500	12,500	130,785	130,785	49,545	49,545

JOHN HENSON

TRADING AND PROFIT AND LOSS ACCOUNT
for the year ended 31 December 2004

	£	£
Sales		122,000
Opening stock	6,250	
Purchases	71,600	
	77,850	
Less Closing stock	8,500	
Cost of sales		69,350
Gross profit		52,650
Add income: Discount received		285
		52,935
Less overheads:		
Vehicle running expenses	1,480	
Rent and rates	5,650	
Office expenses	2,220	
Wages and salaries	18,950	
Depreciation: office equipment	1,000	
vehicle	3,000	
		32,300
Net profit		20.635

BALANCE SHEET as at 31 December 2004

	£ Cost	£ Provision for dep'n	£ Net
Fixed assets			
Office equipment	10,000	1,000	9,000
Vehicle	12,000	3,000	9,000
	22,000	4,000	18,000
Current assets			
Stock (closing)		8,500	
Debtors		5,225	
Bank		725	
		14,450	
Less Current liabilities			
Creditors	3,190		
Value Added Tax	1,720		
		4,910	
Working capital			9,540
NET ASSETS			27,540

continued on next page

FINANCED BY	
Capital	
Opening capital	20,000
Add net profit	20,635
	40,635
Less drawings	13,095
Closing capital	27,540

7.5   A letter incorporating the following points:
- Straight-line method at 20% per year = depreciation of £200 per year
- Reducing balance method at 50% per year = depreciation of £500 for year 1, £250 for year 2, £125 for year 3, £62 for year 4, and £31 for year 5, leaving a small residual value of £32
- Either method acceptable
- The straight-line method will give larger profits for the first two years
- The cash position is not affected, as depreciation is a non-cash expense (this point should be stressed)

7.6   Extended trial balance – see next page

7.6 EXTENDED TRIAL BALANCE

HAZEL HARRIS

31 DECEMBER 2004

Account name	Ledger balances Dr £	Ledger balances Cr £	Adjustments Dr £	Adjustments Cr £	Profit and loss Dr £	Profit and loss Cr £	Balance sheet Dr £	Balance sheet Cr £
Bank loan		75,000						75,000
Capital		125,000						125,000
Purchases and sales	465,000	614,000			465,000	614,000		
Building repairs	8,480				8,480			
Motor vehicle	12,000						12,000	
Prov for dep'n: vehicle		2,400		1,920				4,320
Motor expenses	2,680				2,680			
Premises	100,000						100,000	
Prov for dep'n: premises		4,000		2,000				6,000
Bank		2,000						2,000
Furniture and fittings	25,000						25,000	
Prov for dep'n: furn & fitts		2,500		2,500				5,000
Wages and salaries	86,060		3,180		89,240			
Discounts	10,610	8,140			10,610	8,140		
Drawings	24,000						24,000	
Rates and insurance	6,070			450	5,620			
Debtors and creditors	52,130	32,600					52,130	32,600
Value Added Tax		5,250						5,250
General expenses	15,860				15,860			
Opening stock	63,000				63,000			
Closing stock: Profit & loss				88,000		88,000		
Closing stock: Balance sheet			88,000				88,000	
Accruals				3,180				3,180
Prepayments			450				450	
Depreciation			6,420		6,420			
Net profit/loss					43,230			43,230
	870,890	870,890	98,050	98,050	710,140	710,140	301,580	301,580

HAZEL HARRIS

**TRADING AND PROFIT AND LOSS ACCOUNT
for the year ended 31 December 2004**

	£	£
Sales		614,000
Opening stock	63,000	
Purchases	465,000	
	528,000	
Less Closing stock	88,000	
Cost of sales		440,000
Gross profit		174,000
Add income: Discount received		8,140
		182,140
Less overheads:		
Building repairs	8,480	
Motor expenses	2,680	
Wages and salaries	89,240	
Discount allowed	10,610	
Rates and insurance	5,620	
General expenses	15,860	
Depreciation: premises	2,000	
motor vehicle	1,920	
furniture & fittings	2,500	
		138,910
Net profit		43,230

HAZEL HARRIS: BALANCE SHEET as at 31 December 2004

	£	£	£
Fixed assets	Cost	Provision for dep'n	Net
Premises	100,000	6,000	94,000
Motor vehicle	12,000	4,320	7,680
Furniture & fittings	25,000	5,000	20,000
	137,000	15,320	121,680
Current assets			
Stock (closing)		88,000	
Debtors		52,130	
Prepayment		450	
		140,580	
Less Current liabilities			
Creditors	32,600		
Bank overdraft	2,000		
Accrual	3,180		
Value Added Tax	5,250		
		43,030	
Working capital			97,550
			219,230
Less Long-term liabilities			
Bank loan			75,000
NET ASSETS			144,230
FINANCED BY			
Capital			
Opening capital			125,000
Add net profit			43,230
			168,230
Less drawings			24,000
Closing capital			144,230

CHAPTER 8: BAD DEBTS AND PROVISION FOR DOUBTFUL DEBTS

8.1   (a)   **8.2**   (c)

8.3   •   *Profit and loss account*
        debit bad debts written off, £210
        debit provision for doubtful debts: adjustment, £500

     •   *Balance sheet*
        debtors £20,000, less provision for doubtful debts £500, net debtors £19,500

8.4

Dr	Provision for Doubtful Debts Account				Cr

2004/05		£	2004/05		£
30 Jun	Balance c/d	400	1 Jul	Balance b/d	300
			30 Jun	Prov for doubtful debts:	
				adjustment	100
				(increase in provision)	
		400			400
2005/06			2005/06		
30 Jun	Prov for doubtful debts:		1 Jul	Balance b/d	400
	adjustment	50			
	(decrease in provision)				
30 Jun	Balance c/d	350			
		400			400
2006/07			2006/07		
			1 Jul	Balance b/d	350

2005 *Extracts from final accounts produced for year ended 30 June:*

Profit and loss account: overhead of £100

Balance sheet: debtors £8,000 – £400 = £7,600

2006 *Extracts from final accounts produced for year ended 30 June:*

Profit and loss account: income of £50

Balance sheet: debtors £7,000 – £350 = £6,650

8.5 Extended trial balance – see next page

8.5 EXTENDED TRIAL BALANCE

PAUL SANDERS

31 DECEMBER 2004

Account name	Ledger balances Dr £	Ledger balances Cr £	Adjustments Dr £	Adjustments Cr £	Profit and loss Dr £	Profit and loss Cr £	Balance sheet Dr £	Balance sheet Cr £
Purchases and sales	51,225	81,762			51,225	81,762		
Returns	186	254			186	254		
Opening stock	6,031				6,031			
Discounts	324	438			324	438		
Motor expenses	1,086				1,086			
Wages and salaries	20,379				20,379			
Electricity	876		102		978			
Telephone	1,241				1,241			
Rent and rates	4,565			251	4,314			
sundry expenses	732				732			
Bad debts written off	219				219			
Debtors and creditors	1,040	7,671					1,040	7,671
Value Added Tax		1,301						1,301
Bank	3,501						3,501	
Cash	21						21	
Motor vehicles	15,000						15,000	
Prov for dep'n: vehicles		3,000		3,000				6,000
Office equipment	10,000						10,000	
Prov for dep'n: equipment		5,000		1,000				6,000
Capital		25,000						25,000
Drawings	8,000						8,000	
Provision for doubtful debts				52				52
Closing stock: Profit & loss				8,210		8,210		
Closing stock: Balance sheet			8,210				8,210	
Accruals				102				102
Prepayments			251				251	
Depreciation			4,000		4,000			
Prov for doubtful debts:adj			52		52			
Net profit/loss					103			103
	124,426	124,426	12,615	12,615	90,767	90,767	46,126	46,126

PAUL SANDERS

TRADING AND PROFIT AND LOSS ACCOUNT
for the year ended 31 December 2004

	£	£	£
Sales			81,762
Less Sales returns			186
			81,576
Opening stock		6,031	
Purchases	51,225		
Less Purchases returns	254		
		50,971	
		57,002	
Less Closing stock		8,210	
Cost of sales			48,792
Gross profit			32,784
Add income: Discount received			438
			33,222
Less overheads:			
Discount allowed		324	
Motor expenses		1,086	
Wages and salaries		20,379	
Electricity		978	
Telephone		1,241	
Rent and rates		4,314	
Sundry expenses		732	
Depreciation: motor vehicles		3,000	
office equipment		1,000	
Bad debts written off		219	
Provision for doubtful debts		52	
			33,325
Net loss			103

PAUL SANDERS: BALANCE SHEET as at 31 December 2004

	£	£	£
Fixed assets	Cost	Provision for dep'n	Net
Motor vehicles	15,000	6,000	9,000
Office equipment	10,000	6,000	4,000
	25,000	12,000	13,000
Current assets			
Stock (closing)		8,210	
Debtors	1,040		
Less provision for doubtful debts	52		
		988	
Prepayment		251	
Bank		3,501	
Cash		21	
		12,971	
Less Current liabilities			
Creditors	7,671		
Accrual	102		
Value Added Tax	1,301		
		9,074	
Working capital			3,897
NET ASSETS			16,897
FINANCED BY			
Capital			
Opening capital			25,000
Less net loss			103
			24,897
Less drawings			8,000
Closing capital			16,897

8.6   Extended trial balance – see next page

8.6 EXTENDED TRIAL BALANCE

JAMES JENKINS

30 JUNE 2005

Account name	Ledger balances		Adjustments		Profit and loss		Balance sheet	
	Dr £	Cr £	Dr £	Cr £	Dr £	Cr £	Dr £	Cr £
Capital		36,175						36,175
Drawings	19,050						19,050	
Purchases and sales	105,240	168,432			105,240	168,432		
Opening stock	9,427				9,427			
Debtors and creditors	3,840	5,294					3,840	5,294
Value Added Tax		1,492						1,492
Returns	975	1,237			975	1,237		
Discounts	127	643			127	643		
Wages and salaries	30,841				30,841			
Motor vehicle expenses	1,021		55		1,076			
Rent and rates	8,796			275	8,521			
Heating and lighting	1,840				1,840			
Telephone	355				355			
General expenses	1,752				1,752			
Bad debts written off	85				85			
Motor vehicle	8,000						8,000	
Prov for dep'n: vehicle		3,500		1,125				4,625
Shop fittings	6,000						6,000	
Prov for dep'n: shop fittings		2,000		600				2,600
Provision for doubtful debts		150	54					96
Cash	155						155	
Bank	21,419						21,419	
Closing stock: Profit & loss				11,517		11,517		
Closing stock: Balance sheet			11,517				11,517	
Accruals				55				55
Prepayments			275				275	
Depreciation			1,725		1,725			
Prov for doubtful debts:adj				54		54		
Net profit/loss					19,919			19,919
	218,923	218,923	13,626	13,626	181,883	181,883	70,256	70,256

JAMES JENKINS

TRADING AND PROFIT AND LOSS ACCOUNT
for the year ended 30 June 2005

	£	£	£
Sales			168,432
Less Sales returns			975
			167,457
Opening stock		9,427	
Purchases	105,240		
Less Purchases returns	1,237		
		104,003	
		113,430	
Less Closing stock		11,517	
Cost of sales			101,913
Gross profit			65,544
Add income: Discount received			643
Provision for doubtful debts: adjustment			54
			66,241
Less overheads:			
Discount allowed		127	
Wages and salaries		30,841	
Motor vehicle expenses		1,076	
Rent and rates		8,521	
Heating and lighting		1,840	
Telephone		355	
General expenses		1,752	
Depreciation: motor vehicle		1,125	
shop fittings		600	
Bad debts written off		85	
			46,322
Net profit			19,919

JAMES JENKINS: BALANCE SHEET as at 30 June 2005

Fixed assets	£ Cost	£ Provision for dep'n	£ Net
Motor vehicle	8,000	4,625	3,375
Shop fittings	6,000	2,600	3,400
	14,000	7,225	6,775
Current assets			
Stock (closing)		11,517	
Debtors	3,840		
Less provision for doubtful debts	96		
		3,744	
Prepayment		275	
Bank		21,419	
Cash		155	
		37,110	
Less Current liabilities			
Creditors	5,294		
Accrual	55		
Value Added Tax	1,492		
		6,841	
Working capital			30,269
NET ASSETS			37,044
FINANCED BY			
Capital			
Opening capital			36,175
Add net profit			19,919
			56,094
Less drawings			19,050
Closing capital			37,044

8.7

Dr		Bank Account			Cr
		£			£
J Abel		50			

Dr		J Abel			Cr
		£			£
Bad debts recovered account		50	Bank account		50

Dr	Bad Debts Recovered Account	Cr
£		£
	J Abel	50

Note: As an alternative to using bad debts recovered account, the amount could be credited to bad debts written off account. Bad debts recovered account is used by firms with substantial debtors, where there are a number of recovery transactions.

CHAPTER 9: THE REGULATORY FRAMEWORK OF ACCOUNTING

9.1   (d)

9.2   (a)   Prudence: by making a provision for bad debts the business is recording the possibility that the debtor may not pay.

(b)   Materiality: although the video tapes will be kept for a number of years they are not treated as a fixed asset and depreciated because their cost is not material to the business.

(c)   Consistency: the owner of the business should use the most appropriate depreciation method for the type of asset, and apply it consistently from year-to-year. In this way the accounts of different years are comparable; the accounting policy can be changed – for example, from one method of depreciation to another – provided there are good reasons for so doing, with a note to the final accounts explaining what has happened.

(d)   Accruals (or matching): here the expense of electricity is being matched to the time period in which the cost was incurred.

9.3   (a)   Consistency concept: he should continue to use reducing balance method (it won't make any difference to the bank manager anyway).

(b)   Prudence concept: stock valuation should be at lower of cost and net realisable value, ie £10,000 in this case.

(c)   Business entity concept: car is an asset of John's firm, not a personal asset (in any case personal assets, for sole traders and partnerships, might well be used to repay debts of firm).

(d)   Prudence concept: the bad debt should be written off as a bad debt in profit and loss account (so reducing net profit), and the balance sheet figure for debtors should be £27,500 (which is closer to the amount he can expect to receive from debtors).

(e)   Accruals concept: expenses and revenues must be matched, therefore it must go through the old year's accounts.

(f)   Going concern concept: presumes that business will continue to trade in the foreseeable future: alternative is 'gone concern' and assets may have very different values.

9.4   (c)

9.5   (d)

9.6 (a) Sales for February: 24 tables at £50 each = £1,200

(b) Closing stock at 28 February: 6 tables at £31 each = £186

(c) Cost of sales for February:

		£
•	opening stock	300
•	plus purchases	632
•	less closing stock	186
		746

9.7

		£	
•	seeds	1,450	(selling price)
•	fertilisers and insecticides	2,270	(cost price)
•	tools	4,390	(cost price)
		8,110	

9.8 (a) this year's profit is overstated by £1,000

(b) next year's profit will be understated by £1,000

9.9

> MEMORANDUM
>
> **Cost of computer accounting software**
>
> As the cost of the software is relatively low, I recommend that it is treated as revenue expenditure and shown amongst the overheads in profit and loss account. This is in line with the accounting concept of materiality: at a cost of £99 it is not worth recording it separately. Had the cost been much higher, the software would have been treated as a fixed asset and depreciated over its expected life.

9.10 • The first part of the statement is true – capital expenditure is money spent on fixed assets

• Whilst fixed assets are recorded in the balance sheet, there is a link with profit and loss account in that the annual depreciation will be recorded as an overhead

• As all fixed assets having a known useful economic life must be depreciated (SSAP 12), there is a clear link between such fixed assets shown in the balance sheet and the annual depreciation recorded in profit and loss account

• On disposal of fixed assets the amount of over-provision or under-provision for depreciation is taken to the profit and loss account.

CHAPTER 10: ACCOUNTING FOR CAPITAL TRANSACTIONS

10.1 (a)   **10.2** (b)   **10.3** (a)

10.4

EXTRACT FROM FIXED ASSET REGISTER							
Description/serial no	Date acquired	Original cost £	Depreciation £	NBV £	Funding method	Disposal proceeds £	Disposal date
Office equipment							
Computer, Supra ML	12/3/01	3,000.00			Cash		
Year ended 31/12/01			1,500.00	1,500.00			
Year ended 31/12/02			750.00	750.00			
Year ended 31/12/03			375.00	375.00			
Year ended 31/12/04						500.00	10/2/04

10.5 (a)

Date	Details	Folio	Dr	Cr
			£	£
2001 10 Jan	Machine	ML	32,000	
	Bank	CB		32,000
	Purchase of machine to develop and print films; capital expenditure authorisation number			

Dr			**Machine Account**		Cr
2001		£	2004		£
10 Jan	Bank	32,000	17 Aug	Disposals	32,000
2004					
17 Aug	Disposals (part exchange allowance)	5,000			

Depreciation calculations

Depreciation at 40 per cent reducing balance per year is as follows:

year ended 31 December 2001	£12,800
year ended 31 December 2002	£7,680
year ended 31 December 2003	£4,608

Note: the journal entry for the first year only is shown

Date	Details	Folio	Dr	Cr
2001			£	£
31 Dec	Profit and loss	ML	12,800	
	Depreciation	ML		12,800
	Depreciation charge for year on machine			
31 Dec	Depreciation	ML	12,800	
	Provision for depreciation account – machine	ML		12,800
	Transfer of depreciation charge for year to provision for depreciation account			

Dr				Depreciation Account – Machine		Cr
2001			£	2001		£
31 Dec	Prov for dep'n account		12,800	31 Dec	Profit and loss account	12,800
2002				2002		
31 Dec	Prov for dep'n account		7,680	31 Dec	Profit and loss account	7,680
2003				2003		
31 Dec	Prov for dep'n account		4,608	31 Dec	Profit and loss account	4,608

Dr			Provision for Depreciation Account – Machine		Cr
2001		£	2001		£
31 Dec	Balance c/d	12,800	31 Dec	Dep'n account: machine	12,800
2002			2002		
31 Dec	Balance c/d	20,480	1 Jan	Balance b/d	12,800
			31 Dec	Dep'n account: machine	7,680
		20,480			20,480
2003			2003		
31 Dec	Balance c/d	25,088	1 Jan	Balance b/d	20,480
			31 Dec	Dep'n account: machine	4,608
		25,088			25,088
2004			2004		
17 Aug	Disposals	25,088	1 Jan	Balance b/d	25,088

Date	Details	Folio	Dr	Cr
2004			£	£
17 Aug	Disposals	ML	32,000	
	Machine	ML		32,000
	Provision for depreciation account –			
	machine	ML	25,088	
	Disposals	ML		25,088
	Machine	ML	5,000	
	Disposals	ML		5,000
	Profit and loss	ML	1,912	
	Disposals	ML		1,912
			64,000	64,000
	Part exchange of machine to develop			
	and print films; loss on sale of £1,912			
	transferred to profit and loss account			

Dr			**Disposals Account – Machine**		Cr
2004		£	2004		£
17 Aug	Machine	32,000	17 Aug	Provision for dep'n	25,088
			17 Aug	Machine (part exchange)	5,000
			17 Aug	Profit and loss	
				(loss on sale)	1,912
		32,000			32,000

10.5 (b)

EXTRACT FROM FIXED ASSET REGISTER

Description/serial no	Date acquired	Original cost £	Depreciation £	NBV £	Funding method	Disposal proceeds £	Disposal date
Machinery							
Automated d&p machine	10/1/01	32,000.00			Cash		
Year ended 31/12/01			12,800.00	19,200.00			
Year ended 31/12/02			7,680.00	11,520.00			
Year ended 31/12/03			4,608.00	6,912.00			
Year ended 31/12/04						5,000.00	17/8/04

10.6 **Depreciation calculations:**

	2001	2002	2003	TOTAL
Registration number	£	£	£	£
W704 ZNP	4,500	4,500	–	9,000
W705 ZNP	4,500	4,500	4,500	13,500
Y81 ZUY	–	–	5,250	5,250
TOTAL	9,000	9,000	9,750	27,750

Dr   **Vehicles Account**   Cr

2001		£	2001		£
24 Jan	Bank	15,000	31 Dec	Balance c/d	30,000
24 Jan	Bank	15,000			
		30,000			30,000
2002			2002		
1 Jan	Balance b/d	30,000	31 Dec	Balance c/d	30,000
2003			2003		
1 Jan	Balance b/d	30,000	13 Oct	Disposals	15,000
17 Feb	Bank	17,500	31 Dec	Balance c/d	32,500
		47,500			47,500
2004			2004		
1 Jan	Balance b/d	32,500			

Dr   **Depreciation Account – Vehicles**   Cr

2001		£	2001		£
31 Dec	Provision for dep'n	9,000	31 Dec	Profit and loss account	9,000
2002			2002		
31 Dec	Provision for dep'n	9,000	31 Dec	Profit and loss account	9,000
2003			2003		
31 Dec	Provision for dep'n	9,750	31 Dec	Profit and loss account	9,750

Dr		Provision for Depreciation Account – Vehicles				Cr
2001		£	2001			£
31 Dec	Balance c/d	9,000	31 Dec	Dep'n account: vehicles		9,000
2002			2002			
31 Dec	Balance c/d	18,000	1 Jan	Balance b/d		9,000
			31 Dec	Dep'n account: vehicles		9,000
		18,000				18,000
2003			2003			
13 Oct	Disposals	9,000	1 Jan	Balance b/d		18,000
31 Dec	Balance c/d	18,750	31 Dec	Dep'n account: vehicles		9,750
		27,750				27,750
2004			2004			
			1 Jan	Balance b/d		18,750

Dr		Disposals Account – Vehicles			Cr
2003		£	2003		£
13 Oct	Vehicles	15,000	13 Oct	Provision for dep'n	9,000
13 Oct	Profit and loss		13 Oct	Bank	6,500
	(profit on sale)	500			
		15,500			15,500

10.7 *Hire purchase: accounting treatment*

The van is capitalised and the final accounts show

– in the balance sheet, the cost of the fixed asset (excluding interest), less provision for depreciation

– in the profit and loss account, interest due for the year to the hire purchase company, and depreciation on the asset for the year

– in the balance sheet, a liability for future HP payments (excluding interest), divided between current and long-term liabilities

The reason for the van being shown on Sam Sharma's balance sheet, despite being financed by hire purchase, is that his business has the use of the asset and can treat it as though it is owned (subject to keeping up with the HP payments)

CHAPTER 11: CONTROL ACCOUNTS

11.1   (d)

11.2   (b)

11.3

Dr				Sales Ledger Control Account			Cr
2004			£	2004			£
1 Jun	Balance b/d		17,491	30 Jun	Sales returns		1,045
30 Jun	Credit sales		42,591	30 Jun	Payments received		
					from debtors		39,024
				30 Jun	Discount allowed		593
				30 Jun	Bad debts written off		296
				30 Jun	Balance c/d		19,124
			60,082				60,082
1 Jul	Balance b/d		19,124				

11.4

Dr				Purchases Ledger Control Account			Cr
2004			£	2004			£
30 Apr	Purchases returns		653	1 Apr	Balance b/d		14,275
30 Apr	Payments made			30 Apr	Credit purchases		36,592
	to creditors		31,074				
30 Apr	Discount received		1,048				
30 Apr	Set-off: sales ledger		597				
30 Apr	Balance c/d		17,495				
			50,867				50,867
				1 May	Balance b/d		17,495

11.5 (a)

SUBSIDIARY (SALES) LEDGER

Dr				Arrow Valley Retailers			Cr
2004			£	2004			£
1 Feb	Balance b/d		826.40	20 Feb	Bank		805.74
3 Feb	Sales		338.59	20 Feb	Discount allowed		20.66
				29 Feb	Balance c/d		338.59
			1,164.99				1,164.99
1 Mar	Balance b/d		338.59				

Dr				B Brick (Builders) Limited			Cr
2004			£	2004			£
1 Feb	Balance b/d		59.28	29 Feb	Bad debts written off		59.28

Dr		Mereford Manufacturing Company				Cr
2004			£	2004		£
1 Feb	Balance b/d		293.49	24 Feb	Sales returns	56.29
3 Feb	Sales		127.48	29 Feb	Set-off: purchases ledger	364.68
			420.97			420.97

Dr		Redgrove Restorations				Cr
2004			£	2004		£
1 Feb	Balance b/d		724.86	7 Feb	Sales returns	165.38
17 Feb	Sales		394.78	29 Feb	Balance c/d	954.26
			1,119.64			1,119.64
1 Mar	Balance b/d		954.26			

Dr		Wyvern Warehouse Limited				Cr
2004			£	2004		£
1 Feb	Balance b/d		108.40	15 Feb	Bank	105.69
17 Feb	Sales		427.91	15 Feb	Discount allowed	2.71
				29 Feb	Balance c/d	427.91
			536.31			536.31
1 Mar	Balance b/d		427.91			

(b)

Dr		Sales Ledger Control Account				Cr
2004			£	2004		£
1 Feb	Balance b/d		2,012.43	29 Feb	Sales returns	221.67
29 Feb	Credit sales		1,288.76	29 Feb	Cheques received from debtors	911.43
				29 Feb	Discount allowed	23.37
				29 Feb	Set-off: purchases ldgr.	364.68
				29 Feb	Bad debts written off	59.28
				29 Feb	Balance c/d	1,720.76
			3,301.19			3,301.19
1 Mar	Balance b/d		1,720.76			

(c)

	Reconciliation of sales ledger control account	
	1 February 2004	*29 February 2004*
	£	£
Arrow Valley Retailers	826.40	338.59
B Brick (Builders) Limited	59.28	–
Mereford Manufacturing Company	293.49	nil
Redgrove Restorations	724.86	954.26
Wyvern Warehouse Limited	108.40	427.91
Sales ledger control account	2,012.43	1,720.76

11.6 (a) Extract from stock record:

Photocopying paper

Date	Details	Received	Issued	Balance	Value at £10 per box
2004					£
30 Jun	Adjustment		2	350	3,500

(b)

Date	Details	Folio	Dr	Cr
2004			£	£
30 Jun	Profit and loss	ML	20	
	Stock control	ML		20
	Adjustment of stock valuation following physical stock take			

(c)

Dr			Stock Control Account		Cr
2004		£	2004	£	
30 Jun	Profit and loss account	28,350	30 Jun Profit and loss account		20
			30 Jun Balance c/d		28,330
		28,350			28,350
1 Jul	Balance b/d	28,330			

CHAPTER 12: THE JOURNAL AND CORRECTION OF ERRORS

12.1   (b)   **12.2**   (a)

12.3

Date	Details	Folio	Dr	Cr
2004			£	£
1 May	Motor vehicle	ML	6,500	
	Fixtures and fittings	ML	2,800	
	Stock	ML	4,100	
	Cash	CB	150	
	Loan from husband	ML		5,000
	Capital	ML		8,550
			13,550	13,550
	Assets and liabilities at the start			
	of business			

12.4   (a) *error of omission*

Date	Details	Folio	Dr	Cr
			£	£
	Sales ledger control	ML	150	
	Sales	ML		150
	Sales invoice no .... omitted from			
	the accounts: in the subsidiary (sales)			
	ledger – debit J Rigby £150			

(b) *mispost/error of commission*

Date	Details	Folio	Dr	Cr
			£	£
	Purchases ledger control	ML	125	
	Purchases ledger control	ML		125
	Correction of mispost – cheque no .....:			
	in the subsidiary (purchases) ledger			
	– debit H Price Limited			
	– credit H Prince			

(c) *error of principle*

Date	Details	Folio	Dr	Cr
			£	£
	Delivery van	ML	10,000	
	Vehicle expenses	ML		10,000
	Correction of error – vehicle no			
	invoice no			

(d) *reversal of entries*

Date	Details	Folio	Dr £	Cr £
	Postages	ML	55	
	Bank	CB		55
	Postages	ML	55	
	Bank	CB		55
			110	110
	Correction of reversal of entries on			

(e) *compensating error*

Date	Details	Folio	Dr £	Cr £
	Purchases	ML	100	
	Purchases returns	ML		100
	Correction of under-cast on purchases account and purchases returns account on ....(date).......			

(f) *error of original entry*

Date	Details	Folio	Dr £	Cr £
	Sales ledger control	ML	98	
	Bank	CB		98
	Bank	CB	89	
	Sales ledger control	ML		89
			187	187
	Correction of error – cheque for £89 received on ....(date)....: in the subsidiary (sales) ledger *– debit L Johnson £98* *– credit L Johnson £89*			

12.5

Date	Details	Folio	Dr	Cr
			£	£
(a)	Office expenses	ML	85	
	Suspense	ML		85
	Omission of entry in office expenses account – payment made by cheque no .... on .... (date)			
(b)	Suspense	ML	78	
	Photocopying	ML		78
	Photocopying	ML	87	
	Suspense	ML		87
			165	165
	Payment for photocopying £87 (cheque no .... on ....) entered in photocopying account as £78 in error			
(c)	Suspense	ML	100	
	Sales returns	ML		100
	Overcast on ...(date)... now corrected			
(d)	Commission received	ML	25	
	Suspense	ML		25
	Commission received on .... entered twice in commission received account, now corrected			

Dr   **Suspense Account**   Cr

2004		£	2004		£
30 Sep	Trial balance difference	19	(a)	Office expenses	85
(b)	Photocopying	78	(b)	Photocopying	87
(c)	Sales returns	100	(d)	Commission received	25
		197			197

12.6 (a)

Date	Details	Folio	Dr	Cr
2004			£	£
31 Dec	Stock	ML	22,600	
	Profit and loss	ML		22,600
	Stock valuation at 31 December 2004 transferred to trading and profit and loss account			

(b)

Date	Details	Folio	Dr	Cr
2004			£	£
31 Dec	Profit and loss	ML	890	
	Telephone expenses	ML		890
	Transfer to profit and loss account			
	of expenditure for the year			

(c)

Date	Details	Folio	Dr	Cr
2004			£	£
31 Dec	Profit and loss	ML	23,930	
	Salaries	ML		22,950
	Accruals	ML		980
			23,930	23,930
	Transfer to profit and loss account			
	of expenditure for the year			

(d)

Date	Details	Folio	Dr	Cr
2004			£	£
31 Dec	Profit and loss	ML	1,160	
	Prepayments	ML	80	
	Photocopying expenses	ML		1,240
			1,240	1,240
	Transfer to profit and loss account			
	of expenditure for the year			

(e)

Date	Details	Folio	Dr	Cr
2004			£	£
31 Dec	Drawings	ML	200	
	Motoring expenses	ML		200
	Transfer of private motoring to			
	drawings account			

(f)

Date	Details	Folio	Dr	Cr
2004			£	£
31 Dec	Drawings	ML	175	
	Purchases	ML		175
	Goods taken for own use			
	by the owner			

(g)

Date	Details	Folio	Dr	Cr
2004			£	£
31 Dec	Profit and loss	ML	500	
	Depreciation	ML		500
	Depreciation charge for year on			
	fixtures and fittings			
31 Dec	Depreciation	ML	500	
	Provision for depreciation account			
	– fixtures and fittings	ML		500
	Transfer of depreciation charge for year			
	to provision for depreciation account			

(h)

Date	Details	Folio	Dr	Cr
2004			£	£
31 Dec	Disposals	ML	5,000	
	Machinery	ML		5,000
	Provision for depreciation account			
	– machinery	ML	3,750	
	Disposals	ML		3,750
	Bank	CB	2,350	
	Disposals	ML		2,000
	VAT	ML		350
	Profit and loss	ML		750
	Disposals	ML	750	
			11,850	11,850
	Sale of machine no ....; profit			
	on sale £750 transferred to profit and			
	loss account			

(i)

Date	Details	Folio	Dr	Cr
2004			£	£
31 Dec	Bad debts written off	ML	125	
	Sales ledger control	ML		125
	Accounts in the subsidiary (sales)			
	ledger written off as bad:			
	– Nick Marshall £55			
	– Crabbe & Company £30			
	– A Hunt £40			
	Total £125			
	see memo dated			
31 Dec	Profit and loss	ML	125	
	Bad debts written off	ML		125
	Transfer to profit and loss account			
	of bad debts for the year			

(j)

Date	Details	Folio	Dr	Cr
2004			£	£
31 Dec	Profit and loss	ML		100
	Provision for doubtful debts: adjustment	ML	100	
	Decrease in provision for doubtful debts			
31 Dec	Provision for doubtful debts: adjustment	ML		100
	Provision for doubtful debts	ML	100	
	Transfer of reduction for year to			
	provision for doubtful debts account			

CHAPTER 13: INCOMPLETE RECORDS

13.1   £260,000

13.2   £77,000

13.3   £21,100

13.4   £

   (a) • receipts from sales   153,500
       •   add debtors at year end   2,500
       •   **sales for year**   156,000

   (b) • payments to suppliers   95,000
       •   add creditors at year end   65,000
       •   **purchases for year**   160,000

   (c) • payments for rent and rates   8,750
       •   less rent prepaid at 31 Dec 2004   250
       •   **rent and rates for year**   8,500

       •   payments for wages   15,000
       •   add wages accrued at 31 Dec 2004   550
       •   **wages for year**   15,550

   (d)

TRADING AND PROFIT AND LOSS ACCOUNT OF JANE PRICE
for the year ended 31 December 2004

	£	£
Sales		156,000
Purchases	160,000	
Less Closing stock	73,900	
Cost of sales		86,100
Gross profit		69,900
Less overheads:		
Advertising	4,830	
Rent and rates	8,500	
Wages	15,550	
General expenses	5,000	
Depreciation: shop fittings	10,000	
		43,880
Net profit		26,020

(e)

BALANCE SHEET OF JANE PRICE
as at 31 December 2004

	£	£	£
Fixed assets	Cost	Provision for depreciation	Net
Shop fittings	50,000	10,000	40,000
Current assets			
Stock		73,900	
Debtors		2,500	
Prepayment: rent		250	
Bank*		19,900	
		96,550	
Less Current liabilities			
Creditors	65,000		
Accrual: wages	550		
		65,550	
Working capital			31,000
NET ASSETS			71,000
FINANCED BY			
Capital			
Opening capital (introduced at start of year)			60,000
Add net profit			26,020
			86,020
Less drawings			15,020
Closing capital			71,000

* Cash book summary:

	£
• total receipts for year	213,500
• less total payments for year	193,600
• **balance at year end**	19,900

13.5

JAMES HARVEY
CALCULATION OF STOCK LOSS FOR THE YEAR

	£	£
Opening stock		21,500
Purchases		132,000
Cost of stock available for sale		153,500
Sales	180,000	
Less Normal gross profit margin (30%)	54,000	
Cost of sales		126,000
Estimated closing stock		27,500
Less Actual closing stock		26,000
Value of stock loss		1,500

13.6   (a)

•	receipts from sales	121,000
•	less debtors at beginning of year	36,000
•	add bad debts written off during year	550
•	add debtors at end of year	35,000
•	**sales for year**	120,550

(b)

•	payments to suppliers	62,500
•	less creditors at beginning of year	32,500
•	add creditors at end of year	30,000
•	**purchases for year**	60,000

(c)

•	payments for business expenses	30,000
•	less accrual at beginning of year	500
•	add accrual at end of year	700
•	**business expenses for year**	30,200

(d)

TRADING AND PROFIT AND LOSS ACCOUNT OF COLIN SMITH
for the year ended 30 June 2005

	£	£
Sales		120,550
Opening stock	25,000	
Purchases	60,000	
	85,000	
Less Closing stock	27,500	
Cost of sales		57,500
Gross profit		63,050
Less overheads:		
Business expenses	30,200	
Depreciation: fixtures and fittings	5,000	
Bad debts written off	550	
		35,750
Net profit		27,300

(e)   **BALANCE SHEET as at 30 June 2005**

Fixed assets	£ Cost	£ Provision for depreciation	£ Net
Fixtures and fittings	50,000	15,000	35,000
Current assets			
Stock		27,500	
Debtors		35,000	
Bank		1,210	
		63,710	
Less Current liabilities			
Creditors	30,000		
Accrual: business expenses	700		
		30,700	
Working capital			33,010
NET ASSETS			68,010

FINANCED BY			
Capital			
Opening capital*			69,500
Add net profit			27,300
			96,800
Less drawings			28,790
Closing capital			68,010

* Opening capital:	£
• assets at 1 July 2004	102,500
• less liabilities at 1 July 2004	33,000
• **capital at 1 July 2004**	69,500

CHAPTER 14: PARTNERSHIP FINAL ACCOUNTS

14.1 (b)   **14.2** (a)

14.3

Dr				Partners' Capital Accounts			Cr
	Lysa	Mark			Lysa	Mark
2004	£	£	2004		£	£
31 Dec Balances c/d	50,000	40,000	1 Jan Balances b/d		50,000	40,000
2005			2005			
			1 Jan Balances b/d		50,000	40,000

Dr				Partners' Current Accounts			Cr
	Lysa	Mark			Lysa	Mark
2004	£	£	2004		£	£
31 Dec Drawings	13,000	12,250	1 Jan Balances b/d		420	1,780
31 Dec Balance c/d	–	830	31 Dec Interest on capital		2,500	2,000
			31 Dec Share of profits		9,300	9,300
			31 Dec Balance c/d		780	–
	13,000	13,080			13,000	13,080
2005			2005			
1 Jan Balance b/d	780	–	1 Jan Balance b/d		–	830

14.4 Task 1

Extended Trial Balance – see next page

14.4 Task 1   EXTENDED TRIAL BALANCE   J JAMES & S HILL T/A "GRAPES"   31 DECEMBER 2004

Account name	Ledger balances Dr £	Ledger balances Cr £	Adjustments Dr £	Adjustments Cr £	Profit and loss Dr £	Profit and loss Cr £	Balance sheet Dr £	Balance sheet Cr £
Capital a/c: James		38,000						38,000
Capital a/c: Hill		32,000						32,000
Current a/c: James	3,000						3,000	
Current a/c: Hill		1,000						1,000
Drawings: James	10,000						10,000	
Drawings: Hill	22,000						22,000	
Gross profit		89,000				89,000		
Rent and rates	7,500				7,500			
Advertising	12,000				12,000			
Heat and light	3,500				3,500			
Wages and salaries	18,000				18,000			
Sundry expenses	4,000				4,000			
Shop fittings	20,000						20,000	
Prov for dep'n: shop fittings				2,000				2,000
Bank	29,000						29,000	
Debtors	6,000						6,000	
Creditors		8,000						8,000
Value Added Tax		2,000						2,000
Closing stock: Balance sheet	35,000						35,000	
Depreciation			2,000		2,000			
Partnership salary: Hill					15,000			15,000
Interest on capital: James					3,800			3,800
Interest on capital: Hill					3,200			3,200
Net profit/loss: James					10,000			10,000
Net profit/loss: Hill					10,000			10,000
	170,000	170,000	2,000	2,000	89,000	89,000	125,000	125,000

Task 2

Dr			Partners' Capital Accounts			Cr
	James £	Hill £		James £	Hill £	
2004			2004			
31 Dec Balances c/d	38,000	32,000	1 Jan Balances b/d	38,000	32,000	
2005			2005			
			1 Jan Balances b/d	38,000	32,000	

Dr			Partners' Current Accounts			Cr
	James £	Hill £		James £	Hill £	
2004			2004			
1 Jan Balance b/d	3,000	–	1 Jan Balance b/d	–	1,000	
31 Dec Drawings	10,000	22,000	31 Dec Salary	–	15,000	
31 Dec Balances c/d	800	7,200	31 Dec Interest on capital	3,800	3,200	
			31 Dec Share of profits	10,000	10,000	
	13,800	29,200		13,800	29,200	
2005			2005			
			1 Jan Balances b/d	800	7,200	

Task 3

JOHN JAMES AND STEVEN HILL IN PARTNERSHIP, TRADING AS "GRAPES"
PROFIT AND LOSS ACCOUNT
for the year ended 31 December 2004

	£	£
Gross profit		89,000
Less overheads:		
Rent and rates	7,500	
Advertising	12,000	
Heat and light	3,500	
Wages and salaries	18,000	
Sundry expenses	4,000	
Depreciation: shop fittings	2,000	
		47,000
Net profit		42,000
Less appropriation of profit:		
Salary: Hill		15,000
Interest allowed on partners' capitals		
James £38,000 x 10%	3,800	
Hill £32,000 x 10%	3,200	
		7,000
		20,000
Share of remaining profit:		
James		10,000
Hill		10,000
		20,000

continued on next page

BALANCE SHEET as at 31 December 2004

	£	£	£
Fixed assets	Cost	Provision for dep'n	Net
Shop fittings	20,000	2,000	18,000
Current assets			
Stock (closing)		35,000	
Debtors		6,000	
Bank		29,000	
		70,000	
Less Current liabilities			
Creditors	8,000		
Value Added Tax	2,000		
		10,000	
Working capital			60,000
NET ASSETS			78,000
FINANCED BY			
Capital Accounts			
James		38,000	
Hill		32,000	
			70,000
Current Accounts			
James		800	
Hill		7,200	
			8,000
			78,000

Task 4

- The balance on the partners' current accounts represents the balance owed or owing between the business and the individual partners after transactions such as salaries, interest on capitals, share of profits, and drawings have been taken into account.

- A debit balance on a partner's current account means that the partner has drawn out more than his/her entitlement of salary, interest on capital and share of profits.

- A credit balance on a partner's current account means that the partner has drawn out less than his/her entitlement of salary, interest on capital and share of profits.

CHAPTER 15: CHANGES IN PARTNERSHIPS

15.1 (a)

15.2 (b)

15.3

Dr					Partners' Capital Accounts				Cr
		Jim	Maisie	Matt			Jim	Maisie	Matt
2004		£	£	£	2004		£	£	£
					31 Dec	Balances b/d	60,000	40,000	–
2005					2005				
1 Jan	Goodwill written off	24,000	16,000	8,000	1 Jan	Goodwill created	28,800	19,200	–
31 Dec	Drawings	12,000	12,000	8,000	1 Jan	Bank			28,000
31 Dec	Balances c/d	82,800	51,200	22,000	31 Dec	Share of profit	30,000	20,000	10,000
		118,800	79,200	38,000			118,800	79,200	38,000
2006					2006				
					1 Jan	Balances b/d	82,800	51,200	22,000

15.4   Task 1

Dr				Partners' Capital Accounts				Cr
	Reena	Sam	Tamara		Reena	Sam	Tamara
	£	£	£		£	£	£
Goodwill written off	8,000	–	8,000	Balances b/d	33,000	12,000	30,000
Bank		16,000		Goodwill created	8,000	4,000	4,000
Balances c/d	33,000	–	26,000				
	41,000	16,000	34,000		41,000	16,000	34,000
				Balances b/d	33,000	–	26,000

Task 2

REENA AND TAMARA IN PARTNERSHIP
BALANCE SHEET as at 1 September 2004

	£
Fixed assets	50,000
Current assets	10,000
Cash at bank (£25,000 – £16,000)	9,000
	69,000
Creditors	(10,000)
	59,000
Capital Accounts	
Reena	33,000
Tamara	26,000
	59,000

15.5   Task 1

Date	Details	Folio	Dr	Cr
2004			£	£
1 Oct	Goodwill	ML	45,000	
	Capital account – Dave	ML		22,500
	Capital account – Elsa	ML		22,500
			45,000	45,000
	Goodwill created for the change in the profit-sharing ratio; credited to capital accounts in the partners' old profit-sharing ratio of 1:1			
1 Oct	Capital account – Dave	ML	30,000	
	Capital account – Elsa	ML	15,000	
	Goodwill	ML		45,000
			45,000	45,000
	Goodwill written off for the change in the profit-sharing ratio; debited to capital accounts in the partners' new profit-sharing ratio of 2:1			

Task 2

Dr   **Partners' Capital Accounts**   Cr

		Dave	Elsa			Dave	Elsa
2004		£	£	2004		£	£
1 Oct	Goodwill written off	30,000	15,000	1 Oct	Balances b/d	80,000	50,000
1 Oct	Balances c/d	72,500	57,500	1 Oct	Goodwill created	22,500	22,500
		102,500	72,500			102,500	72,500
				1 Oct	Balances b/d	72,500	57,500

Task 3

DAVE AND ELSA IN PARTNERSHIP
BALANCE SHEET as at 1 October 2003

	£
Net assets	130,000
Capital Accounts:	
Dave	72,500
Elsa	57,500
	130,000

15.6   Task 1

JEAN AND DAVID IN PARTNERSHIP
APPROPRIATION ACCOUNT for the year ended 31 December 2004

	Total	Jean	David
	£	£	£
Net profit	32,700		
Salaries	(22,000)	12,000	10,000
Interest on capital @ 5%	(1,100)	500	600
Balance available for distribution	9,600		
Balance of profit shared:			
6 months to 30 June (six-twelfths)	4,800	3,200	1,600
6 months to 31 December (six-twelfths)	4,800	2,400	2,400
	9,600	5,600	4,000

Task 2

Dr   **Partners' Current Accounts**   Cr

		Jean	David			Jean	David
2004		£	£	2004		£	£
1 Jan	Balance b/d	–	1,250	1 Jan	Balance b/d	2,400	–
31 Dec	Drawings	18,600	14,200	31 Dec	Salaries	12,000	10,000
31 Dec	Balance c/d	1,900	–	31 Dec	Interest on capital	500	600
				31 Dec	Share of profit	5,600	4,000
				31 Dec	Balance c/d	–	850
		20,500	15,450			20,500	15,450
2005				2005			
1 Jan	Balance b/d	–	850	1 Jan	Balance b/d	1,900	–

Appendix:
photocopiable resources

These pages may be photocopied for student use, but remain the copyright of the author. It is recommended that they are enlarged to A4 size.

These pages are also available for download from the Resources Section of www.osbornebooks.co.uk

The forms and formats include:

SOLE TRADER: TRADING AND PROFIT AND LOSS ACCOUNT

This example layout for final accounts is for sole trader businesses; for partnerships, the layout will need to be adjusted to take note of the partners' capital and current accounts (see Chapter 14).

TRADING AND PROFIT AND LOSS ACCOUNT OF .... **(name)**

FOR THE YEAR/PERIOD ENDED ....**(date)**

	£	£	£	
Sales			......	
Less Sales returns			......	
Net sales			......	(a)
Opening stock		......		
Purchases	......			
Carriage in	......			
Less Purchases returns	......			
Net purchases		......		
		......		
Less Closing stock		......		
Cost of sales			......	(b)
Gross profit (a) – (b)			......	(c)
Add other income, eg				
Discount received			......	⎤
Provision for doubtful debts (reduction)			......	⎥ (d)
Profit on sale of fixed assets			......	⎥
Other income			......	⎦
(c) + (d)			......	(e)
Less overheads, eg				
Vehicle running expenses		......		
Rent		......		
Rates		......		
Heating and lighting		......		
Telephone		......		
Salaries and wages		......		
Discount allowed		......		
Carriage out		......		
Depreciation		......		
Loss on sale of fixed assets		......		
Bad debts written off		......		
Provision for doubtful debts (increase)		......		
			......	(f)
Net profit (e) – (f)			......	(g)

SOLE TRADER: BALANCE SHEET

BALANCE SHEET OF .... (name) AS AT .... (date)

	£	£	£	
Fixed assets	Cost (a)	Prov for dep'n (b)	Net	(a) − (b)
Intangible: Goodwill	......	......	......	
Tangible: Premises	......	......	......	
Equipment	......	......	......	
Vehicles	......	......	......	
etc	......	......	......	
	......	......	......	(c)

Current assets
Stock (closing) ......
Debtors ......
Less provision for doubtful debts ......
......
Prepayments ......
Bank ......
Cash ......
...... (d)

Less Current liabilities
Creditors ......
Accruals ......
Bank overdraft ......
...... (e)

Working capital (or **Net current assets**) (d) − (e) ...... (f)
(c) + (f) ...... (g)
Less Long-term liabilities
Loans ...... (h)
NET ASSETS (g) − (h) ...... (i)

FINANCED BY
Capital
Opening capital ......
Add net profit (from profit and loss account) ......
......
Less drawings ......
...... (i)

Note: balance sheet balances at points (i)

Practical point: When preparing handwritten final accounts it is usual practice to underline all the headings and sub-headings shown in bold print in the example layout.

Dr   Cr

Date	Details	Amount £	Date	Details	Amount £

Dr   Cr

Date	Details	Amount £	Date	Details	Amount £

Dr   Cr

Date	Details	Amount £	Date	Details	Amount £

EXTENDED TRIAL BALANCE

EXTENDED TRIAL BALANCE

name.................   date.................

Account name	Ledger balances		Adjustments		Profit and loss		Balance sheet	
	Dr £	Cr £	Dr £	Cr £	Dr £	Cr £	Dr £	Cr £
Closing stock: Profit and loss								
Closing stock: Balance sheet								
Accruals								
Prepayments								
Depreciation								
Bad debts								
Provision for doubtful debts:adjustment								
Net profit/loss								

FIXED ASSET REGISTER PAGE

EXTRACT FROM FIXED ASSET REGISTER

Description/serial no	Date acquired	Original cost £	Depreciation £	NBV £	Funding method	Disposal proceeds £	Disposal date

Index